Mark Kermode is Chief Film Critic for the *Observer* and co-host of *Kermode and Mayo's Film Review* on BBC Radio 5 Live. He is the author of *It's Only A Movie; The Good, The Bad and the Multiplex; The Movie Doctors* (with Simon Mayo) and *Hatchet Job*, which was hailed by Stephen Fry as 'the finest film critic in Britain at the absolute top of his form.' He plays double bass and harmonica in The Dodge Brothers, the award-winning skiffle-and-blues band, who also accompany silent movies. He has written and presented film and music shows on Channel 4 and across BBC radio and television, and currently presents a weekly film soundtracks show on Scala radio. He holds two Sony Awards for his radio programmes, and The Dodge Brothers album *The Sun Set* was voted Blues Album of the Year 2013 by the roots music site Spiral Earth.

www.markkermode.co.uk
@KermodeMovie

Also *by Mark Kermode*
It's Only A Movie
The Good, the Bad & the Multiplex
Hatchet Job
The Movie Doctors (with Simon Mayo)
BFI Modern Classics:
The Exorcist, The Shawshank Redemption, Silent Running

'Wonderful – such a terrific read. *How Does It Feel?* hit me right between the eyes. It brilliantly captures the passion, commitment, searing self-knowledge and dizzy happiness that comes with loving music. An enchanting book'   Stephen Fry

'Oh boy! A rocking whirlwind of a tale. People get into bands originally for the sheer love of the life and the music. Few manage to retain that dizzying adolescent crush like Mark Kermode'

Danny Baker

'[A] witty, self-deprecating account . . . at the heart of this entertaining memoir is a little boy in his back garden in Finchley, banging out a rhythm on saucepans with a couple of wooden spoons'

Daily Mail

'Mark Kermode's wonderful and wry book is a compelling combination of heartfelt enthusiasm, merciless self-analysis and a pleasingly full Rolodex of terrible band names. A true fan, he has the rare gift of making you want to discover things from the margins while never looking down on the mainstream. His writing feels like one of those letters you always wish to receive, one whose sole purpose seems to be to increase your zest for life'   Richard Ayoade

'Mark Kermode deftly and winningly manages to have one foot in knotty film criticism and one in popular entertainment . . . If you enjoyed [Danny] Baker's various volumes of autobiography, Kermode's romp through his own "back story" will appeal too, since he has much of his mentor's style: breezily anecdotal, big on dialogue and set-pieces'   *New Statesman*

'Kermode's insistent perfecting of musical failure is madly funny. I loved this book and cringed at every awful stage fail, but his passion shines through. His unrequited desire to be a rock star in a time when every idiot had a band is bum-clenchingly funny and forensically recalled. How life isn't always the movie in your mind'

Gary Kemp

'Entertaining . . . wry . . . rendered with self-deprecating humour. Overwhelmingly, what comes through every anecdote is the author's genuine enthusiasm for music'   *Spectator*

'A delight. If Nick Hornby's *High Fidelity* and the Kinks' greatest hits had a baby, and that baby could play skiffle, it would be this book'   Hadley Freeman

'An entertaining read by anyone's standards, but if you've ever been in a band, if you understand the idea of throwing yourself body and soul into making music with the absolute surety that what you're doing amounts to genius, even – and especially – when it definitely, definitely doesn't, then it's a book you're going to adore'

Drowned in Sound

'An engaging tribute to the under-sung glories of skiffle, written with the joyful enthusiasm of someone clearly dedicated to making music'   Jonny Greenwood

'From a garden with one person and a cat, to the Barbican Concert Hall. From a cassette recorder in a bedroom in north London to the legendary Sun studios in Memphis, Mark Kermode's self-deprecatory wit exemplifies and celebrates the wonderful unstoppable force of innocence and youthful dreams. Part Spinal Tap, part Nick Hornby, a rock 'n' rollercoaster memoir of never giving up on your passions'   Sanjeev Bhaskar

'You know when you read a biography of your favourite band? And the best bit is the first few chapters where they're chancing it, sleeping on floors, borrowing amps and not believing they've blagged their way onto a bill with Rick Wakeman. Well, imagine that breathless, innocent excitement lasted their whole career. That's what reading *How Does It Feel?* is like. It's the biography of your favourite band who never quite got famous'   John Robins

HOW DOES IT FEEL?
A LIFE OF MUSICAL MISADVENTURES

MARK KERMODE

WEIDENFELD & NICOLSON

First published in Great Britain in 2018
This paperback edition first published in 2019
by Weidenfeld & Nicolson
an imprint of The Orion Publishing Group Ltd
Carmelite House, 50 Victoria Embankment
London EC4Y 0DZ

An Hachette UK Company

1 3 5 7 9 10 8 6 4 2

A CIP catalogue record for this book is
available from the British Library.

ISBN (paperback) 978 1 4746 0899 2
ISBN (ebook) 978 1 4746 0900 5

Typeset by Input Data Services Ltd, Somerset

Printed and bound by CPI Group (UK) Ltd, Croydon, CR0 4YY

'Runnin' around round round . . . ?'

For everyone with whom I have ever played a tune:

Thank you. And sorry.

CONTENTS

INTRO

YOU HUM IT, I'LL PLAY IT

Many people have recurrent nightmares. Some dream of sinking in quicksand. Others are consumed by visions of being unable to escape from an endlessly elongating corridor – or of waking up naked on the underground or accidentally wearing pyjamas to a party.

I have a recurrent nightmare, and it goes like this:

I am standing on the stage of the Royal Festival Hall in London. As I look out, I can see that the auditorium is packed, right up to the very top of the teetering tiered balconies. Behind me, the BBC Concert Orchestra are playing the opening bars of a particularly complicated piece of music, rushing inexorably towards the moment when the solo instrument – the chromatic harmonica – will leap into life and take the tune.

I look down at my hands and realise that I am holding a harmonica. It is big and cold and heavy. I raise it to my mouth, knowing that everyone is expecting me to play the jaunty lead line from this familiar tune, with its distinctive opening ascending phrase, and fiddly semi-tonal twiddles and doodles. But I can't play it. I *know* I can't, because I've already tried, and I just can't do it. I feel the unforgiving metal of the harp against my lips, my mouth parched and dry. I see the faces of the audience, staring and expectant. I see the conductor raising his baton and pointing it towards me. And I feel myself starting to choke . . .

That's my recurrent nightmare, with all its commonplace fears of public exposure and humiliation. The only difference between *my* recurrent nightmare and yours (hopefully) is that mine isn't in fact a dream but a memory. This actually happened, in real life. In the real Royal Festival Hall. With the real BBC Concert Orchestra. The audience were also real. They were there in the packed auditorium. And there were thousands more of them at home, listening to the concert as it was broadcast on BBC Radio 3.

I often ask myself, 'How the hell did I get into this terrible predicament?' The answer is always the same; someone asked me if I could do something and, rather than admitting that I couldn't, I said 'Sure!' After all, how hard can it be? I am particularly guilty of this when it comes to anything musical, despite the fact that I have known from an early age *just* how hard it is to play an instrument – *any* instrument.

As a child, I took piano lessons for several years, during which time I spectacularly failed to learn to read music. My father had long been a fan of the jazz pianist Jelly Roll Morton, and my sister Annie had impressed him mightily by becoming adept at playing the ragtime blues of Scott Joplin. I enjoyed listening to my dad's old 78s (he had a fairly extensive collection of jazz rarities) but I was never able to replicate their fleet-fingered forms. Indeed, my development as a music student was so staggeringly arrested that my piano teacher refused to put me in for any grade exams, knowing full well that I would just crash and burn if put to the test. I've been playing the piano for the best part of fifty years now, and I still don't have a single keyboard qualification to my name. Many primary school children hold more musical honours than I do.

In secondary school, I took French horn lessons, largely because my parents had been told that there was a shortage (local, rather than national) of French horn players, and so I'd make it into the school orchestra no matter how inept I proved. Somehow, I bluffed my way through the Grade 3 exam – which in those days was an entry-level accomplishment that essentially involved being placed in a room with a range of musical instruments and asked to identify which one was the French horn. Seriously, back then a donkey could scrape through the Grade 3 exam.

Sadly, that was as far as I got. Against the better judgement of my music teacher, the school submitted me to take the Grade 4 exam at which point everything went south. I remember very little about the test itself, other than the horror of seeing the examiner wince as I fluffed and farted my way through a couple of horribly unprepared 'prepared pieces'. When it came to the sight-reading section, I started on the wrong note and never regained my foothold. At the end, I rather forlornly asked the examiner if I could 'take another run at it'. To which he replied (sternly, but correctly), 'Well, that wouldn't be "sight reading", would it?'

When the inevitable Fail slip arrived in the post, I flushed it down the loo and resolved never to take another music exam or, indeed, any further musical training. Fired by the arrogance of youth, I convinced myself that the musical establishment was just too damned conservative for my anarchic musical talents. What need did I have of formal training or certification? Hell, I had taught myself to play the thunderous 'Also

3

sprach Zarathustra' theme from Stanley Kubrick's *2001*, on the piano. *By ear!* I didn't need sheet music – I just needed to *play*.

How hard could it be?

Since then, I've spent a lifetime 'playing' musical instruments with a wanton disregard for training or talent. The results have often been far from pretty. Over the years I have 'played' guitar, piano, drums, bagpipes, accordion, French horn, double bass, ukulele, banjo, harmonica, penny whistle, tambourine and (most recently) theremin. To paraphrase John Lennon (or was it Paul McCartney?), I may not be any good at any of these instruments, but if you put me in a room with a euphonium and give me a couple of hours, I'll get you a tune out of it. Just about. Most importantly, I made a decision early on not to be scared of *any* musical instrument – to give it a go, and to hell with the consequences.

On occasion, this has got me into trouble, like the time I agreed to play the theme from *Local Hero* on the bagpipes from the beach at Pennan in Aberdeenshire, and then found myself having to do it in front of BBC television cameras. But more often than not, I've got away with it, through a mixture of luck, goodwill and sheer barefaced cheek. I've played the theremin onstage in some of the most revered music halls of the UK and done enough theatrical arm-waving to distract audiences from noticing that I couldn't hit a single note. I've played banjo in a theatre production where I had to Sellotape the strings to the neck so all anyone could hear was the rhythmic sound of music hall strumming. I once played a trumpet on a recording in which I had to play the piece one note at a time and leave it to the engineer to knit it all together in the edit. Every time, I got away with it.

Which brings me to the Royal Festival Hall. Here's what happened:

Back in 2011, Simon Mayo and I were in the tenth year of our BBC Radio 5Live show, *Kermode and Mayo's Film Review*. Someone decided that it would be fun to do a live show from Salford with the BBC Philharmonic Orchestra which had recently taken up residence in MediaCity. The theme of the show would be favourite film tunes, with conductor Robert Ziegler leading the audience through a guided tour of the orchestra in-between playing hits from the movies. I had first met Robert some years earlier, when I introduced an outdoor screening of Alfred Hitchcock's early silent classic *The Lodger* for which Robert was conducting Joby Talbot's newly composed score.

Robert is that rarest of things – someone who can play music and talk about it with equal ease. Like the composer–arranger Neil Brand, he has a way of demystifying his profession, of making everyone feel included in what is, by nature, a fairly exclusive club. Professional concert musicians can be scary creatures; like brain surgeons or astronauts, they do something which most of us can only *dream* of doing. Yet Robert exudes the kind of enthusiasm for his work which makes everyone feel included – and that includes clueless chancers like me.

At a production meeting to decide which tunes the orchestra should play on the programme, someone suggested John Barry's theme from *Midnight Cowboy*. It's a lovely tune – an instantly recognisable audience favourite – so putting it in the programme seemed like a no-brainer.

'Except that we don't have a harmonica player,' said Robert, 'and we can't do it without one.'

This was clearly my cue to leap into the fray.

'I can play harmonica! I'll do it!'

'You can play the theme from *Midnight Cowboy*?' asked Robert, just to be sure.

'Sure!' I replied. After all, I'd been playing harmonica in my band, The Dodge Brothers, for several years.

How hard could it be?

'Great,' said Robert. 'We'll put "Midnight Cowboy" in the set with Mark on harmonica.' And that was that.

It was only a few days later, when I sat down to listen to a recording of said piece, that I realised I'd made a terrible mistake. The instrument that I'd been merrily playing for years was a 'diatonic harmonica' – the kind of thing you give to small children because they're so easy to play. All you do is blow and suck (or 'draw'), and music magically appears. And brilliantly you have a different harmonica for each different key, so it's basically impossible to play a 'wrong' note.

Blues harmonica players tend to play 'cross harp', in which most of the key notes are on the intake breath. If you blow a diatonic harmonica in C, it will set you off on the major scale of that key. But if you *suck* it (to play 'cross harp'), it will play a blues scale in G, replete with the signature blendable blue notes. Similarly, if someone is playing the blues in A, you simply grab a diatonic D harp and play 'across'. As long as you keep sucking, you *cannot* play a bum note. You may not play all the right ones, but you will *never* hit a wrong one.

The reason this miracle is possible is that diatonic harmonicas don't have *all* the notes – just the ones you want. When I said that I could play the theme from *Midnight Cowboy*, I'd assumed that it was played on a diatonic, with all the safety nets that implied. But listening to it, I realised that it was, in fact, played on a *chromatic* harmonica; a completely different

Playing the diatonic harmonica – an instrument on which it is impossible to play a wrong note.

instrument, twice the size of a diatonic and crucially featuring *all* the notes – including *all the wrong ones.*

By the time I realised my mistake it was too late to back out. Instead, I figured that I could just bluff my way through it – that I could purchase a chromatic harmonica and learn to master it in the two weeks before the programme. So, the next day, I headed to Hobgoblin Music in London, just around the corner from the British Film Institute on Stephen Street, and purchased a 'Chromonica'. It cost a fortune (well over a hundred pounds!) and it proved an absolute bastard to play. For one thing, you had to hit *exactly* the right air hole with your lips in order to produce single notes rather than bluesy chords. For another, this machine had two tiers of notations, between which you were required to jump by pressing a button on the butt end of the harp. Whereas before just blowing and sucking produced randomly reasonable music, now I had to learn to do complicated things with my hands and mouth *at the same time* – an endeavour not aided by the fact that I have hands like slabs of beef and lips that make me look like I've been permanently punched. When my French horn teacher had told me decades earlier that I had a 'problematic embouchure', what he meant was 'you've got a fat mouth', something I was now rediscovering, to my detriment.

Those two weeks leading up to the performance of 'Midnight Cowboy' were hellish for all involved. My family grew sick of hearing me rehearse the wretched piece, squonking and squawking my way through the once-loved tune, now forever tarnished by tuneless repetition. In an attempt to save face, I decided to do a video-blog with Robert demonstrating the level of my ineptitude, hoping that it would somehow win me public sympathy. Robert thought I was kidding when I told him I really couldn't play the piece, but his amusement turned to horror the first time we ran it through in a rehearsal room and he realised I wasn't joking. My friend and colleague, Nick Freand Jones (who had given me my very first harmonica some years earlier), was there to capture the moment on film. Many people assumed that Robert and I were mugging for the cameras, exaggerating my incompetence. But it was all real – and if you don't believe me, ask Robert.

No matter how much I practised, I just didn't get any better. Learning a new tune is one thing; learning to play it on a new instrument is a whole different world of pain. The *Radio Times* had already announced that I'd be playing the piece live on air, so there was no way of backing out quietly. I had put myself in this terrible position. It was all my own fault, and now there was nothing to do except see it through.

The day before the broadcast we all schlepped up to Manchester on the train, then trammed it to Salford where the orchestra awaited. Simon Mayo and I did a couple of media interviews in which we talked about the next day's show and joked about me making a pig's ear of 'Midnight Cowboy'. Everyone laughed along.

Ha-bloody-ha.

Towards the end of the day, Robert had booked a sound-check with me and the full orchestra. They had been playing all day, waltzing their way through a string of memorable themes, from the jazzy melancholia of Bernard Herrmann's *Taxi Driver* score to strident title hits from the Bond movies. They sounded magnificent, and I was certain that no one had hit a bum note all day. When Robert announced that we were going to run through 'Midnight Cowboy', the orchestra welcomed me to the stage by clapping with their feet – a traditional greeting that caught me completely off guard. I stepped up to the microphone next to Robert, and waited in terror as he prepared to cue the orchestra.

There was silence. Followed by music. Followed by me.

It was horrible.

Having never successfully managed to play the theme from *Midnight Cowboy* from start to finish without foul-ups on my own, I came completely unstuck in front of the orchestra. I missed cues, I missed notes, I missed entire sections of the melody. I sounded as if I was gargling machine parts. The chromatic harmonica bumped and squeaked and shrieked and wailed, as if someone was slowly murdering a duck. The more mistakes I made, the more incapable I became. I broke out in a cold sweat, shivering in panic, unable to catch my breath. I wanted the floor to open up and swallow me whole. I thought I was going to spontaneously combust with embarrassment.

And then, quite suddenly, it was over. The piece had finished. The orchestra were silent. Robert thanked them and dismissed them, and they started packing up their instruments. He looked at me in terror.

'We need to go and practise,' he said, quietly but firmly. 'A lot.'

It later transpired that, during that horrendous soundcheck, my microphone had not been turned on. Apparently the orchestra couldn't hear a single note I played. Which was all the better because, as Robert admitted later, if any of them *had* heard what I was doing, they would have simply refused to play with me. And they would have been right. But for now, Robert said nothing; he just led me to a rehearsal room in a quiet corner of the Salford studios where we practised that piece over and over and over and over and over and over . . .

By the time I went to bed at around 11 p.m., my upper lip was bleeding and most of my face was numb. I rang Linda, my wife, from the hotel room and told her to prepare to sell the house because my career was going to end at 3.50 p.m. the next day. I know it sounds like I am exaggerating, but things really were *that* bad. I went for a shower and threw up in the bathroom. I tried to get some sleep, but the terror of the next day kept me wide awake.

Fast forward to Friday afternoon. The 5Live show had kicked off at 2 p.m. and the orchestra had been delighting the listening public with their superbly performed repertoire. Robert had proved to be a huge hit with the audience, swapping erudite quips with Simon, and leading the listeners through the ups and downs of film orchestration. We'd received umpteen laudatory listener emails, and I'd done a bunch of movie reviews, all of which suggested that I was taking this in my stride. But inside, my intestines were tying themselves up in knots, preparing to leap up and strangle my head when the harmonica humiliation began.

About a minute before the moment of reckoning finally arrived, something strange happened. Having been in a state of abject panic for something like twenty-four hours, I started to feel myself floating out of my own body, ready to watch myself go through the ring of fire. Looking back, you could argue that I've simply confused the TV coverage with memory because, along with the radio broadcast, the BBC had decided to live stream the entire show on the Red Button. So not only could people *hear* me destroy my career on live radio, they could *watch* me do it on TV too. In state-of-the-art high definition!

Yet I clearly recall sitting in the audience and watching myself open my harmonica box, pull out the chromatic, walk up to the podium next to Robert and start to play the theme from *Midnight Cowboy*.

With the BBC Philharmonic Orchestra.

And somehow, I got away with it.

Don't get me wrong; it wasn't perfect. Far from it. There were a couple of moments where my notation sounded more than a little hesitant, and there was nothing in the way of style or finesse. But neither were there any proper mistakes as such. I came in at the right place, I ended at the right place and, in between, I played all the right notes in all the right order – something I had never managed to do before. If you think I'm making this up, go look it up on YouTube. The piece is there in its entirety and, against all expectations, it is not terrible. It may not be *great*, but it is definitely passable. And frankly, that is way more than I was aiming for.

As I said, I got away with it.

During the final few bars, with the end in sight, I actually started to enjoy myself, and you can *hear* that enjoyment in the recording. You can also hear the generous applause from the audience (and, indeed, the orchestra) all of which bypassed me in the moment. All I could hear was the sound of the blood rushing in my ears and a voice in my head telling me to call Linda and tell her not to sell the house. As it turned out, she'd been listening live anyway and had figured that our home was safe sometime around bar eight. And then the emails started coming in from listeners saying how lovely it all sounded and I entered something approaching a state of grace.

After that, everything is a bit of a blur. Simon had to dash off to present his daily Radio 2 show, while I was reteaming with Robert for a Radio 3 broadcast in which the Philharmonic Orchestra would play another film-themed selection featuring the music of John Williams, Nino Rota, Erich Korngold and more. Under other circumstances I'd have been mentally preparing myself for the Radio 3 broadcast: reading the script, checking the timings, revisiting the musical ins and outs. But since this time I was only going to be called upon to speak rather than to play, I treated the whole thing as an extended chill-out session. I honestly don't think I've ever been more relaxed about a live two-and-a-half-hour radio broadcast in my entire life.

When the various shows were finished, we all reconvened in the bar, giddy with relief at how well things had gone. Everyone agreed that a particular highlight had been the Philharmonic's boisterous performance of the James Bond theme, so I strode up to the bar, slapped my hand on the counter, looked the barman in the eye and said, 'Three vodka martinis, shaken not stirred.'

The barman looked at me blankly.

'What?'

'Three vodka martinis,' I said again. 'Shaken not stirred.'

Nothing. Then . . .

'Three "vodka martinis"?' he repeated, as if hearing the phrase for the first time.

'Yes!' I replied, adding rather feebly, 'And, you know, shaken. Not stirred.'

He looked at me as if I were mad.

'You want vodka *and* Martini?' he asked, bemusedly. 'In the same glass?'

'Pardon?' I said, unsure if he was taking the piss.

'You want vodka *and* Martini,' he repeated, 'in the same glass? Three of them?'

He wasn't joking.

'No,' I said with a hint of exasperation. 'I want three vodka martinis. You know – like James Bond. Three *vodka martinis*.'

'In the same glass?' he said again.

'What? No! In three separate glasses.'

'But with vodka *and* Martini in the same glass? In three glasses?'

'No! Three vodka mar . . . Oh never mind, just give me three pints of Stella.'

'Coming right up!'

I came back to Simon and Robert bearing the three pints.

'Don't ask,' I said tersely.

'Cheers!' said Simon.

'Cheers!' agreed Robert.

And with that we began a lengthy session of alcohol-fuelled self-congratulation.

Somewhere in the midst of that backslapping bonanza, I started to tell myself a lie that I would come to believe was the truth; that I had always known it was all going to be alright in the end. Gradually, the genuine anguish of the previous few weeks disappeared into the ether (or into a pint glass) and I started to convince myself that failure had never been an option. Even when Robert explained the stark truth of the previous night's microphone failure, and told me that the orchestra would have walked if they'd heard just how poor my playing was, my ability to reinvent the past was working overtime. By the time we all staggered to our beds in a state of advanced refreshment, I had managed to convince myself that there was never any real risk involved at all. I had been doing this sort of thing of thing for years, nay decades. My arrogance had never caught up with me. I had always gotten away with it.

One thing I do remember clearly. In the moments before the madness fully took hold, I seized Robert by the lapels, looked him in the eye, and said, 'Promise me you'll *never* let me do this again.'

Robert just laughed. 'It was great,' he said reassuringly. And somehow I convinced myself that he was right.

Six years later, when Robert was putting together a concert of music from film noir which I was presenting for Radio 3, that conviction would return to bite me in the butt.

'Do you want to play harmonica on the theme from *Touchez Pas au Grisbi*?' Robert asked casually, as if this were no big deal.

'Sure,' I replied blithely.

How hard could it be?

When Robert asked if I was familiar with the piece in question, I just lied, plain and simple. Too ashamed to admit that I wasn't immediately familiar with a fairly famous piece of film music, I simply blustered my way out of a tight spot, figuring that I could work out the finer details later. And so, without ever having heard the tune in question, and with no musical pedigree to speak of, I agreed to play 'Le Grisbi' on the chromatic harmonica, with the BBC Concert Orchestra, in front of a live audience and broadcast on Radio 3.

This is the story of my life; claiming that I can do things which I patently *cannot* do, and believing that good luck and a following wind will see me through. As I said before, music is the area in which this madness has become most prevalent – in which I have ridiculously risked the most, convinced that it will all be alright it in the end.

And so it was that, towards the end of 2017, I found myself onstage in front of a theatre full of expectant music fans and radio devotees, waiting for me to play the theme from *Touchez Pas au Grisbi*, thinking to myself:

'How the hell did I get here?'

1

CAREFUL WITH THAT AXE, EUGENE

As a teenager, I had two ambitions: to watch movies and to become a pop star. In fact, these seemingly disparate goals were inextricably intertwined. I'd always been a huge fan of Elvis, whose movies used to turn up on television with surprising regularity. In general, the movies weren't much good (*Tickle Me* was a low point), but Presley was such a magnetic screen presence that it didn't really matter. I'd watch anything he was in; from *Kissin' Cousins* to *Blue Hawaii*, via *Speedway* and *Roustabout*. It wasn't until years later that I stumbled across earlier offerings like *Jailhouse Rock* and *King Creole*. Those were the films Elvis made in the fifties, when James Dean and Marlon Brando were his idols, and his movies were more than just extended MOR pop promos. But as a child, I wasn't bothered by the inherent naffness of *Girl Happy* or *Easy Come, Easy Go*. Indeed, the soundtrack album of the latter was the first LP I ever bought and I played it to death, dreaming of becoming a star like Elvis.

I started making my first unaccompanied trips to the cinema in the early seventies, a time when British pop stars such as David Essex and Adam Faith could be found in movies like *That'll Be the Day* and *Stardust*. One of the first pop singles I ever bought was 'Sugar Baby Love' by The Rubettes, who promptly showed up in the spectacularly tacky Brit-pic *Never Too Young to Rock*, alongside Mud, The Glitter Band and Peter Noone. Billed as 'The All Family Musical of Today', *Never Too Young to Rock* may have rivalled *Gonks Go Beat* for the title of 'Worst Rock 'n' roll Movie of All Time', but it was a different era and frankly no one cared. Back in the sixties, pop fans had bopped along to The Beatles in *A Hard Day's Night* and The Dave Clark Five in *Catch Us If You Can*, movies that still stand the test of time. By the seventies, we had learned to make do with the sight of Cliff Richard on a barge inventing the 'Brumburger' in *Take Me High*.

Times were tough.

For my money, the greatest British pop movie of the seventies – or, indeed, of all time – is *Slade in Flame*, which opened in the UK in January 1975, when I was just eleven years old. It's an impressively gritty affair; the rags-to-riches story of a band from the north of England who are bought up by a rich London investment company and sold to the public like so many pop fish fingers. Slade played their fictional alter egos, Flame, close to home and it's easy to believe that you're watching a documentary, rather than a drama, as they bicker their way to the top of the charts, becoming more and more disillusioned with the music industry.

Having grown up watching Slade perform misspelled hits like 'Gudbuy T'Jane' and 'Mama Weer All Crazee Now' on *Top of the Pops*, I thought they were pretty much the epitome of homegrown pop stardom. So when *Flame* came to the Hendon Odeon, I went to see it three times in the same week, twice on the same day, always on my own. As it turned

The glam years – thanks to Slade and Bowie, this is what I imagined a budding pop star looked like.

out, the film proved altogether too tough for Slade's teenybopper fans and, on my third viewing, I had the cinema almost entirely to myself. Somehow, the empty auditorium added to the melancholy glamour of *Flame*, making its downbeat dreams of stardom seem that much closer, that much more attainable. '*How does it feel?*' sings Noddy Holder, as the band start to fall apart in the studio. '*Runnin' around round round . . .*' From the last aisle seat on the left of the Odeon, it felt pretty good. All I wanted to do was to form a band.

The first person I managed to persuade to join me in this endeavour was a classmate called Nigel who lived in Harrow and owned a drum kit. Nigel had a friend called Richard, a talented guitarist whose father was a composer and arranger who had done some work for glamorous-sounding movies. Nigel and Richard had been thinking about putting a group together and were on the lookout for a bassist. Spying an opening, and never backward in coming forward, I managed to persuade them that what they *actually* needed wasn't a bassist but a pianist – namely, me.

When I say 'pianist', I am, of course, using the word in the loosest possible sense. As I mentioned earlier, the fact that I had taken piano lessons didn't mean I could actually play the piano. However, there was *one* piece I could play which I was pretty sure would gain me entry into this emerging super-group. A couple of months after *Flame* had opened in UK cinemas, Ken Russell's cinematic adaptation of The Who's rock opera *Tommy* had hit the headlines. Advertised with the slogan 'He Will Tear Your Soul Apart', *Tommy* had spawned hit singles like Elton John's cover of 'Pinball Wizard', the video for which was simply an excerpt from Russell's film, which got shown over and over again on TV.

Having been knocked sideways by *Tommy*, I tracked down a songbook with guitar tabs and piano music for the entire film. After months of practise at home, I'd managed to master the spiralling arpeggios of 'Pinball Wizard' – just about – and Nigel and Richard were impressed enough to let me join their band simply so that they could play that song. We spent an afternoon rehearsing it in Richard's living room and then, later on, we invited a couple of friends around to hear us play it. Always the showman (or show off) and determined to give our performance a spectacular cinematic air, I decided that the song would have maximum impact if we drew the curtains and turned off the lights, so that the opening chords were performed in darkness. Then, the arpeggios would start building to a wild crescendo, awaiting the moment when Rick's guitar would come blasting in . . .

Da–Daaaaa!

At which point, I would reach out with my left hand and . . . turn on a very small table lamp!

Da–Daaaaaaaaaaa!!!!

There were two problems. The first was that, even with the curtains closed, the room wasn't dark. Just a bit dim. And stuffy. The second was that the table lamp was not a Super Trouper spotlight. It was a table lamp.

The first time we played 'Pinball Wizard', no one noticed when I turned the table lamp on. So I stopped the song, turned the lamp off, and insisted that we started again, only this time with everyone *paying attention.*

We played the song again.

I turned the table lamp on again.

Da–Daaaaaaa!!!!

No one paid attention.

Oh well.

Undeterred, Nigel, Richard and I carried on rehearsing together and even wrote a few original songs. Richard's dad had an electric organ out in the garage connected to a Leslie speaker, the rotating horns of which produced a quite sensational sound. It was in this garage that the three of us recorded the homemade hits 'The Last Few Minutes' (a rip-off of David Bowie's 'Rock 'N' Roll Suicide') and 'The Party at 34C', reel-to-reel demos of which have long since been declared lost – forever, if we are lucky.

Looking back on this period, it seems significant that my very first band grew up on the outskirts of the film music industry – or rather, in a living room adjacent to the outskirts of the film music industry. The fact that Richard's dad was a working musician who had broken into moving pictures made me think that such a career trajectory was eminently possible. But we still really needed a bassist and, after a while, Nigel decided that he should fill that gap while new arrival Keith took over on drums. This line-up limped along for a few months until Nigel decided that playing the bass was boring and went back to the drums in another group who ended up auditioning for Stiff Records. Meanwhile, Richard's friend Gavin replaced Nigel as bassist along with new recruit Dave Baddiel (yes, *that* Dave Baddiel) in the band we were now calling The Spark Plugs.

The Spark Plugs never played a gig, but we did manage to record three vaguely presentable tracks on a reel-to-reel tape recorder in one of the music rehearsal rooms at school. Two of those tracks were written by Dave ('Singin' the Blues Again' and 'Down and Out') who turned out to be a prolific songwriter. I remember him carrying around a notebook in

The Spark Plugs (with Dave Baddiel, left, on Strat copy guitar)
recording in the school music room.

which to jot down lyrics and I was so impressed that I went
out and bought my own notebook, which I promptly lost. I
recently found a couple of black-and-white photographs of
that recording session and one thing is apparent; no matter
how good we may or may not have sounded, The Spark Plugs
did not look like pop stars. We didn't even look like we were
trying to be pop stars; we just look like school kids with bad
hair who happen to have stumbled on a room full of cheap
musical equipment.

Back in the mid-seventies, proper pop stars looked like
Slade – a band defined by Noddy Holder's reflective top hat,
with its tower of glittering mirrors, and by Dave Hill's custom-
built guitars, which came in a range of increasingly ridiculous
pointy shapes and sizes. The most infamous of Hill's guitars
was shaped like a giant pistol, with the neck as the barrel and

the body as the revolver mechanism, emblazoned with the legend 'SuperYob'. In *Slade in Flame*, he played a guitar shaped like a huge ball of fire!

The more I thought about it, the more I started to think that I really needed to get an eye-catching electric guitar, abandon the piano and try to look more like Dave Hill. The fact that I couldn't *play* the guitar didn't matter. As I figured at the time: how hard could it be? OK, so I could never quite get my head round the idea of any five-fingered creature deliberately inventing a six-stringed instrument, something which smacked of needless perversity. But as long as I actually *owned* an electric guitar, then surely everything else would just fall into place?

The problem was that, as a spotty teenager, neither my piggy bank nor my Post Office account would stretch to the purchase of a suitably rock 'n' roll instrument. So I decided to build one instead. Out of wood. And glue. And string.

Really.

I was not the first budding musician to try to build their own electric guitar. Indeed, the entire history of the instrument is one of casual experimentation and no-holds-barred kitchen table botchery. Everyone knows that Queen's Brian May built his guitar out of a fireplace (or something), but fewer people are aware of just how much DIY has gone into the evolution of the great rock axe.

Back in the early part of the twentieth century, when musicians were attempting to figure out ways to make the lap-steel guitars used in popular Hawaiian music *louder*, George Beauchamp designed a prototype pickup consisting of two horseshoe magnets and a wire coil which would turn the vibrations of a musical string into an electronic pulse. This pickup was then installed onto a homemade instrument nicknamed

'The Frying Pan' because (guess what?) it looked like a frying pan – something more attuned to cooking your tea than playing a rocking tune.

The Frying Pan had a long neck and tiny circular metal body and was as ugly as hell. But it cost very little and could make a very *big* noise thanks to the copper wire coil wrapped tightly around the six metal poles of the pickup, one for each string. Initially, George used the motor from his family's washing machine to wind the coil. Later, he figured a sewing machine motor was more efficient. Like I said: kitchen table botchery.

Around the same time that George was annoying his wife by taking her washing and sewing machines apart to work on his crackpot musical invention, Lester William Polsfuss was making a name for himself as 'Red Hot Red', playing guitar and harmonica at a drive-in in Wisconsin. Lester had already invented the 'flippable harmonica holder', using a piece of wood and a coat hanger, the latter reportedly stolen from his father's closet. To amplify the sound of his voice and the harp, Lester attached a microphone, cannibalised from the mouthpiece of his parents' telephone, to the top of a broomstick, and connected it to a radio – thereby leaving his parents with nowhere to hang their coats, nothing to listen to, no way to sweep up the mess and no one to call to complain about it.

Having effectively destroyed his parents' house in order to amplify his voice, Lester discovered that his guitar was now too quiet to compete with all the rest of the racket he was making. This was a common problem. As swing bands added more drums and brass to fill the increasingly vast dance halls they now played, so guitars got lost in the mix. Not only could finger-picked melodies no longer be heard by the audience, even strummed chords became inaudible to anyone but the guitarist, with several reporting that they couldn't even hear themselves play. (In light of what came later, this was possibly no bad thing . . .)

With a basic understanding of how his father's electronic record player worked (and clearly eager to destroy yet more of his parents' household appliances) Les ripped the tone arm off the deck and jammed the needle into the guitar, creating an elementary electronic pickup. When the guitar, wired to a radiogram, started to feed back, he stuffed its hollow body with a tablecloth (meaning his parents now had nowhere to eat either). Eventually, he filled it with plaster of Paris, an experiment which effectively 'ended that guitar'.

It occurred to Les that what he really needed was a guitar which had no acoustic soundbox whatsoever. Crossing the street from the house where he lived, to the nearby railroad tracks, he picked up a 2ft piece of steel rail onto which he attached a single guitar string with the aid of three large nails. By fixing his parents' telephone microphone to the rail beneath the string, Les managed to produce an amplified sound which captured the vibration of the string without all the associated clatter of an acoustic guitar. As an extra bonus, the steel rail enabled the string to resonate for longer, producing an unusually powerful sustain. There was just one problem; it wasn't a guitar. It was a guitar string attached to a piece of rail.

Some years later, Les Paul (as he now called himself) designed 'The Log', which was pretty much exactly what it sounded like; a fence-post-shaped piece of pine onto which he attached the neck of a guitar and a pair of homemade pickups. As with the rail, 'The Log' had zero acoustic qualities, but it produced a pure resonant tone when amplified. It sounded great. But it looked like a log. And audiences apparently weren't keen on watching someone playing a fence post. Undeterred, Les simply sawed a hollow-bodied Epiphone archtop in half and attached 'wings' to the log to give it the gently rounded appearance of a traditional F-hole instrument. Audiences went nuts; the modern electric guitar was born.

Most of this history was unknown to me before I started to build my own electric guitar, back in the mid-seventies. Until then, I had no idea who Les Paul was. As far as I was concerned, his name was simply the brand of a fabulously expensive instrument which nobody could afford to buy, let alone play. In fact, almost every band in school had a lead guitarist wielding a cheap import Les Paul knock-off marketed by companies like Kay, Avon and Columbus. But no one talked about Paul's role in refining and marketing something we all now took for granted. Indeed, I remember having an intense conversation with a sixth-former who referred to his instrument as a 'Lay Paul' copy, firmly believing the name 'Les Paul' to be a French phrase meaning, presumably, 'The Paul'.

The Spark Plugs pretty much owed their existence to inexpensive copy guitars – as did every other school band. As I remember, Richard had acquired a three pickup black Columbus Les Paul copy that looked a million dollars, but was actually worth about £120, while Dave had a second-hand Columbus Strat which he had purchased in a Hendon music shop for the knock-down price of £50. Even this was out of my price range, however; my ceiling was closer to £30. At that price, the only guitar available was the Woolworths Audition, a three-toned sunburst abomination available in standard and deluxe versions for £20 and £25 respectively. Today, these monstrous items have become collectible rarities, beloved by enthusiasts of period guitar paraphernalia. But back in the mid-seventies, they were considered to be little more than fire-wood with strings, and nobody would be seen dead playing one in public. Nobody except Wreckless Eric, obviously . . .

As for me, I took a trip to the local library and pulled out a book on the history of amplified guitars. It was thrillingly encouraging stuff, full of stories about people like George Beauchamp and Les Paul making viable instruments out of sewing machines, railtracks and a few planks of wood. I figured that my school's fairly well-equipped Practical Design lab would have all the tools I needed to reproduce such experiments. After all, according to the history books, the only help Beauchamp had was from a skilled carpenter named Harry Watson who had spent 'several hours carving with small hand tools' to make the neck of the prototype wooden version of the Frying Pan. I may not have been a 'skilled craftsman', but if someone could make such a thing in a matter of hours, then surely I could do the same in a few weeks, or maybe months?

In the end it took me two years. But it was worth it.

The design for the guitar which I built came from the October 1974 issue of *Everyday Electronics*. The magazine promised that a decent instrument could indeed be constructed using components totalling no more than £27, all in. The templates seemed manageable enough, and the accompanying text suggested that no complex carpentry or electronics skills were required. This was good news. When I showed the designs to my PD teacher, he agreed that the project was ambitious but manageable, an assessment he would come to regret as he realised the full extent of my technical ineptitude. During one particularly unrewarding session, he pointed out to me that the chisel I was using to cut the pickup holes from the body

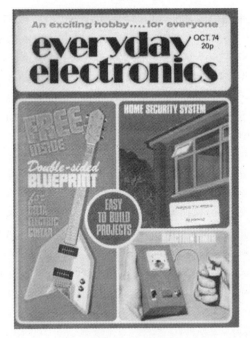

Everyday Electronics –
build your own pop stardom!

of the guitar was in fact a screwdriver, hence its failure to do the job properly. A man of strong opinions and occasionally incautious language, he informed me that the next time he caught me being that stupid he would 'place my size ten boot up your arse!' It was a phrase I would hear many times over the next two years; I knew he was joking, but it still put the wind up me.

The shape of the guitar I was building was peculiar; a cross between an elongated Vox Delta and a stunted Gibson Flying V, with neither the style of the former nor the classic panache of the latter. Dave Hill would doubtless have found it needlessly understated, but I thought it looked suitably starry. It had a vaguely futuristic sci-fi appearance, particularly on the EE front cover illustration, where it was painted gold with a white scratch plate and black lozenge pickups. I had decided to go for a matt black finish with a blue perspex scratch plate, but that aesthetic modification aside I pretty much followed the design to the letter – at least initially.

The body of the guitar was solid and therefore required no luthier skills whatsoever. Constructed from a piece of chipboard, with template holes for the pickups and wiring, glued onto a piece of hardboard which formed its surprisingly hefty back side, it soon started to take shape. The neck was altogether more problematic (where was Harry Watson when I needed him?). Indeed, as I write this, I have that very neck lying on the desk next to me, and it astonishes me that I ever managed to construct something so oddly beautiful. I have no idea what kind of wood it's carved from; suffice to say that both the neck and fingerboard are blond, and both have been chiselled and sanded into shape over months of hard labour. It has 22 frets (including a so-called 'zero fret' up by the nut) and each piece of fret wire has been individually flattened before fitting because I didn't know how to make a curved fingerboard, and nor apparently did the people at *Everyday Electronics*. Buried deep inside that neck, hidden from view, is a solid steel bar functioning as an elementary (and wholly unadjustable) truss rod, preventing the neck from warping and bowing under the tension of the strings. I remember that I acquired this weighty steel bar from a scrap metal merchant in Edgware, something which made me feel a little like Les Paul lugging that old hunk of rail back to his house.

The only things on the neck which I didn't build myself

are the machine heads and the nut, which I purchased from a music shop in North Finchley. Many years later, I would buy my first 'proper' electric guitar from that same store for the princely sum of £180 – a Westbury Deluxe with DiMarzio SD pickups for which I paid a tenner a week for the best part of five months. They wouldn't let me take the guitar away until I had paid the full sum, but they did let me come into the shop of a Saturday lunchtime and play it, which made a welcome break from mashing up frozen slabs of mince and 'cow fat' in the supermarket where I was earning the necessary money.

While the main body of the EE Delta seemed in general to be shaping up quite nicely, the metal tail-plate was proving to be a potentially lethal weapon. A spiky shape with jagged, pointy edges, it threatened to slash the wrist of anyone approaching the guitar without gardening gloves, and required endless hours of filing and buffing to take the bite out of its snappy form. The blue perspex scratch plate was more fun, cut with a hot wire which sliced through the plastic with ease. Everything was coming together. Except for the pickups . . .

According to the EE article, homemade pickups were actually a fairly straightforward proposition involving (as we have seen) a magnet, six small metal poles and a lengthy piece of wire wrapped around the whole in a coil formation. The problem was that winding the coil required a level of precision which was way beyond my clumsy capabilities. God only knows how George Beauchamp did this with a sewing machine! Imagine if you had a reel of cotton which you first unwound and then attempted to rewind by hand. Chances are that by the time you'd gotten all the cotton *back* on the reel, it would be four times its original size, an ungainly, unwieldy ball of raggedy intertwined thread. The same was true of my botched attempt at building a homemade pickup; by the time I'd got the right length of wire wrapped around the magnets, it was the size of a football and simply wouldn't fit into the hole allotted for it by the designs. Worse still, it was pathetically quiet, yet still extremely buzzy, making it sound as though you were trying to play 'Don't Fear the Reaper' on a food blender. After months of winding and *un*winding and then *re*winding the wretched thing, I simply gave up and bought a pair of cheap pickups, thereby doubling the cost of the guitar. The extra expense hurt, but at least the guitar *worked*. In fact, it sounded pretty damned good. To me, anyway.

By the time the guitar was finished, The Spark Plugs had long gone their separate ways. According to Dave, it all got a bit messy. He remembers being told that the group was disbanding, only for us to reform the next day *without him*. I have no memory of this happening, but it's definitely a trick that school bands pulled on a fairly regular basis. My own memory is that no one in The Spark Plugs wanted to be in a band with me playing electric guitar – particularly not a *homemade* electric guitar built by someone who was clearly desperate to be in Slade. This was perfectly understandable: while the Delta shape had seemed like a really cutting-edge idea when I started building my axe, by the time I finished it two years later, it just looked a bit naff. By then, the world had turned its back on glam rock and adopted the stripped-down ethos of punk. There I was, brandishing an instrument that was out of date before it was even finished.

I couldn't play it either.

So that was that.

The only surviving photo of my home made Delta.
Note the art easel microphone stand.

The first band in which my homemade Delta finally made an appearance went by the improbably upbeat name of The Tigers. The driving force in the group was a wry young man called Chris who played piano far better than I ever could and read exotic literature by foreign authors of whom I had never heard. Inevitably, Chris had no time whatsoever for my childish infatuation with Slade, preferring the altogether hipper sound of The Doors, whose music I was duly instructed to study. The first song The Tigers learned to play was 'I Looked at You', a poppy Doors hit over which I played an almost comedically simple guitar riff. We rehearsed it at the home of Chris's best friend Hugh whom we'd roped in on vocals because he looked great and had a very sharp sense of humour. It was Hugh who first introduced me to Yachts, the band whose snappy pop songs I would shamelessly attempt to rip off for decades to come. I remember very clearly sitting in Hugh's living room and listening to the first Yachts single 'Suffice to Say' and wondering how many of the notes and words I'd have to change in order to pass it off as an original composition. A few years later, I wrote a song called 'Something to Say' which sounded *nothing* like 'Suffice to Say', but *everything* like 'Easy to Please', a track from the eponymously entitled first Yachts album. To this day, Yachts remain one of my favourite bands of all time. Their career may have been comparatively short-lived (they broke up in the early eighties) and their fame less than stellar, but I'm pretty sure that almost every song I have written since 1977 has stolen *something* from their immaculate back catalogue.

As for The Tigers, Chris remained the band's primary songwriter and I was in awe of his talent. I struggled to get my clumsy fingers around the fiddly guitar parts he wrote for songs like 'Kiss You' and 'Patricia', but it seemed worth the effort because both were clearly going to be Top Twenty hits. Our bassist, Jon, was much quicker at picking up riffs and also became a dab hand at writing catchy hooks. I remember spending a day with Jon washing cars in order to help raise the money to buy the second-hand, red semi-acoustic bass he would play in The Tigers. As with so many of my musical memories from this period, that one is bathed in sunshine and laughter and the certainty that pop superstardom was just a couple of muddy hubcaps away.

The first step on the road to chart-topping success was obviously to go back to the trusty school rehearsal rooms and record another reel-to-reel demo. We did this one Friday afternoon, during which we recorded a pretty decent version of 'Kiss You'. But after struggling with the complexity of that song for several hours we decided that it all felt too much like hard work. So, instead, we started recording the sounds of us knocking over piles of school furniture while everyone took turns beating up the drum kit. I have no idea what ever happened to the tape of 'Kiss You' that we worked so hard to perfect, but I have a suspicion that, if pushed, I could still probably locate the cassette of us smashing up the music room.

As with previous bands, we never actually played any gigs. Eventually, Hugh and Chris lost interest and The Tigers gradually mutated into a mod band called The Vi-Brogues who threw me out for not being cool enough. 'It's not that we don't think you can play,' they explained during one school lunchbreak. 'We just don't like you.' This was fair enough. I didn't really like me either, and if I'd found myself in a promisingly hip band with someone farting around on a homemade guitar that looked as ridiculous as mine, I would have thrown them out too.

And so I went back to my bedroom. On school nights, I'd shut the door and practise by playing along to records by The Clash, David Bowie and (of course) Slade. At some point during the construction of the Delta, I had made a startling discovery. If I recorded an LP on my reel-to-reel tape recorder at 15 inches per second, and then replayed the result at 7½ips, the track would re-emerge at half-speed, but with all the same notes played at exactly an octave below. Using this process, I was able to replay extremely complicated Mick Ronson-guitar solos at a speed which made the notation decipherable. In effect, I could play along with the band as if they were running through their entire repertoire *very slooowwwwwwly,* but crucially in the same key – albeit an octave lower. This is basically how I learned to play the guitar; jamming along with records running at half speed, bodging around with mechanical recording equipment I didn't understand, on an instrument which I would never master, but which I had nevertheless managed to build from scratch.

Years later, sometime in the mid-eighties, when I was living in Hulme in Manchester, my flat was burgled and I lost a few precious possessions. Among the items that were stolen was that all-but-valueless EE Delta electric guitar which it had taken me so long to construct. As chance would have it, I'd replaced my original homemade neck with a commercial neck salvaged from a Squire Stratocaster copy which the mod band Purple Hearts had smashed up onstage at the Marquee Club on Wardour Street in 1979. So the burglars stole a homemade guitar, with a cheap copy neck, presumably because they liked the look of its ridiculous shape.

They left behind a black Fender Stratocaster – a *real* one.

Who said criminals were clever?

So now, I just have the neck of the guitar which I built all those years ago. It lives in my office, a relic from a bygone age. I look at it from time to time, trying to remember what it felt like to build it, to play it, to dream it. Like the long-lost Delta body, the headstock is angular and sharp, and it makes the neck look like an arrow, pointing towards . . . who knows where? I keep thinking that at some point the guitar itself will resurface, and find its way back to me. In the age of Twitter and social media, anything is possible. If you ever happen to stumble across a battered old instrument that looks like it was knocked together by a teenage Slade fan, please do let me know. I'd love to get it back. And I'd be willing to pay for it.

How does £30 sound?

2

SCHOOL OF (SIXTH FORM) ROCK

Some people tell you that your school days are the best days of your life. Those people should be made to go and stand in the corner until they've learned to stop telling lies. Seriously, if you thought being at school was as good as life was ever going to get, you'd lose the will to live. Even by the time you hit the relative freedoms of the sixth form, usually around the age of sixteen, things can still be dispiriting. If you happen to be reading this while still at school, then please take my word for it – your life will get *infinitely better* once you get out into the world. Trust me.

My own formative educational years were made infinitely more grim by the fact that my school considered sport, at which I proved particularly spineless, to be a character-building activity. I was always utterly rubbish at any form of sports. I couldn't catch or throw a ball if my life depended on it, and the one time I scored a try in rugby was the time I got confused and ran the entire length of the pitch the wrong way, all the while wondering why the opposition seemed so keen to let me through. The only sport at which I showed any aptitude at all was cross-country, which I basically viewed as an organised form of running away – something of which I had experience. All this was in stark contrast to the achievements of my younger brother Jonny who was basically a sporting star – captain of the rugby team, a whizz at cricket, a dab hand at athletics and a general all-round high-school hero. As somebody once memorably explained to me: 'Jonny is basically the Sports GT version of you; faster, leaner, fitter, and generally more fun.' Some people might imagine that this would become a source of rivalry or bitterness. On the contrary, the fact that Jon and I are so entirely different has always been our greatest sibling strength. Unlike some battling brothers, we have *never* competed against each other. I would never attempt (as he once did) to rejoin a rugby match after being kicked so hard in the head that my vision became temporarily occluded. And he would never do something as silly as try to build an electric guitar.

So, while Jonny was out winning trophies for the various school teams, I devoted my energies to becoming a driving force in the soon to be forgotten Sixth Form Common Room Music Festival. Spreading itself over five days in 1980, during which gigs took place both in the lunch hour and the after-school 4.15-to-5 p.m. 'study period', the festival was basically a thinly veiled attempt to get myself a much-needed gig. There were a number of groups at school, and I sold the festival as a chance to celebrate this huge wellspring of homegrown creativity. A contemporaneous article in the school magazine *Skylark* filled two pages with details of the bands clamouring for pupils' attention. These included Gene Frequency and The Features who had reportedly 'prompted great interest from St Albans record company Waldo's'; The Geoffrey Split ('always a guarantee of fun on stage'); Secret Agents ('they achieved the unique distinction of ALMOST playing support to Linda Lewis'); and The Switchblades, whose frontman 'Gari' (nee Gary) Tarn went on to direct the brilliant 2005 documentary *Black Sun*. But the real rising stars were Small Change, a jazz-funk combo in which (according to *Skylark*) 'each member's technical aptitude is considerable'. Small Change included former Spark Plugs' members Richard, Keith and Gavin, at least two of whom went on to become renowned professional musicians – making me all the more ashamed of having wasted their time in Richard's front room all those years ago. They also had a keyboard player named Andy who reappeared on *Top of the Pops* some years later as part of Sade's hit-making band.

As for me, having been unceremoniously thrown out of one band, I had answered an advert pinned to a school noticeboard to join another. The advert had been posted by Simon Booth who was in the process of putting together a group called The Basics and was looking for a guitarist/singer. I met Simon during a lunchbreak and we bonded immediately. He had thick, wiry hair, which he wore cut short, and he stomped around in big lace-up Doc Martens boots which made him look very imposing. He was incredibly smart, a little bolshy and could run intellectual rings around pupils and teachers alike. He loved The Clash and Gang of Four and read erudite literature *for fun* (my own reading habits back then were confined exclusively to pulpy horror novels). Before I met Simon, I don't think I'd ever heard of Marxism, feminism, or anarcho-syndicalism. He introduced me to the works of Hunter S. Thompson and also to the joys of the Harrington jacket, to which I have remained passionately devoted ever since. He also agreed to come with me to the Phoenix cinema to watch a midnight screening of

"SURREY BY NIGHT"

I

A Deathscape,like milky tea
Stretched across a sulphur sky
Of features warm to number 10
Cemented on to hazel eyes.

Down alleys,in bus-shelters
Bodies stretched along the sands
Warm and wet between the waves
Rough and smooth between the hands

"twenty quid for all the night"
Or fifty Francs with ice
A promised automatic act
For the lampshade and the lice.

Angostura with your gin?
(If you're running from the law)
A one-piece on the patio
(Don't tell th em   what you saw)

II

Jackie stayed out late last night
With Mummy pacing in the hall
IFor just a look or just a taste
#Or just a touch,but not it all

But Jon was strong and firm and there
And liked the answer 'Yes'
And who was she to be a prude
To curl up tight,and not to guess?

It comes to all of us,you know—
So why not let it happen,see?
And boast of it to all your friends?
Of how you did it naturally.

A Deathscape,like milky tea
Bodies stretched along the sands
A promised automatic set
For Him and Her in adult lands.

Duncan Cooper June 1980

Acknowledgements too vague and/or numerous to mention.

This probably isn't what you want, as it has no specific chorus, and part I is well... ...well... different to part II in terms of comprehensibility... Still, I prefer part I on a purely aural/poetic level, and If you're going to choose one verse as a chorus, make it number 2. Anyway, it's better than nothing... isn't it?... (It isn't?).

Duncan.

*Duncan Cooper's lyric sheet for 'Surrey by Night',
with typically self-effacing hand-written notes.*

Pink Flamingos. After we both walked out in protest at the chicken-cruelty scene, I knew we would be friends forever.

Simon's older brother, Paul (sometimes confusingly called Harry), was in the year above me and had an altogether more laid-back demeanour. They lived in St Albans, and played guitar and bass respectively. Simon had a dark red Columbus SG copy, Paul a cheap Chinese Precision knock-off. Together, they'd been rehearsing in their downstairs garage and had become very tight. All they needed was a drummer and a singer and the world would be theirs.

Brilliantly, The Basics also had a secret weapon – a lyricist named Duncan Cooper (author of that *Skylark* article) who had been writing song-style poetry for months and just needed a band to put tunes to his couplets. Duncan had a terrific way with words and an encyclopaedic knowledge of music – there wasn't an album he hadn't heard or a rock review he hadn't read. He didn't play an instrument, and had little desire to sing. All he really wanted to do was to write, which he did – prolifically. His songs could be poignant or punky; I remember marvelling at the melancholy imagery of 'Surrey by Night' and the political anger of 'Infiltration'. Crucially, Duncan's input meant that The Basics had a seemingly infinite supply of lyrics around which to build songs – something Simon and Paul had been doing in their St Albans hideout.

In the absence of a drummer, The Basics started rehearsing in a music room at school. Between us, we wrote an infectiously catchy earworm called 'The Mirror'. Duncan had written a particularly enigmatic lyric; to this day I have no idea what that song was about, although I suspect that drugs and death (evergreen pop themes) were in there somewhere. A few weeks later, at my home in Barnet, we recorded a demo tape on my dad's Sony cassette recorder, which (for reasons which seemed hilarious at the time) we called 'Spot the Bastrd'. The tape opened with a recording of 'The Mirror' that was subsequently featured on a compilation entitled 'A Suicide in St Albans', alongside tracks from other local bands like Snatch 22, The Seen, Fae Jane and the Burning Docs and more. I no longer have a copy of that tape, but, to my utter astonishment, I recently discovered that someone had uploaded it to the internet. I listened to it for the first time in forty years. It sounds scratchy and awful, as if it was recorded underwater. But it is unmistakably us, and I think it's pretty much the only surviving recording that features my homemade guitar.

'A Suicide in St Albans' was very well received (in St Albans) and the local paper ran an article about it, accompanied by a large photo of all the bands – a picture opportunity which I missed thanks to an inconvenient bout of glandular fever. Also absent from the photo was the drummer we still didn't have – a gap which needed to be filled forthwith. So I came up with a solution. I had a friend called Nick Cooper, a brilliant pianist, who played in a jazz combo in which he delighted and amazed everyone with his wizard-like keyboard skills. There wasn't anything Nick couldn't do with a keyboard; he could make it soar, make it sing, make it swing, make it weep. One night, decades later, the film producer Steve Woolley would be reduced to tears by the brilliance of Nick's piano playing. He was (and still *is*) the best piano player I have ever known.

So I asked him to play drums.

I mean, how hard could it be? The piano has hundreds of notes, all of which have to be played correctly, and *in time*. A drum kit is just a couple of drums and a high hat, and all you have to do is to hit them . . . *in time.* A monkey could do that. If Nick could play the piano, it stood to reason that playing the drums would be a piece of cake.

I explained this to Nick who thought it made some kind of sense. Unfortunately, Nick didn't have a drum kit. Fortunately, I knew someone who *did.* Even more fortunately, this someone didn't have any use for his drums anymore, since (like me) he'd been thrown out of his previous band. So we rang him up and agreed to buy them off him for a knock-down price.

Now we had a drummer! With a drum kit!

By the time we got to do our first gig in the Sixth Form Common Room, Simon had upgraded from his SG copy to a shiny black Aria Pro II axe which looked like the one Andy Summers played in The Police before they became rubbish. Paul had landed himself a very glamorous-looking bass with a cut-out in the headstock and black-coated strings. Meanwhile, I had moved from my Delta guitar to that Westbury Deluxe with DiMarzio SD pickups with which I was going to conquer the universe. Sadly, I was so nervous that I broke two strings during the first song and had to borrow Gavin's white Fender Telecaster for the rest of the gig – a superior instrument, yes, but not one which I was accustomed to playing. It was the first in a long line of onstage string breakages which would eventually convince me to abandon the guitar and move on to the thicker-stringed double bass, on which I could do less damage – in theory at least.

That first gig had its ups and downs. We were so excited about being onstage that we chased through everything too fast, too loud and with too little attention to tuning (I have the occasionally wince-inducing tape to prove it). But we basically got away with it, and we couldn't wait to play again. Our first

The Basics play the Sixth Form Common Room. Before breaking the strings on my Westbury . . .

. . .and after, with Gavin's white Telecaster.

'proper' gig (i.e. one at which we played to people we didn't know) was at the St Albans Civic Hall, on a line-up which reunited some of the stars of the 'Suicide' tape. Backstage, we shared a dressing room with Stern Bops, whose line-up included a pre-fame Tracey Thorn (yes, *that* Tracey Thorn). Decades later, I found myself in a dressing room at the Albert Hall with a woman who had been in Marine Girls – the band with which Thorn recorded some classic tracks for Cherry Red Records in the early eighties. I told her that I had been in The Basics. She said that she had never heard of us. Hey-ho.

The Basics continued to gig around north London, sharing a stage with Dave Baddiel's new band Room 101 at the Bernays Institute in Stanmore, and travelling to a sixth-form college in Bournemouth, where we explored some profound ideological differences with the rugger-bugger audience, all played out in the key of F-You Minor.

At some point, I ill-advisedly decided that the name The Basics was too basic, insisting that we change it to the altogether less punchy Basic Rhythms. This was a mistake, as was changing it again to the excruciatingly pretentious Culture Over Here – a phrase which I had lifted, ad hoc, from one of Duncan's lyrics in the belief that it made us sound more mysteriously multicultural. It didn't – it just made us sound silly. It was also irrelevant, since everyone just kept on calling us The Basics anyway. However, it did give me the chance to make an eye-catching gig poster mimicking the front cover of a hokum book about alien invaders. A few years later, I would run off band posters based on an image from Ken Russell's *Altered States* – my favourite film of the moment. Even then, I thought I was the star of my own movie.

Eventually, Nick and Paul left school and went their separate

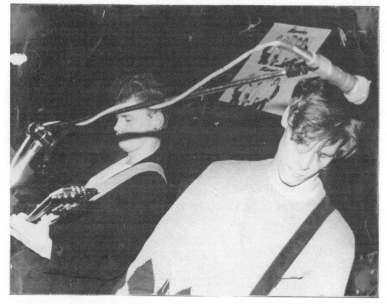

Fifth Incident sound-checking at the Moonlight.
Simon Booth wielding his mighty Aria axe.

ways. But Simon and I wanted to keep playing together, so we teamed up with Saul Rosenberg and Simmy Richman to form Fifth Incident – a band whose primary mission was to make aggressively complicated cubist rock music that would frighten people away in droves.

Fifth Incident played their first gig at The Moonlight Club in West Hampstead, supporting a band called Paint, whose line-up I believe included former members of Wayne (later Jayne) County and the Electric Chairs. Our soundcheck was thrillingly loud; the gig itself was even louder. Somewhere, there's a cassette tape of that gig; all you can hear is screaming feedback, thunderous drums, booming bass, and the sound of people crying in pain. I *loved* it. It really was impressively intolerable. By this time, I had become very fond of Tom Verlaine's band Television, and Simon and I had discovered that turning the treble up to eleven on our guitars had a genuinely startling effect on the audience. Our songs were long and unnecessarily angular and hearing them being played live was like being smacked around the head with a frying pan by an Einstürzende Neubauten fan.

Like I said, I loved it.

Along with playing real gigs in real venues, Fifth Incident went to a real eight-track recording studio in Edgware to record a real demo tape. The studio was owned and run by a Greek guy called Dimitri who had a warm, welcoming smile and owned an impressively soppy Alsatian which padded around amiably while we were trying to set up Simmy's drum kit. Dimitri insisted it was a 'guard dog' but it seemed altogether too friendly to scare off any potential burglars. We recorded four songs at Dimitri's studio, basically a converted garage in his back garden. One of these songs, 'So They Say' (as opposed to 'Suffice to Say' or 'Something to Say' – noticing a pattern here?), welded a flange-ridden atonal verse to a poppy chorus ripped off the old Motown classic 'Back in My Arms Again' – a pleasing juxtaposition. Later, we recorded a version of the old Belle Epoque standard, 'Black Is Black', which sounded like it had been put through a Moulinex mincer. This was where I felt most at home – taking a cheese-grater to bubblegum pop songs and turning them into something twisted and malformed, but still oddly catchy. The other members of the band weren't so sure, and drew the line when I suggested doing a mangled version of 'Sugar Baby Love'. I still think it would have been a hit.

Fifth Incident used to rehearse in Walm Lane Synagogue, in Willesden, on Sunday afternoons, after which we would retire

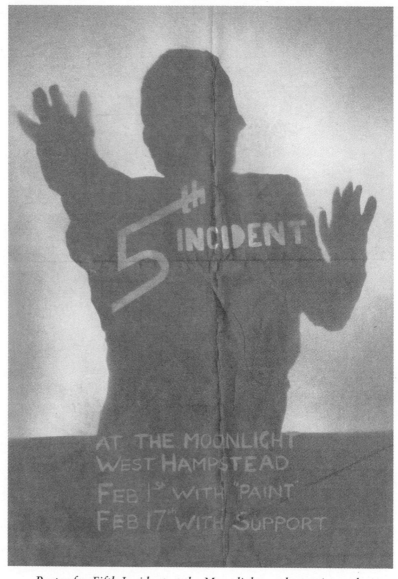

Poster for Fifth Incident at the Moonlight, and upstairs at the Starlight, stealing an image from Altered States.

to Saul's house to listen to records by The Comsat Angels and Television and talk about taking over the world. We weren't popular or successful, but we really believed in what we were doing, and we loved how alarming we sounded.

And then academia took over again. Simon and Saul were both on course for Cambridge and had more pressing matters to attend to than frightening the horses at The Moonlight, or its upstairs counterpart The Starlight. For a while, Simmy and I soldiered on together under the new name Meanwhile Back at the Barracks, but it wasn't the same. Instead, determined to strike out in a different direction, I started playing music with an old friend called Simon Blair who, by remarkable co-incidence, had also built a Delta electric guitar at school. A Stanmore soul boy with a fondness for baggy suits and Buggles-style glasses, Simon was both a bassist *and* a drummer – the two things every band needs but can never find. Simon and I used to drink in a pub near Bushey which (it later turned out) was a sometime watering hole of the young George Michael. We'd also frequent The Orange Tree and The Rising Sun on Totteridge Lane, both of which became our unofficial offices.

Simon's dad was a hairdresser named David Blair, whose 'Changing Room' salon had once catered to the likes of Mott the Hoople. I remember going to the Barnet Odeon in the seventies and watching a short supporting film in which he featured heavily. Despite the fact that he lived in Stanmore, David drove a Cadillac and occasionally he would take us riding in it up the A1, eight-track blazing Bruce Springsteen, bomber jacket dressed to kill. My mind was blown.

Simon had played drums in a school band called The Bystanders who I'd always rather admired. They were boisterous and uneven, but what they lacked in terms of polish, they made up for in sheer tenacity and enthusiasm. They had cut a 4-track 7-inch EP featuring a terrific song called 'True Blue' which included the memorably angry couplet '*A German name sounds enigmatic and equality's out of fashion*' – a swipe at the trend for dodgy crypto-fascist imagery with which some bands were casually flirting in those post-Joy Division days.

One evening in The Orange Tree, I suggested to Simon that we should form a band that didn't actually exist – that we should go to Dimitri's studio and cook something up on which Simon could play drums *and* bass while I played guitar and sang. As far as I can remember, we didn't have any material, and simply wrote a song in the studio which lacked either a verse or a chorus. But it was weirdly funky, and it was fun working with just the two of us. Around about this time, there were a plethora of two-piece bands on *Top of the Pops* who used drum machines and synthesisers, augmented by reel-to-reel tapes which would whirr impressively in the background. Back in The Orange Tree, I hit upon an idea; what if we used tapes to play a recording of Simon *actually playing the drums*? Like a drum-machine, but with a *live* drummer – on tape! We could go into Dimitri's studio and record Simon playing an entire drum set and then play along to that live.

It seemed like a skills-on-toast idea. And it was. After an intensive week of writing poppy songs with verses, choruses and middle-eights, we retired to Dimitri's studio to record the drum tracks. I played along as a guide, but all that was on the tape was Simon's rhythm section and a few random bits of keyboards and backing vocals. When we'd finished, Simon picked up his bass and we played live through the whole set which Dimitri recorded for us on a cassette. We took the cassette to The Moonlight, who listened to it and booked us on the spot.

We were going to be bigger than Wham! So we decided to call ourselves Brag!

Then we dropped the exclamation mark, because it was just silly.

So we were just Brag.

Which sounded brilliant!

Thrilled by our recording success and armed with our fab new name, Simon and I decided to drive straight to Radio 1 and deliver our tape into the hands of a top radio DJ. We weren't sure which one, but we figured any of them would do. Our tape was clearly so brilliant that it would soon find its way into the hands of a top controller. As we drove towards Broadcasting House, just up from Oxford Circus, we turned on the radio to see who was on air. As luck would have it, David 'Kid' Jensen was in the final half-hour of his show, so we knew he'd be leaving the building soon. Striding into the BBC foyer, I waved blithely at the person behind the desk and announced, 'We're here to see Mr Jensen. We're a little early, so he's asked us to just wait here in the foyer. He knows we're coming. He'll be out shortly.' The man behind the desk shrugged and gestured towards some spectacularly uncomfortable furniture. I have no idea whether he believed my story (probably not) but it didn't matter. We were *in*. We were sitting in the foyer of Broadcasting House, waiting for a top Radio 1 DJ to come out so we could slap a cassette into his hand. He would be here any second.

We had arrived!

Unlike Mr Jensen.

Seconds turned to minutes and the minutes turned to hours but still, no sign of 'The Kid'. Had he slipped out the back? Was there even a back out of which one might slip? Perhaps that's what he always did – nipped out quietly to avoid any weirdos waiting for him in the foyer. Like us. I looked around. We were the only weirdos in waiting. The guy behind the desk had finished his shift and someone else had taken over – someone who kept peering sternly in our direction. He clearly didn't like the look of us – and who could blame him? I was starting to feel awkward, squirming in my uncomfortable seat, pretending to read the *New Musical Express*. Simon was altogether more nonchalant, and I wondered how he managed to seem so cool. After a while, I began to think that maybe he'd fallen asleep. I wanted to nudge him to see if he was awake, but doing so would have been a giveaway; a signal to the guy behind the desk to come over and ask us who we were and what the hell we thought we were doing.

Ah, damn it . . .

I nudged Simon.

'What?'

'Are you awake?'

'Of course I'm awake. Why?'

'I just thought maybe you were asleep.'

'Why would I be asleep?'

'Well, because we've been here so long, and I'm starting to feel antsy.'

'Antsy?'

'Yeah, you know, *antsy*. Anxious. Uptight.'

'Why?'

'Because I thought we were going to get thrown out.'

Simon looked up.

'We are,' he said, nodding towards the desk. As I looked up, I saw the security guy get up from his chair, walk round the side of the desk and make a beeline for Simon and me.

'Alright, lads,' he said. 'What are you doing here? You've been here for over an hour.'

'We're waiting for someone,' I said, sounding less than certain.

'Oh yeah, who?' said the guard, preparing to move us towards the revolving door.

'Erm . . .' I said. 'Well, you see, we're waiting for . . .'

He stared at me.

'For . . .'

I was floundering badly.

'For . . .'

The security guy folded his arms across his chest and nodded his head knowingly.

'We're waiting for . . .'

'David Jensen!' said Simon suddenly and triumphantly. And as he did so, the doors from the inner sanctum swung open and out walked The Kid. He had a scarf draped casually over his shoulders, blue jeans and a very suave leather jacket. His hair was . . . blond. But not blond like ordinary blond. Like David Soul blond. Or like David Bowie in *Merry Christmas, Mr Lawrence*. It shone. And bounced. Bounced and shone. In blond. For a moment, I was utterly dazzled, and a little dizzy.

Simon was less star-struck; he headed straight for our prey.

'Mr Jensen,' he said, extending his hand in a businesslike fashion.

'The Kid!' I squeaked, sounding like a twelve-year-old teenybopper.

He stopped and smiled.

'David,' he said, shaking Simon's hand, marvellously unfazed.

I ran towards him, desperate to receive a similarly warm greeting.

'Mister The Kid David!' I squealed.

'David,' Simon corrected me.

'Sorry, *David*,' I mumbled.

'Can I help you?' Mr The Kid David asked politely.

'We've brought you a tape,' said Simon.

The Kid continued smiling politely. Presumably this happened to him all the time.

'And you are . . .?' he asked.

'Brag!' I barked, suddenly reinstating that excised exclamation mark.

'Pardon?' said Mr The Kid.

'Brag!' I said again. 'We're Brag!'

I held out the cassette tape, upon which was scrawled the word 'Brag' (without the exclamation mark).

'See?' I burbled. 'Brag!' (It was back again.) 'We're Brag! Him and me. Simon and Mark. We're Brag!'

Mr The Kid smiled and nodded.

'Brag!' I said again, sounding like someone with Tourette's. 'Br . . .'

Simon cut in.

'We're a new band,' he explained. 'Called Brag [gone again]. And we've just recorded a demo and we really wanted you to hear it first because we really love your show and we know how much you love new music. So we'd really like you to listen to our tape . . .'

'By Brag!' I interjected.

'Yes, by us, and then maybe see if you like it.'

Mr The Kid David looked down at the scruffy cassette, of which he had doubtless seen millions.

'Well, thank you,' he said, in a voice that sounded even more wonderfully transatlantic in person than it did on the radio.

'Thank *you*,' said Simon.

'And you,' The Kid said, nodding towards me.

'Brag!' I said again.

'Right,' said The Kid. 'I look forward to listening to it.'

'You can play it in the car,' Simon suggested. 'You know, things always sound better in the car.'

The Kid smiled, and said, 'Yes, they do.'

There was an awkward pause.

'Brag!' I said again.

'Well, nice to meet you,' said Mr The Kid. He started walking towards the revolving doors, exchanging some pleasantries with the security guy and generally oozing confident charm. Without asking, Simon and I started walking towards the door with him and I would have squeezed myself into the same revolving compartment as The Kid had Simon not pulled me back. Out on the street, we continued to stay close, seeing the star safely to his car and into his seat. I'm sure he appreciated it.

'Well, bye now,' he said, as he started the engine, which purred in impressively successful tones.

'Bye!' we said, not moving.

He put the car in gear; as he pulled away, he waved the cassette at us out of the window.

'Do you think he'll listen to it?' I asked.

'He's sure to,' said Simon.

And with that, we headed off to The Orange Tree, aglow with our success, and ready to rock the world.

Brag at the Moonlight.

Brag's first gig was the best gig we would ever do. The tape worked perfectly, the songs were short and sweet, and the audience heaved a sigh of elated relief that we were playing music you could actually dance to. As an encore, we did the Box Tops standard, 'The Letter', and everyone cheered and whooped with delight. After the gig, an old friend came up to me and said, 'That's brilliant. You've dispensed with the issue of ever having to soundcheck a drum kit ever again. Genius!' I hadn't realised it at the time, but he was absolutely right. The best thing about Brag was that we'd been able to spend thirty minutes soundchecking the vocals and bass, rather than scrabbling around in the few remaining seconds left after miking and checking an entire bloody drum kit. We'd already done that – back in Dimitri's studio. All we had to do was give the soundman a jack lead out of the back of the reel-to-reel tape recorder and tell him to plug it in and turn it on. This took ten seconds tops. After which, we could concentrate on making everything else sound lovely.

If you've never heard a drum kit being soundchecked, think yourself lucky. It is a peculiarly horrible form of torture which involves the drummer methodically hitting every skin and cymbal one by one, over and over again, while the soundman attempts to make each thud sound like the drum solo from Led Zeppelin's 'Rock and Roll'. It can go on for hours and the result is always the same – it sounds like a drum kit, only louder. As if anyone ever needed a drum kit to be *louder*!

Because of the horror of drum soundchecks, rock music is full of anti-drummer jokes, such as:

Q: What do you call someone who hangs around with
   musicians?
A: A drummer.

Q: What do you call a drummer without a girlfriend?
A: Homeless.

Q: How do you know if there's a drummer at your
   door?
A: They knock three times then come in late.

Q: How do you know if the drum-riser is level?
A: Equal amounts of drool come out of either side of
   the drummer's mouth.

Q: How do you make a drummer happy?
A: Who cares?

And so on.

Frankly, this is all a bit rich when one considers how much a good or bad drummer can make or break a band. But sound-checks are always stressful, and there are only so many times you can hear someone hitting a floor-tom without wanting to do them physical harm. It's hard being a drummer. But it's even harder being *with* a drummer.

Anyway, for a brief moment, Brag seemed to be a brilliant solution to a perennial problem. Then we played a 'top London venue' and it all fell apart.

The venue in question effectively operated a 'pay-to-play' system – a racket upon which the Musicians' Union had quite rightly clamped down. The way it worked was that you got a booking, but *you* had to sell the tickets. If you sold enough tickets, you'd make a minuscule profit. But if you sold less than fifty, you'd have to pay the venue to cover their alleged 'loss'. Either way, the management made a profit at zero financial risk.

Looking back, I knew it was a lousy scam. But my senses were dulled by the prospect of playing a prestigious 'top London venue' and I was convinced that we could sell fifty tickets. Which, indeed, we did, after spending weeks running around begging friends and acquaintances to come along and support us. I promised them the show would be great, and they wouldn't be disappointed. As it turned out, we were *all* to be disappointed . . .

Problems started when the day of the gig arrived and Simon and I rocked up to the venue nice and early, ready to sound-check. We'd been told that the headline band would be checking from 6 to 7 p.m., and we would then have forty-five minutes before they opened the doors. But when we arrived at 6.30, it soon became evident that the headliners had a much more casual attitude towards timekeeping than we did. By 6.45, their roadies were still messing about onstage, erecting drum kits and fart-arsing around with synthesisers, with no sign of the band themselves. Come 7 p.m., and the headliners were still nowhere near ready to soundcheck, and were now starting to eat into our time. The minutes ticked by, and Simon and I were starting to panic. We had to set up the reel-to-reel and at this rate we weren't going to get the chance to do a proper line-check, let alone a balance check. At 7.30, I made my way up to the manager's office and asked him if he could kindly tell the main band to get off the stage so we could do the soundcheck which our contract guaranteed. He looked at me, laughed and went back to scratching his scrotum through the too-tight Levis over which his saggy beer belly hung. 'Not my problem,' he explained dismissively. 'Sort it out between yourselves . . .'

I went back downstairs to where the headliners were still making a nuisance of themselves and tried to explain that they needed to finish because they'd already taken up most of our soundchecking time. 'Who are you?' asked someone who may or may not have been in the band.

'We're the support band,' I explained.

'Support band?' he exclaimed. 'We haven't got a support band.'

'Yes you have,' I replied. '*We* are the support band. We have sold a load of tickets and there's a bunch of people coming to see *us* in about twenty minutes so we need to soundcheck. *Now!*'

He laughed. 'Yeah, well we're not finished yet. So get lost . . .'

By 8 p.m., they were still not finished, and as the doors opened, a group of around sixty of our staunchest supporters filed into what now looked like the pit it actually was. For half an hour, they were treated to the headliners soundchecking their drum kit, an endurance test I would not have wished upon anybody. Then, at around 8.30, they shambled offstage, announcing, 'We'll be back at 9.' And that was it.

With a mixture of embarrassment and rage, Simon and I shuffled our meagre equipment onto the stage, plugged in the tape recorder and attempted to play.

One of the great things about live musicians is that they can usually manage to play along whatever the circumstances and work round unforeseen hiccups and mishaps. But a tape recorder is just a tape recorder and no matter what's happening onstage, it just plays what's on the tape. So by the time the PA guy finally got the machine wired to the speakers, it was halfway through the third song of our seven-song set. Also, it sounded awful because we hadn't had the chance to balance it. Plus, Simon's bass didn't work because it hadn't been plugged in. Plus, my guitar was out of tune because we hadn't had time to tune up. Plus, I was really pissed off . . .

And so, in what would be a harbinger of how the rest of my life was going to go, I decided to down tools, mount a soapbox and call for a revolution.

I cannot remember exactly what I said, and to the best of my knowledge, there is no taped evidence of that terrible gig. But in a nutshell, I told the audience that they had all been ripped-off by the bastard management of this bastard club who were running a bastard racket which needed to be shut down. Bastards. I instructed them to head directly to the bastard box office and demand their bastard money back. I also threw in some colourful descriptions of the bastard headliners who were about to come back onstage and bore the bastarding shit out of everyone with their perfectly soundchecked bastard drum kit. In a final flourish, I told everyone the name of the bastard venue manager and advised them to express their displeasure to him in bastard person.

Bastard.

In my head, I sounded like Leon Trotsky, but in real life I probably sounded more like Vyvyan from *The Young Ones*.

The minute we got offstage, Simon grabbed me with a look of sheer terror. 'What was that? *What was that?* What were you thinking?!'

'They're a bunch of bastards and they deserved it,' I replied.

'They are a bunch of bastards with *bouncers*!' Simon replied. 'We are in the basement of their club and they have *huge bouncers* between us and the door! We are going to *die*!'

This hadn't occurred to me before, but as soon as Simon said it I realised that he was right; that we were, indeed, going to die.

'Grab the tape recorder,' I said in a panic. 'I'll get the amp.'

We scurried back onstage to collect our equipment, and it was immediately apparent that I had made a very big mistake indeed. Most of our friends were filing out of the venue, their heads hung in shame. I didn't know what had happened, but it was clear that none of them thought that going to demand their money back was a good idea. Had one of them tried? Had one of them tried and *died*? Good lord, what had I done?

As we came back offstage, a very large bouncer grabbed my guitar and yanked it out of my hand. 'I'll take that,' he said. 'Come with me.'

'Come where? Where are we going? We're leaving!'

'You're not leaving,' he said. 'You're coming with me. To the manager's office . . .'

And with that he marched me up the flight of stairs to the office where the rat-faced scumbag who had told me to 'sort it out between yourselves' was waiting to continue our conversation. The bouncer opened the door, and laid my guitar on the manager's desk. The manager glared at me, daring me to make a grab for it.

'Who the *hell* do you think you are?' he seethed. 'You come into *my* club, on *my* stage and you incite a riot using *my name*!'

This seemed a little harsh. For one thing, there clearly had not been a riot. Our audience were, in fact, fantastically well-behaved, middle-class kids, most of whom were from Stanmore and Bushey. The chances of them rioting were less than zero. One of them might have politely asked for a refund, but if so they had clearly been told to get stuffed and had promptly obliged. It wasn't as though they were smashing the place up, like those British teen audiences of the fifties who responded to the sounds of Billy Haley in *The Blackboard Jungle* by slashing the seats and cavorting in the aisles. The last time I looked, our crowd were leaving the venue in an orderly, if somewhat downcast, manner. If anything, I wished they'd been a bit angrier. But like upset parents, they seemed merely disappointed.

'What riot?' I asked, and then immediately regretted it.

Mr Bastard Beer-belly Manager got up from his seat and stood rocking slowly back and forth on his fists which were placed squarely alongside my guitar on his desk.

'Don't get cocky with me, you little prick,' he hissed.

We stared at each other over the guitar. I noticed that he seemed shorter standing up than he did sitting down – an absurdity which made me giggle in fear.

'What are you laughing at?' he stormed. 'You think this is funny? You think it's funny to come into *my* club and tell *my* audience to demand *my* money back?'

It wasn't grammatically correct, but I got the general gist. Now would probably have been the right time to say sorry. I didn't. Instead, I said: '*Our* audience.'

Silence.

'What?'

'They were *our* audience. *We* brought them along. They bought tickets to see *us*. And we were meant to have a sound-check. It was in the contract. But we didn't because that other band took so long setting . . .'

'SHUT UP!' he screamed, cutting me off in my complaint. 'SHUT YOUR MOUTH YOU PIECE OF SHIT. SHUT THE *FUCK* UP!'

I shut up.

The bouncer, who had been standing behind me the whole time, moved half a pace closer. This is it, I thought. Simon was right . . .

Hang on, a minute.

Simon.

Where was Simon?

I thought he'd been frogmarched into the room with me. But it was only now that I noticed he wasn't here. I was sure he was here a minute ago, but a quick glance over my shoulder revealed that I was, indeed, alone with Mr Bastard Beer-belly Manager and the bouncer. If Simon wasn't here, then where the hell was he?

I looked up at the manager and felt a hand on my shoulder. Time to die.

'You,' said the manager, 'are . . . *banned.*'

'What?'

'That's right,' he growled. 'Banned. *Forever!* You and your poxy band. Banned! Got it? *Banned!*'

Silence.

'BANNED!' he shrieked.

Oh, for heaven's sake!

'Banned?' I said, unable to suppress a snigger.

Mr Bastard Beer-belly Manager looked outraged.

'*Banned?*' I repeated.

'Yes, *banned*, you little shit. You will never play in this club again. You and your mates will *never set foot* in this club again. Never. Understand? All of you. You're all banned! *Banned!*'

'Suits me!' I replied, delighted to learn that I wasn't going to die after all. 'Can I have my guitar back now?'

'*Throw him out!*' the manager yelled at his bouncer. 'Him and his poxy little friend.'

'Oh, he's already gone,' said the bouncer.

'He's banned too!' screeched the manager.

'Yeah, I know. I told him downstairs.'

'What did you tell him?'

'I told him to clear off.'

'But did you tell him he was *banned*?'

'Yeah, I told him to clear off. Because he was banned. So he did.'

So, Simon had already 'cleared off'. Which presumably meant that he'd cleared the stage – taken our equipment and loaded it into the car outside. Which meant there was nothing to lose.

I looked back at the manager who no longer looked frightening. He just looked a bit pathetic, waddling around in his faded Levi's, desperately trying to act like a rock 'n' roll big shot, while actually being just a bit of a wanker. He wasn't terrifying. He was a twat.

In that instant, I felt a moment of sublime realisation – that we were all just faking it, playing at being things we weren't. I was trying to pass muster as a pop star, he was trying to convince me he was Peter Grant. Both of us were frauds, way out of our depth, dreaming of being someone else.

I looked him in the eye, and for a moment I saw myself – older, fatter and more embittered.

Then I reached down, grabbed my guitar from the desk, span on my heels, rushed past the bouncer, down the stairs, through the loading doors and out into the cool night where Simon was waiting in the car.

'Got your guitar?' he said, gunning the engine.

'Just drive,' I said – and off we went.

A few months later, in the autumn of 1982, I moved to Manchester, where I'd managed to scrape my way onto an English Literature degree course (they had rejected me twice before finally caving in). The first thing I did was to blag a gig for Brag at Manchester University's Solem Bar, with posters proudly proclaiming us to be a 'Top London Band'. The gig went well, but the band didn't last – the 200 miles between Simon and me put paid to our musical ambitions. But it was fun while it lasted.

Simon went on to join a band named The Flowers who had a brief moment in the sun as a New Romantic pop combo with a catchy tune called 'Living in America'. I haven't seen Simon in a while, but I hope he's still playing. He was a good musician, a very good friend and proved an absolute rock in times of crisis.

As for that 'top London venue', I never went back – so Mr Bastard Beer-belly Manager was right about that. In fact, I thought of being banned as a badge of honour which I would work into conversation whenever possible. 'Banned from a top London pay-to-play venue.' Take that, capitalist pig-dogs.

Recently, in a moment of nostalgia, I decided to look up that venue up on the internet. Here's what I got:

Yelpers report that this venue has closed.

Vive le Revolution!

3
HIT THE NORTH

Before moving to Manchester in the autumn of 1982, I only really knew the city from what I had read in the pages of the *New Musical Express*. I'd devoured umpteen articles about its thriving music scene, and marvelled at photographer Kevin Cummins' iconic pictures of earnest young men looking alienated against its darkening metropolitan skies. Those pictures seemed like something out of a science-fiction movie, and I was desperate to escape my drab north London past and embrace something altogether more . . . epic.

In my first year at Manchester University, I lived on the fourteenth floor of the Owens Park tower block, which by night gave me a spectacular view of what I imagined to be a *Blade Runner*-style landscape. I loved the idea of being in a new town, making a new start, forging a new identity. This 'new identity' manifested itself in a peculiar name change (the first of many) which meant that almost everyone I met in Manchester ended up calling me 'Henry'. I'm not sure exactly how this happened. I think that it began as a joke. When I was in The Basics, I occasionally used to refer to Simon Booth as 'Strummer' because his favourite band were The Clash. In response, he called me 'Henry' after Yachts frontman Henry Priestman – the gag being that while Strummer sounded cool, one struggled to think of a less rock 'n' roll name than Henry. Someone in Manchester got wind of that being my nickname (which it wasn't really – at least not until then), started using it and it stuck. The reason was simple; every other person I met was called Mark, but I was the only Henry in town. Take that as you wish.

Shortly after the demise of Brag, I'd met up with Pete whom I knew vaguely from school. Pete was the guy The Vi-Brogues (or Vibrôge, as they became) had drafted in to replace me after I'd been thrown out for being insufficiently likeable (he was later replaced by Gavin from The Spark Plugs and Small Change). Pete had a Columbus copy of a Gibson SG ('Solid Guitar') which he later replaced with something called a 'Bamboo' – a model I had never heard of before or since. He was playing in a band called The Herbs, fronted by another ex-schoolmate named Andrew. A former member of The Switchblades (according to that *Skylark* article) Andrew was now going by the name of 'Ralph', for reasons as obscure as my own change from Mark to Henry. Ralph was a huge Gerry Anderson fan, and his band played songs which took their lead from kids TV shows of the sixties and seventies. The Herbs had a gig booked at a hall of residence on Halloween night, but at the last moment Ralph had discovered that he had a prior engagement and the band would have to do the gig without him. Eager to play whenever the opportunity arose, I suggested to Pete that I could stand in for Ralph.

I think we managed one rehearsal before the gig, which went off well enough to convince us that we should do it again. So we formed a band called Border Incident (a name we stole from our mutual former bandmate, Jon), and I wrote a couple of new songs, including one which was completely ripped off from a Comsat Angels B-side. Then, at my insistence, the band with a stolen name and a ripped-off song decamped to a local studio in Stockport and made a demo tape, which turned out surprisingly well. At one point our bassist, Phil Gladwin, ran his bass through a fuzz box which made it sound absolutely *massive*, almost drowning out drummer Stuart's impressively monolithic pounding. I was convinced that we were going to be the next Echo & the Bunnymen (whose daft wardrobe tendencies and haircuts I had also 'borrowed') and I promptly blagged some free radio publicity by spreading baseless rumours about an impending record contract.

These kind of shenanigans were to become a key part of my subsequent music career, and it was a technique that I like to think I learned from Marc Bolan – albeit indirectly. I had read somewhere that Bolan regularly exaggerated the extent of his success when speaking to the music press, conjuring film projects and collaborations out of thin air, a few of which actually came true. It proved to be a brilliant ruse that had helped catapult him to stardom. So the day after we went into the studio, I phoned Piccadilly Radio and told them that my band had a top level meeting with an unnamed A-list London record company who were about to sign us on the strength of our demo. This was all top secret, of course, but I could let them borrow the tape for an hour, on condition that they interviewed me on my return from the meeting. Obviously, the name of the (non-existent) record company would have to remain hush-hush for the moment, but this was a chance for the station to get the jump on their London counterparts.

Astonishingly, it worked. That demo with the Comsat

Border Incident in supremely unglamorous surroundings, Manchester.

Angels rip-off song got played on the radio in Manchester; people heard it and we immediately started booking gigs at fairly decent venues. Even more remarkably, we landed a support gig with (guess who?) The Comsat Angels – the band to whom we essentially owed our entire thieving existence. On the strength of that radio exposure, we'd already wound up supporting bands like The Higsons and New Model Army. But the Comsats were a step up because they were one of my favourite bands in the whole world. When I wasn't pretending to be in Yachts, I was desperately trying to imitate the Comsats and their bleakly cinematic landscapes. Despite the fact that international superstardom proved elusive, I always considered them to be the very pinnacle of post-punk pop music. As I kept telling anyone who would listen, 'The Comsat Angels are the band Joy Division could have been if they could sing and write songs.' The fact that few others seemed to share this opinion just made me all the more militant.

Indeed, I became so obsessed with the Comsats that I pretty much created a fanzine (*The Golden Man*) dedicated 'to science fiction and music', with the sole intention of landing an interview with lead singer–guitarist Stephen Fellows whose primary interests were . . . science fiction and music. The fanzine didn't really exist in any meaningful sense – I just dreamed it up out of nothing and then attempted to make it 'real' by typing up a few random pieces on the politics of author Robert Heinlein and a review of the soundtrack album for *Silent Running*, and then stapling them together. Somehow it worked. After ringing the Comsats' management agency from a phone box on Oxford Road and insisting that I was writing for a cutting-edge futurist publication, they agreed to let me interview Fellows in a hotel in Maida Vale. They even offered me free tickets to the Comsats gig at the Lyceum. With guests!

Despite the weirdness of the situation, Stephen Fellows was lovely when I met him. I was utterly star-struck; he was fantastically generous and self-deprecating. We talked for an hour or so about everything and nothing and I went away clutching a cassette recording of our conversation. I duly transcribed the whole thing – several thousand words, which made up the entire second issue of *The Golden Man*. I illustrated the article with line drawings of Fellows and co., copied from photographs of the band which I nicked from the music press (yet more theft). Then I added a glowing review of the Lyceum gig as a sidebar. The homemade mag looked pretty good and I felt really proud of it – proud enough to photocopy and staple *twenty* copies of *The Golden Man* Issue 2, most of which then sat forlornly in the corner of my bedroom, never to be read by anyone. After an extensive hunt through the clutter which now resides in my attic, I could find no trace of *The Golden Man*, so presumably they all went in the bin at some point.

I presumed that Stephen Fellows would promptly forget about the strange young man from the non-existent fanzine who had pursued him to Maida Vale. But I kept in touch with the Comsats' management company, constantly promising to send them a copy of *The Golden Man*, Issue 2, but somehow never quite getting round to doing so. Then, in September 1983, I rang them to see if I could blag tickets for a gig the band had booked at a venue in Manchester. As it happened, the venue had closed unexpectedly and there was now a Manchester-sized hole in their touring schedule.

'I can fix that!' I blithely announced. 'I'm involved in putting on gigs at the Students' Union and I'm sure we could find space in the schedule for the Comsats – maybe in the main hall.'

This was all utterly untrue. I had no role whatsoever in organising anything anywhere in the Students' Union, let alone in the main hall, a sizeable venue with a balcony and everything. But I knew the people who *did* organise it and I figured that bluffing had got me this far, so why stop now? As soon as I'd put the phone down, I legged it down to the Union, and somehow sold them on the idea of rebooking The Comsat Angels pronto – on *one* condition; that we got to support them.

To my amazement, they agreed. So I ducked out of the Union to the nearest phone box, called the management company, told them I'd fixed the gig ('Hooray!') and then – almost as an afterthought – mumbled something about a local support band. The Comsats already had their own support band, The Group, who'd been opening up for them for the entire tour. Frankly they didn't need or *want* a second support, but at this stage in the proceedings it was clearly too late to argue, so the management just heaved a sigh and said OK.

And there it was: I was going to support The Comsat Angels. And not just in my head, but in real life.

So, come 12 October 1983, the Comsats arrived at Manchester University to be greeted by that weird bloke from the non-existent fanzine who they'd once met in Maida Vale, setting up his equipment, with his ragtag bunch of mates ready to rock.

To their infinite credit, the Comsats in general (and Stephen Fellows, in particular) took all this on the chin. That said, I don't think that either The Group or their hardworking soundcrew were in the least bit thrilled by the disruption caused by this last minute intrusion. Yet having somehow willed this gig into existence, I honestly didn't care what anyone thought about it. We were going to support the Comsats, whether they liked it or not.

Looking back on it now, Fellows would probably have been within his rights to take out a restraining order against his most annoyingly enthusiastic fan. Instead, he just smiled pleasantly, made friendly small talk and even sat quietly at the side of the stage when we performed our mercifully short set. We weren't bad, but we weren't good either – we were just a perfectly adequate local band performing songs which Fellows must have recognised as straight rip-offs of his own greatest hits. After the gig, he made helpful noises about us being 'promising', but questioned our decision to attempt 'Waiting for the Man', on the grounds that 'The Velvet Underground are sort of sacred'.

We dropped the song from our set immediately and never played it again.

*Proof that Border Incident(s) did, indeed,
support The Comsat Angels.*

Years later, when I had actually become a 'proper' journalist, my Comsats-mania continued unabated. By the early
nineties, I was presenting BBC radio shows that could actually
play The Comsat Angels' records like 'Shiva Descending' and
'Field of Tall Flowers'. I also persuaded the Radio 1 arts show
The Guest List to let me do a feature about the studio that the
Comsats had built in Sheffield. Then when I took over from
Mark Radcliffe as the programme's presenter, I got Steve to
come on and perform a live acoustic set, and introduced him as
a 'god-like genius'. After years of harassment, I felt like I finally
had the chance to repay him for putting up with me so politely
for all those years. I'm not sure it did the band any good, but
hey – it's the thought that counts, right?

One evening, sometime in 2002, I was in Sheffield making a documentary about the film *The Full Monty* and Steve and I met up for a drink after the shoot was finished. After years of touring and recording with the Comsats, Steve had wound up managing the band Gomez whom he had steered to remarkable success. Having spent decades in the industry, he was perfectly placed to help these rising stars avoid the pitfalls of pop, a task he had performed with drive, enthusiasm and fearsome determination. Now that the band were doing well (they won the Mercury Prize in 1998) he was finally reaping some well-earned rewards. He'd also been doing some solo recordings under the title Mood X and he seemed to be happy and contented.

After a while we started talking about guitars, and the strange joy of taking them apart and then putting them back together again. Over the years, Steve had cannibalised and rebuilt several Fender Strats to make better instruments. I wondered which guitar he had used on the Comsats' first three Polydor albums, *Waiting for a Miracle*, *Sleep No More* and *Fiction*.

'Oh, that was a real Frankenstein job,' he told me. 'It had a Jazzmaster neck bolted onto a Strat body, and then I put a brass bridge on it to stop it going out of tune. It looked terrible, but it was great in the studio.'

'What happened to it?' I asked.

'It's in bits now,' Steve replied. 'For a while it was in the National Centre for Popular Music, on display as a bit of local heritage. Then it ended up in my loft and I took it apart to reuse for other instruments. So it's just a heap of spare parts now.'

'But it's a piece of history!' I exclaimed.

Steve snorted derisively into his pint.

A couple of weeks later, I was at home in Southampton, when the postman arrived with a large parcel. The label said simply 'A piece of history'. Inside was the neck and body of that guitar and a note which read:

> I thought you should have this, since you're probably
> the only person who understands its significance. Steve.

I just sat staring at it, as if it were the Holy Grail. The body was blue and battered; the neck and frets needed work. But to me it looked perfect. I remembered fiddling around with the constituent parts of the Delta guitar I had built at school and wondered whether I'd be able to rebuild this beauty. But I didn't have the nerve to start tampering with it so, instead, I just put it on display and proudly showed it to anyone who came to the house. In the end, my friend Paul Simpson offered to take it away and get it rebuilt. I agreed on the strict understanding that he couldn't make any alterations – that it be rebuilt *exactly* as it would have been in the studio when the Comsats recorded those albums. So Paul took it away, and a year later he presented me with the restored instrument – fully functioning in all its Frankensteinian glory. He'd done a brilliant job, tracking down the right pickups, getting the correct machine heads and steadfastly refusing to make any of the changes or improvements suggested by everyone he enlisted to help with his sacred project. The guitar was magnificent.

Inevitably, the first thing I did was to plug it in and play along to my vinyl copy of *Sleep No More*, imagining this beautiful monster playing those very notes in the studio all those years ago. I'd learned to play the guitar noodling along to the sound of *this very instrument* back in the early eighties. Now, here I was in the twenty-first century, playing a piece of living history, answering the record with riffs which I had studied and copied all those years ago. I felt like I was in an episode of *Doctor Who*; as if I had somehow created a warp in the time–space continuum and was being sucked back into the past at a speed of thirty-three-and-a-third revolutions per minute.

If you want proof that time travel is possible, just listen to a record you first heard as a teenager. If that's not a time machine, I don't know what is.

Anyway, back to Manchester in the 1980s.

Border Incident were still knocking around on the edges of pop visibility, playing a string of solid support gigs but never finding our own spotlight. Inevitably we fell apart, and Phil and I (who now shared a flat in Hulme) formed a new band with drummer Steve Hiscock which we named Russians Eat Bambi after an absurd headline ripped from the pages of the US paper *Weekly World News*. Russians actually did quite well, our line-up variously expanding and contracting depending upon the weather, but with Phil, Steve and me as the stable members. There were some disagreements over what we wanted to sound like: I was thinking along the lines of Echo & the Bunnymen and, naturally, the Comsats; Steve said he wanted us to sound 'like Wham!'. On reflection, we probably should have gone with Steve's instincts. Instead, we followed our own tails up a series of exciting musical dead ends.

At one point, in a desperate attempt to make us sound 'different', I decided that we should ditch the guitar and use *two basses*! As far as we could tell (in those heady days before

Russians Eat Bambi – with Phil on the left, Steve on the right, and someone trying to be Kevin Rowland in the middle.

Google searches), this was something that had never been done before (even though it had). And with good reason. To paraphrase Oscar Wilde, one bassist is unfortunate, two looks like carelessness. But that didn't stop me from rushing down to the local music shop and purchasing a cheap black Ibanez electric bass which I still own to this day.

I didn't have a bass amp, but I had somehow acquired a rickety old Marshall valve amp, with a spring reverb and two 12-inch speakers which I figured could take the strain. I was wrong, and eventually it blew up. But for a brief period, Russians became 'the band with two basses', one of which sounded like an under-strung ukulele. We recorded a couple of demo tracks with this line-up at a flat in Hulme which had been converted into a sixteen-track studio. Later, that same flat would become a nightclub of some notoriety. But when we recorded there, it was just a mixing desk with a toilet and a kitchen.

It was called 'The Kitchen'.

Really.

If memory serves, the best gig Russians ever played was at Whitworth Park on Oxford Road, where we were briefly augmented by backing singers and a makeshift brass section (I think this was in my Dexys period). We sounded absolutely brilliant – and for a moment I thought we'd made it. But then someone spilled their pint on the mixing desk which promptly expired and that was the end of that. So, we went back to trying to sound like Echo & the Bunnymen performing a set of Wham! tribute act songs.

Those were heady days, and at any one time most of us were in two or three different bands. When I first arrived in Manchester, I knocked around for a while in an unnamed band with Andrew Hussey, a charismatic Liverpudlian who went on

to become a celebrated cultural historian, academic and journalist. Back in his hometown, Andrew had played in a band
called The Last Chant whose claim to fame was that a reviewer
from the *NME* said that they had given him a headache. The
Last Chant had been associates of Pete 'Wah!' Wylie, which
made them almost magical in my eyes. As for Andrew, he
seemed incredibly cool and dazzlingly clever – largely because
he was.

One summer, a group of us travelled to Paris (a city with
which Andrew had long been infatuated) and busked Velvet
Underground songs on the Metro, spurred on by Andrew's
belief that it was exactly the kind of thing that young guns like
us *should* do. Years later, he was awarded an OBE for 'services
to UK/France cultural relations' and wrote an acclaimed book
called *Paris: The Secret History*, in which he kindly credited
me with providing 'backing vocals'.

Shortly after we got back from Paris, I was asked by a bassist friend in London named Simon Clarke to stand in with his
band who were short of a guitarist. Originally called White
Noise, the renamed Sketch for Summer (after the noodley
Durutti Column track) were a pop-reggae band with a pleasingly political edge. Simon was a fine bass player and a prolific
songwriter, and the band had a number of gigs lined up at
impressive venues like the Embassy Club in Mayfair. More by
accident than design, I found myself becoming their regular
lead guitarist, travelling down from Manchester on the midnight 'milk train' for gigs or rehearsals and then schlepping
back up the next night to pick up again with Russians. I quite
liked this arrangement, which seemed wistfully romantic –
alone on a train in the middle of the night with nothing but
a guitar – like something out of a Tom Waits song. Although

Tom Waits never stared out the window of his downtown train and saw the concrete cows of Milton Keynes drifting slowly by.

I may well be mistaken, but I seem to remember that at some point Sketch for Summer became involved with someone from a well-known rock combo who offered to co-manage us. This might be nothing more than a wish fulfilment fantasy – I have told so many exaggerated stories about my musical escapades over the years that occasionally I start to wonder if the whole thing was simply a dream. But I do recall that one sunny afternoon, we were taken to Peter Cook's flat (yes, *that* Peter Cook) in Hampstead where we did a photoshoot up on the roof, all wearing silly dark glasses. We also recorded a demo tape in Dimitri's studio in Stanmore, a copy of which I can no longer locate. Perhaps Simon has one. He was always the driving force of that band and I really liked playing with him, although we have since lost touch.

After Sketch for Summer broke up, Simon reassembled the disparate remnants of the group and took us into a recording studio to cut a record. To this day, that record remains the only piece of vinyl on which I have actually played. While at school, a couple of the more ambitious bands like The Wimps and The Bystanders had pooled their resources and made 7-inch singles, some of which wound up being reviewed in the pages of the *NME*. But I had never scaled those heady heights. So when Simon announced that he was going to make a record and needed some people to play on it, I made absolutely bloody certain that I was on the disc!

The record was an oddity, because there was no band as such. Simon just had some songs he wanted to record and needed people to play them. My primary contribution was to suggest that we included a cover version of 'Slow Hand', the Pointer Sisters' song which I loved in much the same way that I loved 'Black Is Black' by Belle Epoque. I had a little Tascam 4-track mini-studio recorder that I'd been playing around with in Manchester, and I'd knocked together an arrangement of the song which sounded very little like the original. For one thing, I didn't know any of the words (other than the chorus) so I'd just made up some new verses which sounded fine to me. Simon liked the recording and agreed that we should redo it for the record. A couple of years later, I found myself in a miserable club in Manchester, feeling lonely and pathetic, propping up the bar as last orders were called. There was a tiny dancefloor on which a handful of male couples had been bopping around all night without much conviction, when the DJ announced the last song of the evening. At which point, a familiar bass riff came wafting over the speakers and I realised that the night was closing to the sound of 'Slow Hand' by the Mighty Jungle Beasts. I was so bewildered that I burst into tears.

Officially, the record was called *The Trumpeting of Mighty Jungle Beasts*, a phrase which Phil Gladwin had used to describe the noise made by his favourite pinball machine in the Students' Union when the player hit a high score. The record was produced by Tim Worman, singer of The Polecats, who had been a lifelong friend of Simon's, and who also provided the cover artwork. After Rough Trade agreed to distribute the record (a 4-track, 12-inch EP), we got favourably reviewed by Dave Haslam in the *NME*, and made 'Second Single of the Week' in *Sounds*. John Peel chose one of Simon's original compositions, 'Kick in Windows', to play on his show and we all thought we'd made it. We hadn't, but it was fun while it lasted. And then it was over.

In between juggling bands in Manchester and London (while nominally continuing my English Literature university studies), there also was a brief period when I decamped to Birmingham, albeit only for a few weeks. I'd seen an advert in the back pages of the *NME* seeking a guitarist to play with a bassist called Alice Marsh. I knew Alice because she'd previously been one half of a brilliant two-piece post-punk band (along with Heather Joyce) called Toxic Shock who had released a couple of records on Robert Lloyd's Vindaloo label. Lloyd had made his name in The Nightingales, and his record label would later strike gold with the excellently named We've Got a Fuzzbox and We're Gonna Use It. They were also the label who gave the world Ted Chippington, for which we should all be eternally grateful. But to my mind, the jewel in Vindaloo's back catalogue was the Toxic Shock EP *A Dubious Deal*, which still ranks among my favourite records of all time. It's a brilliantly stripped-down affair – at once angry and beautiful, balanced on the knife-edge between jazz, poetry and punk. I think the band had formed at Greenham Common and they had something of the revolutionary spirit of anarcho-legends Poison Girls.

When Toxic Shock split up, Al decided to go solo, but being a bassist (and a brilliant singer) she needed someone to stand in the background and strum a few jazzy guitar chords when she played live. I could do that! So I answered the ad, borrowed a black Stratocaster from a friend in Hulme, and booked a ticket on the first bus to Birmingham. When I arrived, Al met me off the bus and took me to her bedsit flat where she played me all the new songs she'd written. They were terrific. They were also bloody complicated – way beyond my cack-handed abilities. Despite the fact that I'd been playing guitar for years,

I still wasn't actually any good at it. For one thing, you need nimble, flexible fingers to play guitar properly. I have hands like boxing gloves – big and clumsy – and my playing style was once accurately described as 'All the strings, all the time'. This was fine for horse-frightening rock music, but something of a hurdle if you actually wanted to hear the notes that were being played.

I realised I had to do something.

So I went out and bought a black turtleneck jumper with a zip.

This was the kind of garment that I had seen proper jazz-types wearing on the television, and it was clearly an essential part of playing music which involved augmented chords and complicated major/minor modalities (whatever the hell *they* were). There was no way I could ever learn to *play* that kind of complicated stuff. But if I looked the part, I figured I might just get away with it.

I didn't.

I played one gig with Al, at which I think I let her down badly. She was extremely gracious about the whole thing, but the percentage of bum notes that I hit was alarmingly high and we never played together again. Still, at least I got to play with another of my musical heroes, so I didn't regret the experience, even if I had fallen flat on my face. In public.

Back in Manchester, I'd fallen into conversation with an enigmatic young man named Frank who worked at the Haçienda. Frank had charisma to spare and a trunkload of song lyrics for which he needed some music. I introduced Frank to Charlie Baker, a sometime architecture student and a very close friend, who was also a budding photographer and a bit of a musical all-rounder. Charlie had been singing and writing songs for Russians Eat Bambi, and had a double bass and an impressive array of percussion instruments in his flat in Charles Barry Crescent in Hulme. He was extremely charismatic, had a fantastic record collection and was an absolute demon on the dance floor. The first time I saw Charlie dance I thought his hips must have been made of rubber. He was also a jack of all trades who was never backwards in coming forwards in offering forthright advice on any and every subject, from tuning your bongos to rebuilding your house – a habit to which I affectionately referred as 'The Charlie Baker Do-It-Better Method'. He was fiercely committed to making the world a better and more egalitarian place, a commitment which (unlike so many of us mouthy student activists) he never abandoned. For that, he will always have my undying admiration.

For a while, the three of us rehearsed together under the name No Sons of Mine, and some of what we did sounded fairly decent. I liked that band a lot, not least because I was able to hide behind Frank. Despite the fact that I'd spent most of my life desperately attempting to hog the limelight, I was slowly starting to realise that I was much happier with somebody else standing front and centre. The more I thought about it, the less I wanted to be a lead singer or a lead guitarist. What I really wanted to do was to stand at the back.

After a while, the line-up of No Sons of Mine changed and we ended up recording a demo tape at a studio in Barnet with Steve Hiscock on drums and Matt O'Casey on guitar (more of whom later). But it was Frank's band all the way, and it didn't really matter who else was playing. I thought he was a star – and, all these years later, I still remember just how sparkly he seemed and how witty his lyrics were (*with thoughts steamy as the midden, I crossed my fingers, lay back and did as I was bidden*' sticks in the mind). Like Duncan Cooper, Frank just sneezed and songs came out.

As for Phil and Steve, it turned out that *they* were the real talents in Russians Eat Bambi. After the group had gone their separate ways, Phil persuaded Steve to go into business with him – making music. Due to a weird and oft-forgotten anomaly, the Tory government funded several wannabe pop stars under the auspices of the Enterprise Allowance scheme. This scheme aimed to reduce unemployment figures by encouraging entrepreneurial types to start their own businesses. In return for staying off the dole, the government would give you a moderate financial stipend, along with some amorphous 'business advice' and the promise of expert mentoring. Brilliantly, the rubric of the scheme didn't dictate the nature of the business – you could pretty much do what you wanted as long as you weren't actually signing on. Some enterprising types, like Soul II Soul founder Jazzie B, took advantage of this scheme to set up thriving sound-system businesses. Others, like Phil and Steve, managed to convince the authorities that pop superstardom was a viable professional path – or at least it was no *less* viable than any of the other options open to them. And so, for a couple of years, the dynamic duo holed up in The Kitchen and recorded demo tapes under the name Fatspeak.

I know it sounds unlikely, but those demos were some of the best experimental music recordings I have ever heard. Ever the pragmatist, Phil insisted that Steve was the musical maestro, and his own job was to get Steve to the studio and then arrange instruments and recording equipment around him so that he could work his magic. This rang true. Steve *was* a brilliant musician, but he could also be a tad disorganised. One day, he arrived at our flat for a Russians Eat Bambi rehearsal. It was the wrong day, at the wrong venue and he had arrived without his drum kit. This was typical drummer behaviour. But Steve was much more than a drummer; he could play umpteen instruments, sing, and write songs. And those Fatspeak demos really were extraordinary. After all those years of tramping around trying to be pop stars with Russians, hearing the stuff Phil and Steve recorded in The Kitchen made me want to weep. How come I'd never done anything that good? How come I'd never managed to make music to which people *wanted* to listen. What the hell was I playing at?

Fast-forward to 2009. After a lengthy absence, the now-defunct Comsat Angels had decided to reform for a one-off gig in Sheffield, at which they would exclusively play material from their first three albums – the three albums recorded on that guitar which had now become my most prized possession.

I got a call from Steve Fellows asking me if I would introduce the band onstage. I jumped at the chance, and then immediately hesitated and said, 'What about Simon Armitage?' Simon, who was fast becoming one of the UK's most celebrated poets, was also arguably its most famous Comsat Angels fan. A year earlier, I'd interviewed Simon for *The Culture Show* about a book he'd written called *Gig* in which he waxed lyrical about *Waiting for a Miracle*. During the course of the interview, we'd gotten into a friendly fight about who was the greatest Comsats devotee. He had declared that he had a red vinyl copy of their first 7-inch single 'Red Planet', to which I replied that I had Steve Fellows's blue Stratocaster. In the end we called it a draw.

Steve admitted that they had, in fact, asked Simon to introduce the band, but being an essentially humble soul, he had politely declined. Which was why they were now asking me. Unshackled by humility, I agreed.

Reviewing the gig in the *Guardian* on 5 May 2009, Dave Simpson reported that 'Kermode is here, introducing "the most exciting night of the year" as the Sheffield post-punk quartet reform, playing the "extraordinary" songs that "invented the future".' I said a bunch of other things as well, about how the Comsats had long been 'our secret' and how the band's real fans would never 'give it up' – a reference to the final track on *Sleep No More* which had become something of an anthem. As I spoke, Simon Armitage stood in the crowd, silently egging me on, oozing encouragement.

'Kermode's claims are over the top,' the *Guardian* reported, although the reviewer went on to concede that the gig was really something special. 'Once the music kicks in,' wrote Simpson, 'it is amazing how effectively the greying men on stage transform back into their youthful selves, with clattering drums, eerie keyboards and powerful angst.' He concluded that 'The Comsats' 1980-vintage fear of the future sounds weirdly current . . .'

See? Time travel!

After the gig, I sat in the bar with Steve, basking in the warm afterglow of the evening's entertainment.

'I still can't quite believe it,' I said.

'Can't quite believe what?' Steve replied, his voice still slightly hoarse from singing.

'I can't quite believe that I *know* you,' I burbled like an idiot. 'That we've become, well . . . friends I suppose. It still astonishes me. I think back on all the times that I sat in my bedroom figuring out how to play *your* songs. And then I played in bands who tried to sound like the Comsats, because I was desperate to know how it would *feel* to be in a band making that kind of music. I would spend hours imagining what that would be like. And now, here we are, having a drink. And I just can't quite believe that I actually know you.'

Steve thought about this for a while.

'It's funny,' he said. 'All those years, you were running around after the Comsats. And nowadays, because you're on the telly, I find myself having to convince people that *I know you.*'

And then he laughed. And in his laughter I could hear the sound of my foolish childhood dreams coming back to greet me.

4

NO LAUGHING MATTER

The huge, golden pint pot hung in the air in almost exactly the way (as Douglas Adams would say) a brick doesn't. A stream of lagery froth followed in its wake, glinting in the spotlights. I'd heard people say that during moments of trauma, time appears to stand still, but I'd never really understood what they meant. Until now. Looking up above the angry crowd, whose fancy had clearly not been in the least bit tickled by my act so far, I could see the plastic glass of what I hoped was beer at the very top of its trajectory arc. It had apparently been lobbed by someone at the back of the auditorium – someone with surprisingly good aim, very probably a rugby player. There were a few of them in tonight – beery rugger-buggers – and they were particularly unimpressed with my hilarious blend of mahoosive quiff, long red Burton drape coat, oversized red brothel-creepers and repertoire of songs about falling in love with the milkman, having a vasectomy and voting for revolutionary communists. I was appearing under the name of Henry One Hundred, a persona I had cooked up with the aim of becoming a top flight purveyor of radical musical comedy, combining fifties tunes with old Trot politics and a belief in Truth, Justice and the Inevitable Decline of Capitalism. I thought it was funny. The crowd begged to differ.

The whole idea of becoming a musical comedian had been fuelled by alcohol. After years of playing in somewhat po-faced bands who saw it as their mission to 'challenge' (or, let's be honest, antagonise) their audience, I found myself wondering what it would be like to make people laugh. One evening, towards the end of my first year at Manchester University, I came across a flyer for a talent show which was being staged at Owens Park – the tower block in which, as I mentioned, I lived on the fourteenth floor. I had no desire to be involved in any form of talent show, such nonsense clearly being below a budding rock star of my stature. But then I noticed that in the small print at the bottom of the poster it said: 'Expenses up to £25 will be provided for each competing act.' Suddenly I was interested. After all, £25 divided four ways would net each member of my current band a tidy £6.25 apiece, enough for three pints of lager and several packets of crisps at the heavily subsidised student bar. Bingo!

And then a greedy thought occurred to me: what if I entered on my own? The prospect of pocketing £25 without having to share it with three other people was tempting indeed. But what would I do? Up there, onstage, alone? A couple of bars of 'Streets of London' perhaps? A painful ramble through 'The Bewlay Brothers'? No, the thought was just too humiliating. I needed an accomplice – someone else to share the shame. Someone who could command the stage. Someone I could hide behind. Someone larger than life . . .

Kevin!

Kevin was all of the above. Tall, gangly and blessed with hair that made him look like he'd just stuck his toe in an electrical socket, he was something of a cult figure. It was Kevin who had first introduced me to the obscene majesty of The Fugs, the anarcho-pranksters whose legendary 1969 album *Golden Filth*, recorded live at the Filmore East, was just about the rudest and most disreputable thing I had ever heard. (I could quote you some of their lyrics, but propriety forbids it; I think that song titles such as 'Slum Goddess' and 'Saran Wrap' speak for themselves.)

Kevin (or 'Kevin Big Hair' as he was sometimes known) had a fondness for lager, James Joyce, Gnosticism and the poetry of William Blake, and strode around campus looking like an escapee from a nightmarish production of *The Rocky Horror Show*. He also owned a genuine Gibson SG – cherry red and a bit battered round the edges, adding to its rock star charm. If I could rope Kevin into this endeavour, he could do all the hard work entertaining the crowd and I could earn £12.50 without having to do anything other than turn up and take the cash.

I went round to see Kevin.

'Er, Kevin, do you fancy forming a band to do a one-off concert at the Owens Park talent show?'

'No.'

'You'll get £12.50.'

'In that case, yes.'

'Great.'

'When is it?'

'I think it's tonight.'

'OK, who else is in the band?'

'Me.'

'And . . .?'

'You. Me and you. We are in the band. We *are* the band.'

'I see.' He seemed to hesitate momentarily, weighing up the prospect of going onstage with just me.

'£12.50?' he checked.

'Yes, £12.50. *Each*.'

'OK. What will we play?'

'What do you know?'

'Um, "Sweet Transvestite"? "Waiting for the Man"?'

'Great, those will do. Both in E right?'

'No idea.'

'Excellent. Can I borrow your guitar?'

'Sure.'

'Great, see you at 7.'

And so at 7 p.m., Kevin and I rocked up at the Owens Park bar armed with his guitar, my Washburn amp, a very short lead and a large amount of hairspray. When asked to provide a name for our act, we opted for Herpes One Hundred – a particularly childish combination of a modern popular music group (Haircut One Hundred) and a modern unpopular sexually transmitted disease. Together, we watched the other acts, all of which were slick and rehearsed. When it was our turn to take to the stage, Kevin strode purposefully towards the microphone stand. I tried to follow him, but my guitar lead was too short to make it all the way to the front of the stage and it pulled my amp off its stand so it came crashing to the ground with an awful smashing, groaning roar. Silence. Followed by laughter. Lots of laughter. Kevin and I looked at each other. This was going to be easy. I shambled around putting the amp back on its stand (more laughter), while Kevin recited some William Blake. Finally, we got round to playing a song. At some point we attempted to get into the *Guinness Book of Records* with a twenty-second version of 'White Riot' during

Ripping it up with Kevin in the mercifully brief-lived
Herpes One Hundred.

which the amp fell off its stand again and Kevin broke the microphone stand in half. The crowd lapped it up. Figuring we should quit while we were ahead, I did a big twiddly-diddly guitar finish, Kevin shouted something demonic-sounding, and we exited stage left, less than ten minutes after making our entrance.

Brevity is a virtue: always leave them wanting more.

'That'll be twenty-five quid please,' said Kevin to the bemused stage manager who handed us a brown envelope marked 'Expenses' as we made our way past him towards the bar. Amazingly, we appeared to have got away with it. But now we wanted *more* . . .

Flushed with success, and giddy with the thrill of all that loose change in our pockets, we rashly decided to go professional – to form a proper band. A band that could actually *play*. Sort of.

Some months later, while fiddling around with my Tascam 4-track recorder, Kevin and I knocked together a collection of songs with names like 'Infectious Diseases' and 'Stripey Bananas Go Round Corners'. Because we were short on cassettes, I recorded the session over an interview I had done with *Hitchhiker's Guide to the Galaxy* creator Douglas Adams for *City Life*, the Manchester magazine for which I had started freelancing. At the end of one of the songs, you can hear me asking Adams, 'Do you ever get the feeling that the whole thing's a cosmic joke, and it's horrible?' It seemed to fit quite well.

Always the entrepreneur, Kevin (who had done this sort of thing before) decided that we should 'release' these songs as a limited-edition cassette EP, entitled *Psycho Slippers Ate My Toes*, aka *I Sold My Brain*. Before I had time to disagree, he had whipped up some exotic magick-style artwork featuring a two-headed beast. He also renamed the band Hopeless, although for comic purposes this would be misspelled on the cassettes as 'HOPLESS'. Inexplicably, the Hopeless EP proved a (very) local hit; we sold about forty copies of that tape, some of which are presumably still lurking out there to this day. I don't have one myself, but I did put a pleading post on Twitter which read:

> Serious enquiry; does anyone out there still have a cassette tape of 'Psycho Slippers Ate My Toes' by 'Hopless'? Asking for a friend.

So far, no one has come up trumps but hey, you never know. Twitter has already turned up a photo of Kevin and me onstage at Owens Park as Herpes One Hundred, and considering how brief-lived our appearance turned out to be, anything is possible.

Anyway, having achieved fame beyond our wildest dreams with the 'Psycho Slippers' tape, Hopeless started to get offers of gigs. And not just piddly little parties, but proper gigs in proper venues – with proper fees, in excess of ONE HUNDRED POUNDS! This was great. The problem, however, was that outside of me and Kevin farting around with a tape recorder in an upstairs flat in Hulme, Hopeless didn't actually exist per se. Like The Archies (although obviously *not* like The Archies), we existed only as cartoon drawings of creatures with two heads. In order to play live, we would need to rope in some more people. And we would have to figure out how to play some songs.

Getting the other musicians was simple, since I have yet to meet either a drummer or a bassist who would turn down a gig for which the fee was £25 cash in hand and all the beer they could drink. This was what we were offering for the first Hopeless outing, which was booked to take place either in the usually sedate surroundings of the Postgraduate Society or downstairs in the Students' Union – eye-witness accounts offer oddly conflicting testimony. Having lured Phil and Steve (later of Fatspeak) away from other projects, Kevin and I booked a rehearsal which never actually happened. Instead, as the day of the gig approached, we simply entertained ourselves by thinking up stupid things to do onstage while remaining supremely confident that the music would just take care of itself. After all, we told ourselves, no one who came to see a band called Hopeless would be expecting virtuosity. They wanted something else – and we were going to give it to them.

If only we could figure out what 'it' was.

One afternoon, as I was attempting to squeeze a third cup of tea out of an anaemic looking tea bag in the SU canteen, Kevin bounded up to me with a strange glint in his eye.

'I've got it!' he declared loudly, before realising that he was in a very public place, and downshifting to a conspiratorial whisper.

'I've *got* it!' he said again, rummaging around in the vast pockets of the spectacularly spacious coat into which he seemed permanently welded. Out came keys, tissues, cigarette papers, coins, bus tickets, a ring pull, and a dog-eared copy of *The Bhagavad Gita*. All were scattered on the table in front of me until finally . . .

'Aha!'

Kevin pulled out a blue-and-white-striped paper bag from which he tipped what appeared to be a collection of Mexican jumping beans, only without the jumping. (So, just Mexican beans, presumably.)

'What are those?' I asked, unimpressed.

Kevin smiled – a cracked, wicked smile.

'Those,' he whispered, 'are stage-blood capsules.'

'Right. And what are we going to do with them?'

Kevin's grin became so wide that it looked like his whole face would crack in half – like Heath Ledger playing the Joker in *The Dark Knight*, but twenty-five years earlier.

'We are going to *bleed* with them,' Kevin explained. 'Can you play "Seasons in the Sun"?'

'You mean the Terry Jacks song?'

'Yes.'

'The one about him having joy and having fun with the chorus about it being hard to die when all the birds are singing in the sky?'

'The very same.'

'Didn't Terry Jacks die like a week after it went to Number One?'

'No. Everybody in school thought he did because the song was about dying. But he didn't. He was fine. Is fine. Is *still* fine.'

'Well, that's a relief. I think there's an earlier version by Jacques Brel which is meant to be much better.'

'Quite possibly,' said Kevin, 'but not half as good as the version we are going to do. Which is going to be *magnificent*!'

And it was . . .

Fast-forward to the night of the gig. The room was packed, the air was sweaty, and the crowd was pleasantly drunk. Backstage, Kevin put a motorcycle crash helmet onto his head and prepared to skateboard his way into legend. Someone had managed to procure a Mole Fogger which produced copious amounts of smoke, from the midst of which came the sounds of me murdering 'Also sprach Zarathustra' on the French horn. Phil and Steve lurked in the gloom, fiddling with drums and amplifiers, turning everything up to eleven.

Enter Kevin!

He removed the motorcycle helmet. His hair looked madder than ever. He scanned the skies with rainbow eyes, presumably seeing machines of every shape and size.

'Good evening!' he boomed. 'WE. ARE. HOPELESS!'

At which point (and to our great surprise) the band launched into a surprisingly tight and excruciatingly loud rendition of 'Since You Been Gone', the Russ Ballard chugger which had become an unexpected hit for Rainbow during their delight-fully naff (and inevitably short-lived) Graham Bonnet era. We hadn't rehearsed the song; in fact, I don't think we had ever played it before. But everyone knew it since it was on hard rotation on the Students' Union jukebox, along with David Bowie's 'Modern Love' and Bruce Springsteen's 'Dancing in the Dark'. All of these were guilty pleasures – tunes for which I professed a hip *NME*-style disdain ('commercial crap'), but which I secretly enjoyed every time they came on the jukebox. And having bashed out the first few chords of 'Since You Been Gone', I was delighted to find everyone else dutifully joining in, as if we'd been playing it for years.

To be honest, we could have been playing anything. My guitar was so loud and the PA so horrible that all the audience heard was an eardrum-busting shriek of white noise drenched in feedback and awash with distortion. No one cared; they were just transfixed by the sight of Kevin spider-walking around the stage in his massive boots and generally being splendidly strange. As the song ended, I realised that at least *some* of the awful racket was not us but the sound of the crowd, laughing and shouting and having a beery good time. They all seemed happy.

We would soon put a stop to that.

Stomping heavily on the tremolo pedal of the groaning Marshall valve amp which would blow up only a few weeks later, I played the first few notes of 'Seasons in the Sun'.

Dang Dang Dang Doooong (wobble wobble wobble).
Dang Dang Dang Doooong (wobble wobble wobble).
Dang Dang Dang Ding!

'*Goodbye to you my trusted friend,*' sang Kevin, in an oddly affecting and melancholy baritone.

The crowd was momentarily hushed at this quieter turn of events. Then a few titters of recognition broke out as Kevin proceeded to groan his way through the verse of this maudlin classic, with its wistful tales of climbed trees and skinned knees, leading up to the fateful line:

'*Goodbye my friend it's hard to DIE!*'

And that was when it began. Under Kevin's evil instructions, I had been copiously salivating into a stage-blood capsule that I had secreted at the back of mouth just before we came on. The capsule was small, but when moistened in the warm caverns of one's gums, it allegedly produced a sufficient amount of the old red red krovvy to be visible from the back of the stalls. Personally, I doubted that the effect was going to be as impressive as advertised, so not only had I used two capsules rather than one, I'd also been industriously chewing all the way through 'Since You Been Gone' in order to work up a full theatrical display. I had planned to just open the side of my mouth and allow a trickle of blood to drip down my chin as Kevin sang about how hard it was to die. But at the last minute, I decided it would be more effective to cough, thus adding drama to the moment.

So as Kevin made his mournful way towards the chorus, I came and stood alongside him, gazing balefully at the audience . . . and I coughed.

The result was quite spectacular. Imagine that moment in *Jaws* when the shark devours the kid on the lilo and the water turns a frothy red. Now take away the shark, the kid, the lilo and, most importantly, the water. Just hold the image of frothy redness in your mind. Then imagine that foamy spray spewing explosively out of my mouth, and then splattering its way through the air above the stage and straight onto the faces of the front row. There was an audible intake of breath, as if the whole audience had gasped in unison. A few squeals of 'Ewww!' and 'Eurghh!' and 'Aargh!' But mainly, just stunned silence.

And then Kevin started bleeding too. Having deftly palmed a blood capsule into his mouth between lines, he began to haemorrhage his way through the chorus of the seventies chart topper. As the lyrics told of birds singing sweetly in the sky, blood splashed down Kevin's front, covering his chin. Words like 'spring' and 'pretty' proved particularly splashy, the letter 'p' producing spectacular explosions of crimson spray.

'*We had JOY, we had FUN, we had SEASONS IN THE SUN!*' screamed Kevin and I in unison, now looking like extras from some horrible Italian cannibal movie. The floor was awash with slimy red drool, a sea of sticky nastiness. Some of the audience sang along; others turned away in disgust. I think I saw someone weeping.

I honestly don't remember much else about the gig after that. I am reliably assured that we did play some other songs, including The Fugs' Country and Western heartbreaker 'My Baby Done Left Me (And I Feel Like Homemade Shit)'. But all anyone talked about afterwards was 'that Terry Jacks moment' – the moment when Hopeless did something outrageous enough to ensure that their next engagement would be in a larger venue to an even more expectantly pissed-up crowd.

'What the hell did you *do*?' asked Rob, the events manager who had booked us, before insisting that we did it again as soon as possible. Although my memory is now cloudy, I am reliably informed that for our second gig, Hopeless shared a bill with Julian Clary who was then performing as The Joan Collins Fan Club with Fanny the Wonder Dog. By the time we got to our third outing at the Solem bar, the moment had passed – at least for me. We certainly played better, but somehow that just undermined the gag. At one point, during a particularly rousing version of 'Smoke on the Water', I climbed up on the PA stack, ripped open the front of my bloodied T-shirt, and then stood there with my fist in the air – full guitar hero – while the drunken crowd cheered. Later, I admitted ashen-faced to Kevin that this was the moment when I thought: 'Oh my God, I'm not taking the piss – I actually *mean* this!' It was time for me to stop.

The one thing that does still make me laugh about that Solem Bar gig is the memory of our good friend Mike, a bearded mature student who had served as a journalist in Northern

Ireland and whom we had roped in to spice up the act. Mike was cast as our roadie (codename: 'Useless Hopeless') whose job it was to crawl around onstage with the crack of his arse showing above the waistband of his Levi's, knocking over microphone stands and unplugging amplifiers at moments of great inconvenience. Mike was very good at doing this and Kevin and I found his performance absolutely hilarious, although I think the subtleties were lost on the wider audience.

As the gig came to an end, I decided to grab my very own Ziggy Stardust moment. 'Not only is this the last show of the tour,' I announced, 'but it's the last show we'll ever do!'

Silence.

'No it isn't!' said Kevin.

Huge cheers!

Oh well.

As it turned out, it was simply the last show that I would do with Hopeless. The band carried on very successfully without me, playing a number of increasingly large gigs to adoring crowds. Crucially, they got in a guitarist named John Pardue who could actually play (he went on to become an award-winning cinematographer) and got quite slick, in an anarchic way. As for me, I decided to retreat to my bedroom and try to write some material that I could perform on my own, in smaller venues, with less noise and fewer blood capsules.

And more politics.

In retrospect, the politics may have been a mistake. But it seemed very important to me at the time. Around the edges of making music, watching films and studying English Literature, I had become something of an old Trot. This was not unusual in Manchester in the mid-eighties; years of hard-line Tory rule had driven many towards the far left, eager for something – *anything* – that offered an antidote to the cocktail of greed and prejudice upon which our leaders seemed drunk. My political education had begun when Simon Booth gave me a copy of George Jackson's prison letters, *Soledad Brother*, when we were in The Basics. By the mid eighties, I had become actively involved in a number of equal rights battles and anti-deportation campaigns, and felt a burning need to change the world through the medium of showing off in public. I'd seen an alternative theatre/cabaret act called The Joeys who did musical stand-up deconstructing masculine stereotypes. Trust me; it was a lot funnier than that sounds. The Joeys played sell-out shows at the Edinburgh Festival and wound up being interviewed by Joan Bakewell on *Newsnight*. One of their members was Robert Llewellyn who would go to star as Kryten in *Red Dwarf*.

Years later, I would fall in love with The Panic Brothers, a duo who looked and sounded like The Everly Brothers but with a post-punk twist. One summer, I shared a performance space with The Panic Brothers at Edinburgh, alternating shows at the Pleasance Theatre. Night after night, I would sit there studying their act, marvelling at their musical brilliance, mesmerised by their comic timing. Each night, they would end their show with a song called 'I've Forgotten What It Is That I Was Drinking to Forget', which was both beautiful and heartbreaking – in equal measure funny and sad. I loved that song, and after several tequila slammers with Reg and Richard (the brothers Panic) I told them that I adored it above all other songs.

'Then *have* it!' said Richard – an offer that I was inclined to take at face value. To this day, I still play that song when sitting alone at home with a large whiskey and it never fails to work its melancholy magic.

Meanwhile, back in Manchester, I set about concocting my own alternative cabaret/musical comedy act in the vain hope that I could become as witty as The Joeys and wind up being interviewed by Joan Bakewell. I listened to *True Love Stories*, the album that Manchester Polytechnic alumnus Graham Fellows had recorded under his Jilted John persona, deciding that I needed to create a fictional character. This would give me something to hide behind, but more importantly it would elevate whatever nonsense I was serving up to the level of 'theatre'. No longer would I be just someone prancing around in pursuit of a cheap laugh. This would be performance art. I might even get an equity card.

My first instinct was simply to stand onstage dressed as an old ted (I owned an extensive collection of drapes and brothel creepers) and sing six verses of 'The Internationale' a capella – in Russian! This struck me as both hilarious and provocative, and I probably would have done it had fear not got the better of me. In the end, I was just too scared to give that idea a go, something I still regret.

Instead, I bought an old-fashioned-looking red Epiphone guitar from some bloke in the Students' Union and started writing songs that combined whimsical romance with hardline revolutionary communism – and jokes. Charlie Baker took photographs of me dressed as a member of Showaddywaddy, pulling open my shirt in a Superman style to reveal a hammer and sickle logo beneath, and making ironic peace-signs with the aforementioned guitar. *Et voila!* Henry One Hundred was born!

My first gig as Henry One Hundred was at the Solem Bar in the Students' Union, the same place that Hopeless had gone down a storm only a few months earlier. The audience were

*The 'Superman' shot – vest
(and pic) courtesy of Charlie Baker.*

pliable, enthusiastic and essentially onside. A satirical ballad about Manchester Police Chief James Anderton (who was famously on first-name terms with God and thought people with HIV/AIDS were 'swirling in a human cess-pit of their own making') proved a crowd-pleasing highlight, after which I figured I had gotten this musical stand-up comedy thing nailed. I did a few more gigs in Manchester, again to wholly sympathetic crowds, all of whom seemed to share the same right-on socio-political views and affiliations.

At a gig in London, I expanded my repertoire to include a version of the tear-jerking standard 'Old Shep', featuring an Action Man, his plastic dog and a bucket of water. Having always had a soft spot for ludicrous sentimentality, I figured it would be fun to sing this Red Foley classic (a favourite of Elvis, Hank Williams, Johnny Cash et al) while illustrating the song line by line through the medium of puppetry. The song itself is an irresistible tale of a young boy and his faithful hound, gaily bounding over hills and meadows, both so full of life. But danger lurks in verse two, as we learn of an incident 'at the old swimmin' hole' where the boy would have drowned had his trusted mutt not jumped in and rescued him. To illustrate this dramatic turn of events, I produced a bucket of water into which Action Man and his dog were duly plunged, amid much theatrical splashing.

Things take an even darker turn in verse three as the ageing Shep's eyes start growing dim, and the doctor (portrayed in my version by a Ken doll dressed in hospital whites) tells the narrator that '*I can do no more for him, Jim*'. The fact that it's a doctor who says this rather than a vet reminds us that life was rather different in rural Kentucky, and anyone with a working knowledge of medicine was expected to negotiate their way around people and livestock alike. (Apparently the same is still true of Somerset.) What's more alarming is the fact that, in the tradition of Steinbeck's *Of Mice and Men*, our narrator immediately feels duty-bound to reach for his firearm.

> '*With hands that were tremblin' I picked up my gun,*
> *And aimed it at Shep's faithful head.*'

Much pantomime-style business ensued as I tried to get the Action Man's fingers to fit round the trigger of his rifle, something which any small boy will know is totally impossible, unless you had the rubberised 'gripping hands' model, which was basically cheating. Despite the fact that Action Man's fingers were welded into a position which made it look like he was performing some quasi-Masonic handshake gesture, there seemed to be no single accessory which actually fitted the bizarre finger-pointy signals into which our hero was permanently locked. Hold a bazooka? Not a chance! Grab that bayonet? In your dreams! Indeed, the only thing Action Man's pointy fingers were any good at was preventing you from putting his arms through any of the strapping militaristic costumes on which you had just spent all your saved-up pocket money. Whereas Barbie and Cindy *loved* to play dressing up, Action Man stuck one finger up at such girlie pastimes – literally.

So, plenty more cheap laughs would be generated by trying to get Action Man to hold his gun and point it somewhere in the vicinity of his loyal friend, before Shep was saved by the lyrical bell as our narrator finds himself unable to pull the trigger – just like Action Man!

They don't write 'em like that anymore – thank God.

Anyway, the song about James Anderton and the puppet-show performance of 'Old Shep' went down a treat, and I was starting to feel ridiculously confident about my new-found musical direction.

And then everything went to Hell.

Or, more precisely, to Hull.

I'd blagged the Hull gig by convincing some very talented theatrical performers who'd gained a cult following that they really needed a regular support act. They were doing loads of gigs up and down the country; I figured that if I hitched my wagon to their star, I would soon be stealing the spotlight and basking in the glory of a life on the road.

The problem was that I had only ever performed as Henry One Hundred to wholly sympathetic audiences – people who were always going to give me the benefit of the doubt. Sure, I'd played loads of gigs with bands in which there was an active sense of hostility between us and the audience, but that was different. That was like facing down a rival gang when you had all your best mates beside you. This was just me standing up onstage, making an arse of myself and assuming that every-one would smile and wave. It never occurred to me that they might not like me and that I would have nowhere to hide.

The Hull gig was at a venue which I had fondly imagined would be every bit as counter-culturally welcoming as Man-chester's Solem Bar. I had lived for so long inside the bubble of Manchester's 'alternative' scene that I had all but forgotten that most venues were actually frequented by people who didn't find jokes about Chinese agrarian reform amusing and wanted only to drink, shout and occasionally throw things. To be fair to Hull, there was probably an equally sizeable amount

Henry One Hundred publicity shot,
taken by Charlie in his Hulme flat.

of people in Manchester who thought I was an unfunny lefty wanker. I just hadn't met any of them.

The minute I walked out onstage, I realised I was out of my depth. Jokes about the Communist Party Manifesto which had elicited warm, smug chuckles elsewhere didn't fall *upon* deaf ears – rather, they fell several yards *short* of them. Clearly, the guy handling the PA didn't like the look of me either; he had decided that the quieter I was the better. Despite learning at an early age that the first thing you should do upon arriving at a venue was to buy the sound engineer a pint, I had completely failed to make a friend behind the mixing desk. Now, he was getting his own back. Fair play to him.

I'm pretty sure that, for the first five minutes of my act, no one in that already rowdy crowd knew that I was onstage. When they finally realised that the clapped-out old ted fumbling around behind the microphone wasn't the janitor but the 'turn', they could hardly have been less pleased. Mumbles of 'Who's that wanker?' and 'Fuck off, grandad!' wafted through the room at a volume considerably louder than my own whimsical musical comedy warblings. For a moment, I wondered whether the PA guy had actually put a microphone on the crowd, just to ensure that their voices were more clearly heard.

Of course, this was the moment when a more experienced performer would have singled out a particular heckler and witheringly put them in their place as an example to the rest of them. I'd seen this done before, but I had neither the skill nor the confidence to pull it off. Instead, I decided that the only thing to do was to carry on regardless – to block out the growing anger of the crowd and just play the set *exactly* as I had rehearsed it, as if none of this was happening. Maybe my sheer plucky persistence would win them over. Perhaps they'd be so impressed by my quiet professionalism that they would be stunned into hushed reverence. They may even change their voting habits.

Nope.

The Action Man dolls came and went, as did the song about James Anderton and the joke about how many Manchester policemen it took to change a lightbulb (three – one to smash the lightbulb, and two to stand up in court and swear the lightbulb started it. *Boom-tish!*). The crowd grew noisier – so much so that not only could *they* not hear me, but I couldn't hear myself. I was sweating badly, and I think my fear was evident. I had discovered that by staring directly into the spotlight which illuminated the stage I could effectively blot out the sight of the crowd, which provided some form of comfort. You know that bit in *Poltergeist* where the little girl disappears into the television and has to be persuaded against going 'into the light'? Well, that was where I was headed.

And then the flying pint pot appeared and time stood still . . .

For perverse reasons, I have long believed that a person is not defined by the things they do, but by the things that they *don't* do. For example, it's not the jobs you take that matter – it's the jobs that you turn down. I'd love to imagine that if someone offered me a huge amount of money to voice an advert for, say, cigarettes, I would turn them down flat, on principle. Luckily, no one has ever offered me a huge amount of money to advertise anything at all, so it's been a fairly easy task keeping my conscience clear. After all, selling out is only a problem if someone wants to buy you in the first place.

So, as that pint-pot appeared before me, I was faced with

a simple yet (to my mind) deeply profound question. Should I run, and face the horror of knowing I had thrown in the towel onstage? Or should I stand my ground, and get covered in what I hoped was beer, simply to prove a point – to demonstrate my moral superiority?

To be honest, neither option seemed particularly tempting. Whatever I did, my act was a disaster, and no gesture of fool-hardy defiance was going to make it seem any funnier. Comedy is a very binary medium – the audience are either laughing or they're not. And in my case, the absence of laughter thus far had pretty much sealed my fate. There are few things more painful than watching somebody failing to be funny onstage, and the audience at Hull had clearly suffered enough. Out of respect for them, I probably should have left the stage.

Which is exactly why I didn't.

Instead, I had what I later realised was an Excalibur moment (as opposed to a Eureka moment) – a moment when, to para-phrase Monty Python, some moistened bint lobs a scimitar at you and you feel the full regal force of a farcical aquatic cere-mony beckoning. Like Rupert Pupkin, if I was to become the next King of Comedy, then I would have to undergo a baptism of fire. Or, in this case, a baptism of beer.

Or maybe piss. As anyone who's ever experienced the warm blessings that often fall from on high amid revelling festival crowds knows, beer and piss are pretty much indistinguishable when lobbed from a distance. You *hope* it's nothing more than watery Carling, which it very probably is. The only problem is that the Carling may well have passed through someone else before ending up all over your head and then trickling gently down your back.

Ah festivals. What fun they are!

Anyway, back in Hull, the 'Is it beer or is it piss?' debate was rattling around inside my head, along with all the other conflicted thoughts about staying or going – of bottling it or being bottled.

A feeling of immense calm descended upon me that, with hindsight, I recognise as traumatic distraction. Apparently, if a bird is faced with some irreconcilable conflict between two possible courses of action, its brain will go into meltdown and it will perform a third utterly irrelevant action in order to distract itself from the conflict at hand. For example, if the bird sees both a tasty worm and a scary cat in roughly the same vicinity, rather than either going for the worm and risking the cat, or flying away and missing the worm, it will stay where it is and start to clean its feathers. This usually results in both the worm getting away and the cat getting fed, so as an evolutionary strategy it's not that effective. But up there onstage in Hull, it made perfect sense to me.

So I decided to tune my guitar.

Dang. Dang. Dang.
Ding-ding-ding!
Dang . . .
Dang . . .
Ding-ding-ding!
Dangy-dangyy . . .
Dangyyyyy . . .
Ding!
Ding-Ding-Ding!
Booomffff!

The pint pot of whatever it was hit my guitar with a thump,

followed by a hot, sticky kersplosh as its contents splashed themselves over me, over my instrument and (most importantly) over the microphone. This was a problem. Everyone knows the story of Les Harvey, guitarist of Stone the Crows, who died in 1972 after touching an unearthed microphone with wet hands. It's just one of a number of stories (many doubtless apocryphal) of musical equipment turning into lethal weapons, and although such electrocutions are rare, they loom large in rock mythology. They were clearly very much in the mind of the PA guy who reacted to the sight of me standing in a puddle of indignity by cutting the power, thus neutralising both the sound and the lights onstage and leaving me not only utterly dampened, but also sorely under-lit.

With lightning reflexes, I said something really witty and withering that immediately cut my assailant right down to size. Except of course it *didn't* because the power had been turned off, so no one heard me. All they heard was a brief moment of silence, then a few nervous titters, followed by booing laughter – a tidal wave of derision. I looked down at my guitar as something unpleasant dripped into the F holes. It was an interesting guitar. The bloke who sold it to me had insisted that it had been made by Gibson; apparently he'd read an article about how the guitar giant had produced their own bargain-basement competition instruments for a while, and this was one of them. I didn't believe him – it was clearly just a cheap Japanese knock-off of a Gibson ES-335 – but I admired his cheek and I liked the look of the guitar. It was a bugger to play – always going out of tune, thanks to some particularly tacky machine heads and a bridge which wasn't so much 'floating' as 'sinking'. But it made a nice twangly sound. And, as it turned out, it was impressively resistant to being drenched in piss and/or beer, which is what you really want from a gigging instrument.

I decided to finish my set. Since no one could hear me anyway, I thought I might as well. So I just started up where I left off, brushing the horrible yellow fluid off the strings, dusting down my drenched drape coat, and generally carrying on with the crazy communist singing.

I don't know how long I stayed up there. I felt as if I had ascended onto some alternate plane of reality – unamplified, invisible, and apparently impervious to pain. I'd love to say that it was a glorious victory, but the reality is far more mundane. After realising that I wasn't going away and there was nothing to see or hear, the crowd lost interest and starting talking and squabbling among themselves. Occasionally the word 'wanker' would float above the general hubbub, but I paid no attention – neither did anyone else.

Eventually, it was over. I walked slowly offstage and headed towards the dressing room, still trying to figure out whether I had won or lost in my battles with the audience. Like the Vietnam War, I think technically it was a draw. But I didn't care. I hadn't run away. Yes, I had been terrible. Yes, I had woefully misread the crowd. Yes, my songs were nothing like as funny as I thought they were, and yes everyone had had a pretty rubbish time all round. But I didn't bottle it. I had been bottled, and I had carried on.

I am nothing if not persistent.

A year or so later, I found myself back in London again, playing to a home crowd, all of whom were decidedly on message. Since the Hull affair, I'd decided that stand-up musical comedy wasn't my forte after all. So I'd stuck Henry One Hundred into retirement, to be brought out only among friends, if the moment absolutely demanded it. The songs were duly raising chuckles and I felt a wave of nostalgic warmth as I remembered how much fun it was to make people laugh. It was something I didn't want to lose entirely.

So, although I was never going to make it in comedy, I promised myself that whatever I did from here on in, it wouldn't be po-faced. I'd had it with playing music which gave people headaches. I was finished with songs about the deep wellsprings of misery which lurk within the soul of a tortured artist. Instead, I wanted to play something that people actually *enjoyed*. Something that made them feel good. Something like . . .

Skiffle!

Yes, *that* was it! Skiffle!

Skiffle was going to save my soul! And the world – probably.

From here on in, everything was going to be fun fun fun till Daddy took the T-Bird away.

Or, perhaps more appropriately, till the chewing gum lost its flavour on the bedpost overnight.

All I needed was a washboard . . .

5
KIN YE NO' SLAP IT?

'Hello. My name is Mark Kermode. I play skiffle. And I am not ashamed.'

According to the official BBC website covering the event, that statement was one of 'Eight moments that defined the Folk Awards 2017'. The glitzy ceremony had been staged at the Royal Albert Hall in London and featured performances by such notaries as Billy Bragg, Al Stewart, Ry Cooder and Shirley Collins. Bragg had just published a book called *Roots, Radicals and Rockers: How Skiffle Changed the World*, a wonderfully exhaustive volume detailing the rebellious power of what was now being hailed as 'proto-punk'. I knew Billy was a hardcore skiffle devotee; some years earlier I had made a film for BBC Two's *The Culture Show* in which he had defined the genre as utilising 'three chords and the truth'. But I'd been more surprised to hear Al Stewart announce that 'I *love* skiffle!', while receiving his lifetime achievement award. Suddenly, it seemed, everyone was jumping on the skiffle bandwagon, although some of us had been aboard this train longer than others . . .

Like so many people, I started playing skiffle by accident. At the age of about seven or eight, long before I started trying to build my own electric guitar, my brother Jonny and I formed a skiffle band in our back garden in Finchley. Since Jonny is a couple of years younger than me, it's probably fair to assume that the whole thing was my idea and he just got corralled into co-operating. But that's not how I remember it. In my mind, we both simultaneously decided to stop messing around with bikes and Action Men and do something more expressive, more *creative*. Like forming a band.

OK, so it wasn't a 'band' in the traditional sense – we didn't have any musical instruments and, even if we did, neither of us would have been able to play them. But that wasn't going to stop us. Instead, we got an old trestle table out of the garage at the end of the garden and covered it in kitchen implements (pans, colanders, metal draining racks, etc.) which made a loud noise when struck with a wooden spoon.

Having tested each implement for its particular resonant tone (*Bong! Boing! Crash!*), we carefully arranged them in front of us, and then stuck some glittery tinsel around the edge of the table to give it a hint of glam. Grabbing a piece of paper and a pencil, we wrote a couple of songs in about ten minutes – it's amazing how easy it is to write hits when you can't read music and you don't have to worry about a tune. One of the songs was about a car crash, for which our instruments were perfectly suited. The other was about . . . another car crash! We busked them through a couple of times and they sounded bloody awful. But we didn't care. We had formed a band and we were ready to rock – although to the casual observer it looked more like we were ready to cook. Or do the washing up.

I put a poster on the garden gate announcing the super hit

rock event of the year and we waited for the crowds to roll in. At 4.30 p.m., Mum came home from work around the same time the neighbour's cat wandered into the garden to do its business in our flowerbed. Not a sell-out, perhaps, but a 'select crowd', nonetheless.

Good enough for us. Lady and gentle cat – let's rock!

If you'd asked us what we were playing, we wouldn't have known that it was called skiffle. All we knew was that it was a joyous racket and that all our 'instruments' would have to be returned to the kitchen before we could have our tea.

Skiffle as we know it today had its heyday in Britain in the mid-fifties thanks to the efforts of British jazzmen like Ken Colyer, Chris Barber and Tony (later 'Lonnie') Donegan. According to legend, Colyer, a trumpet player, jumped ship from the merchant navy in Alabama and hitched to New Orleans, where he heard the music of so-called 'spasm' bands – dirt-poor musicians knocking out tunes on anything they could lay their hands on, from china moonshine jars to tin bathtubs. After a credibility-enhancing spell in jail (he was 'detained by the authorities'), Colyer was deported back to Blighty where he and Barber started showcasing rag-tag DIY blues between more formal jazz sets. They preferred the term 'skiffle' because 'spasm' sounded too rude. The music became a national craze when an upbeat reworking of Lead Belly's 'Rock Island Line' hit the charts. Overnight, the British public were introduced to the wonders of the washboard and Lonnie Donegan became the UK's first genuine pop superstar. To this day, if you say the word 'skiffle' on British soil, it is Donegan's warbling voice, thrumming guitar and gor-blimey trousered dustman-dad that spring irresistibly to mind.

In fact, skiffle has its roots in turn-of-the-century Mississippi, in the informal house jam sessions at which all comers would play blues, gospel and work songs. Essentially, it was a mix of American ragtime, jazz, minstrelsy and medicine shows, which built upon the legacy of jug and string bands. Early skiffle bands featured kazoos, comb and paper, washboards and bathtubs, taking their lead from Doc Malney's Minstrel Show, in the 1890s, which featured 'Slew Foot Pete', on cigar box guitar, 'Warm Gravy', on cheese-box banjo, and 'Whiskey', on a bass made from a half-barrel. Plentiful recordings from the twenties and thirties reveal the earliest roots of skiffle, including those by the Mound City Blue Blowers and the Memphis Jug Band, paving the way for popular acts like Dan Burley's Skiffle Boys in the forties. Crucially, no matter how talented the musicians were, the underlying message was simple – anyone can play these songs and you don't need proper training or fancy instruments to do so. (All of which made it the perfect medium for two under-tens from Finchley to spread their fledgling rock wings.)

In Britain, Lonnie Donegan's success inspired a whole generation of proto-rockers to take to the stage, from The Quarrymen (who later mutated into The Beatles) to young guitarist Jimmy Page, later of Led Zeppelin. In his terrifically quaint 1958 article, 'What is Skiffle?', clergyman and musicologist Brian Bird attempted to define the parameters of this new musical craze and to instruct his readers on how to form their very own 'skiffle combo'.

'It is perhaps wrong to talk about "forming" a skiffle group,' notes Bird earnestly, 'as these usually develop spontaneously and naturally. So a group of instrumentalists gets together and decides to Skiffle!' Despite this free-form philosophy, Bird goes on to lay down some quirky ground rules for budding 'skifflists', namely that any group 'should not exceed seven members' and should stick to 'guitar, banjo, mandolin, string bass, drums and washboard', with the possibility of adding 'harmonica, fiddle, mandolin, or even electric guitar' if absolutely necessary. 'And remember to keep the instruments in tune . . .'

Good advice, Your Reverence.

It was in Edinburgh in the mid-eighties that I really got the skiffle bug. Having grown tired of rock guitar bands and stand-up musical comedy, I'd started to redirect my energies towards theatre. Most of the cool people I knew at Manchester University were either drama students or people who *wished* they were drama students. I fell into the latter category. While the English students were attempting to plough their way through Edmund Spenser's *The Faerie Queen*, the drama students were showing off onstage and having earnest political arguments in the coffee bar, interspersed with drunken partying and loads of casual sex. At least, that's how it looked from the outside. I'm sure the reality was very different. Yet despite my attempts to become one of the beautiful people (I played Brad in a production of *The Rocky Horror Show* in which Kevin had a starring role as Riff Raff) I never got invited to any of those hedonistic parties, so I only have my imagination to go on.

Having no discernible talent as an actor, I had somehow managed to reinvent myself as a 'musical director' – this despite the fact that I could neither read music nor direct, let alone do both at the same time. More through luck than talent, I got roped into an undergrad production of Caryl Churchill's *Vinegar Tom*, a *Crucible*-style play about seventeenth-century witch trials, for which I was asked to provide musical accompaniment. I'd bought a second-hand Boss echo pedal from Johnny Roadhouse on Manchester's Oxford Road, the store through which all Manchester bands passed at some point. Specialising in 'new and used guitars, drum kits, and unusual instruments and pedals', Johnny Roadhouse was a Manchester institution which is still thriving today. I dropped in there a few months ago and very nearly bought a vintage Tube Screamer distortion pedal like the one I owned in the eighties, and which (it turns out) is now *very* valuable. If only I'd known that when I lent it to someone and then forgot to ask for it back, all those years ago . . .

As for the echo pedal, I discovered that it was possible to use it to make some eerie looping noises by running the Epiphone semi-acoustic through it. Crucially, this didn't involve playing notes – merely banging the guitar around and twisting the neck and the whammy bar while allowing the instrument to feed back through my old Washburn amp. It was all very 'ambient', and needed something a little more concrete to give it some oomph, so I enlisted a percussionist called Ant who made a very big noise with some equally large congas.

There were a couple of songs in the play, such as 'Something to Burn' and 'Nobody Sings', which were meant to sound folksy and weird. By the time Ant and I had finished with them, they sounded more like outtakes from Lou Reed's famously unlistenable *Metal Machine Music* – a wall of modulated noise with some pagan weirdness going on in the background. Bafflingly, this got a big thumbs-up from the theatre critic in the student rag. And that was it – I was now a 'musical director'.

From there, I worked on a few more shows, including an original play by Ed Jones (who went on to become an acclaimed author and playwright) called *Transforming Ricky Nixon*. This required writing a trio of songs that were meant to be from the fifties, sixties and seventies, respectively, and then recording them at The Kitchen in Hulme. I had great fun writing those pastiche tunes, and then conducting the assembled cast through the recording process. The end result was pretty good and I managed to convince myself that my future lay in theatre. I even started wearing a hat (a battered old brown trilby) on the basis that it felt . . . theatrical.

I have always been a bit of an arse.

All of this brought me to *The Death of Joe Hill*, a prize-winning student play by upcoming Liverpudlian writer John Fay, which started to get some reasonable reviews and attention when it opened in Manchester. Based on the life of the 'Wobbly' activist and songwriter, *The Death of Joe Hill* had loads of musical numbers like 'The Preacher and the Slave' and 'Casey Jones', all of which could be knocked out on an acoustic guitar which I played from the side of the stage – still wearing the hat. When the play went to the Edinburgh Fringe, it was described by one reviewer – disparagingly, I think – as having an 'off the back of a lorry' flavour. Certainly there were a number of tea chests involved, some employed for percussive purposes in the musical numbers. But one of them I converted into a skiffle-style tea chest bass by attaching it to a broom handle with a piece of string, and that was all it took . . .

Between shows, we figured it would be a good idea for the *Joe Hill* cast to go out on to the streets and sing a couple of tunes to drum up support for the performances. This was standard practice at the Edinburgh Fringe and frankly you had to fight to find a piece of pavement that wasn't being used to showcase some obscure piece of performance art, playing daily at 9.30 a.m. in Venue 73. Seriously, there were probably more fringe theatre shows on than there were people in Edinburgh, meaning that most shows ended up playing to one man and his dog. Of course, this was nothing new for me, since I had started out quite happily playing to one woman and her (neighbour's) cat.

At some point in the middle of the *Joe Hill* run, I met Alison Armstrong-Lee, a boisterous young woman from Belfast, with a smile as broad as the horizon and an attitude which said, 'Don't mess with me or I will punch your lights out.' Introduced to me as 'The Queen of the Washboard', Al had taught herself to make a fantastic din with nothing more than a portable domestic appliance, some gardening sticks and a rubber band. Brilliantly, she brandished her washboard as if it were a weapon, exuding rocking confidence as she bashed her way through any song you wanted to play.

Al had been trying to put a band together with Matt O'Casey, the aforementioned Manchester guitarist with whom I would later play in No Sons of Mine. Matt owned a battered Martin acoustic that had once been played by B.B. King. His parents were both actors and, as a kid, he'd been sent on hippy-dippy Woodcraft Folk holidays where he'd learned to hold his own at singalongs around the campfire. Matt knew hundreds of songs, as I'd discovered when we first met a year or so before. Both of us were going out with drama students, and we'd essentially been thrown together as supporting players in their lives. One evening, as our respective girlfriends discussed how to smash the patriarchy downstairs in the lounge of my Hulme flat, Matt and I retired upstairs and started pootling around with some old blues standards. Gradually we became 'guitar buddies' and so I was delighted to learn that Matt was up at the Edinburgh Fringe with Al, where the pair had gone to busk.

One of the lead actors in *Joe Hill* was Olly Fox who played clarinet and dressed like Tom Waits in his *Looking for the Heart of Saturday Night* period. Olly was close friends with a trumpet player called John Preston (also part of the *Joe Hill* cast) who had played with The Forest Hillbillies, Bad Manners and The Bhundu Boys. One morning during the Festival, the three of us were approached by the manager of a local venue who had a 'jazz lunch' booked, from which the jazz band had pulled out at the last minute. Seeing that we had a guitar, a clarinet and a trumpet, he offered us £50 to step into the fray – to play 'jazz' for an hour while people ate some suitably hep food. We didn't know a jazz tune from a hole in the ground, but fifty quid *was* fifty quid, so we agreed – to the annoyance of the paying customers who did *not* get what they had paid for.

For reasons of self-preservation, my mind has pretty much blanked out most of that hour. I know that we started with me at the piano, playing a fairly terrible version of 'Mr Siegal' from Tom Waits' *Heartattack and Vine* album. I suspect that we had a run at 'Summertime', since this was one of the songs I had recorded with The Spark Plugs back in the seventies, and for which I could still remember the words and the chords. And I recall (with a sinking feeling in my stomach) that at some point we tried to entertain the crowd with a selection of South African freedom songs which we had all learned while keeping vigil at the Church of the Ascension in Hulme, in which Viraj Mendis had taken sanctuary to avoid being deported back home to Sri Lanka. Those songs were stirring, passionate and politically important. But they weren't jazz, in *any* way, shape or form.

The audience weren't happy. A few of them walked out. Many more demanded their money back. I certainly would have done so. But after my experience in Hull, I wasn't about to walk off and call it a day. So we kept going. *For a full hour.* At the end of which we got paid, as promised.

Result!

After surviving the horror of the 'jazz lunch', Olly, John and I started wondering about other ways to turn our musical talents into hard cash. Having spent several afternoons trying to drum up support for *Joe Hill* by playing songs on the street, wouldn't it be better to do the same thing in support of our own pockets? After all, if you were going to sing for your supper anywhere, then the Edinburgh Fringe was the place to do it. So we teamed up with Al and Matt, figured out five songs that we could busk our way through and took to the streets.

The results were impressive. Although our first set was necessarily short, we managed to make about ten quid in loose change. A second set, further up Princes Street, bagged about the same amount. By the time we had to pack up and head for the theatre to do the evening performance of *Joe Hill*, we'd made around forty quid – which seemed pretty good at the time. There was a problem, however. During the course of the afternoon, I had broken every single string on the acoustic guitar I was using, and the cost of a replacement set came to around ten quid – so I was actually a couple of quid down.

This was to prove an ongoing problem. Having never been a light-handed player, my tendency to hit 'all the strings all the time' was only worsened by the demands of playing outdoors where no one can hear you over the noise of passing traffic. Somehow I had got it into my head that simply hitting the strings *harder* would make them *louder* – something which is only true up to a point. In fact, the volume of a guitar is defined by the resonance of the instrument rather than the force with which the player attacks the strings. Also, *hitting* the strings isn't the best way of getting a sound out of them. You have to pluck, strum and generally fondle the notes out of the instrument, something which requires a level of musical skill which I lacked then and still lack today.

You could hear Matt's guitar all the way across the street; you could barely hear mine as far as the edge of the pavement.

It wasn't until we were back in Manchester and regularly losing money, thanks to my incredible ability to break strings as fast as I could put them on the guitar, that we started to think I was probably playing the wrong instrument. While busking in Edinburgh, we'd seen a rockabilly band draw a huge crowd largely by virtue of the fact that they had a double bass. The instrument sounded fine, but it was how it *looked* that was most impressive. Even when you couldn't hear it (which was frequently), the sight of the bassist spinning his instrument around and merrily running up the side of it was eye-catching enough to make the crowd part with their loose change. Moreover, even from a distance, it was clear that the strings on the bass were big and thick and bruising – hardly the kind of thing that I could break.

So, one Saturday morning, Matt and I drove down to Johnny Roadhouse in his clapped-out white Beetle, and purchased a knackered plywood bass for about fifty quid, which we then took straight out to St Anne's Square in the centre of town for a road test. It didn't seem to matter that I had never played a double bass in my life – people literally started putting money in the hat as soon as we got there, clearly impressed that someone had bothered to lug such an impractically unwieldy instrument out onto the street in the first place. Over the next few years, I would get used to the string of witticisms ('You've

Busking with The Railtown Bottlers in Castlefield, Manchester.

been over-feeding that violin!'; 'How do you get that under your chin!'; 'Bet you wish you'd taken up the harmonica!') which people feel positively compelled to utter when faced with someone carrying a bull-fiddle. But that same compulsion also seemed to ensure that they wouldn't walk by without chucking a few coins in your direction, so I never had any cause for complaint.

The first day we busked in Manchester with the double bass, we broke £100. Part of the key to our financial success was having a 'bottler' – somebody who would walk round the crowd with a hat while the band were playing, ensuring that no pocket went unemptied. Legend has it that the word 'bottler' came from an old tradition whereby someone would go from table to table in pubs collecting money for the musicians, with a hat in one hand and a bottle in the other. In the bottle was a fly, which the bottler would keep trapped in there by placing their thumb over the end of the bottle. If they took their thumb *off* the bottle (in order to reach into the hat and steal some of the money), the fly would escape and they would be undone.

It's a fanciful story, but one which we all enjoyed telling when explaining the origin of our band name, 'The Railtown Bottlers'. There's a lot of storytelling involved in playing skiffle – always has been and always will be. Mike Hammond, with whom I now play in The Dodge Brothers, loves to regale audiences with the story of American banjo legend Charlie Poole, who played the bluegrass classic 'Goodbye Booze', which we skiffled up for our own purposes. According to this oft-repeated tale, Poole worked the mills in the Carolinas, benefiting from his employers' benevolent policy of hiring European music teachers to enhance the lives of their struggling workers. Charlie achieved fame prior to the Depression years, churning out everything from bawdy vaudeville songs to Civil War ballads with his old-time string band the North Carolina Ramblers. One of his best-loved tunes was 'Goodbye Booze', an old 'temperance' song warning about the evils of drink, which Charlie would sing with a bottle of moonshine at his elbow and a sozzled twinkle in his eye. As one close friend put it, 'Charlie only ever said "Goodbye Booze" between drinks', and by the time the thirties rolled around, he was back in the mills, his health and career both failing. Then, just when it seemed it was all over, Poole got a call from Hollywood asking him to come to California and record the music for a new motion picture. Charlie was thrilled – so thrilled that, to celebrate his new-found success, he went on a thirteen-week bender and died, the train ticket to California left propped forlornly on his dresser.

I love this story (which involves a degree of artistic licence) because it combines all the themes which recur throughout the music that means the most to me: namely trains, heart-break, alcohol and death. These were certainly touchstones for The Railtown Bottlers, who started to develop a surprisingly enthusiastic following in Manchester. Every Saturday, we'd play on the steps of the Royal Exchange Theatre in St Anne's Square, alternating sets with Rob Gray's Little Big Band – a one-man-band whirlwind of Dobro guitar, blues harmonica and thumping bass drum. In the evenings, we'd go back to John's house and count the day's takings, after which we'd usually decamp to a party, where we'd be paid in booze for our musical services.

The next summer, we returned to Edinburgh, eager to capitalise on our success. We rented a single room in which all five band members slept on the floor and we kept a pretty tight timetable. In the morning, we'd head out onto the streets to play, turning anything from ten to fifteen sets a day. Then, as the sun was setting, we'd decamp to the Pachuca Cantina, a chilli-in-a-bowl establishment on Leith Walk which played old blues music and didn't mind us spreading the day's takings out on the table and paying the bill with assorted shrapnel. Then we'd go back to the flat and tend to the blisters and blood sores which had blown up during the day, ready to head back out the next morning.

Injuries were always a big part of busking. The first day that I played the double bass in Manchester, I split the ends of the fingers on my right hand and proceeded to bleed all over the instrument – something which seemed to impress the crowd mightily. For a while I tried playing while wearing gardening gloves. There are pictures of the Bottlers competing at the

International Street Entertainers of the Year festival in Covent Garden, in the late eighties, at which I appear to be dressed for a bout of extreme horticulture, gaffer tape round my wrists in the manner of a mad rose-gardening boxer. By the time we got to Edinburgh, I had got into the habit of rubbing surgical spirit into my hands and binding my fingers with micropore surgical tape, but I still finished every day looking like an extra from *Casualty*.

None of this impressed the bassist of the rockabilly band whom we had seen busking there the year before, and who turned up one afternoon to watch us play with an air of great disdain. At the end of the set, as I attempted to clean and re-bandage my bleeding hands before we started again, he came up to me and said five words which would become a band mantra.

'Kin ye no' slap it?'

'Pardon?' I said, fiddling with the strands of ragged micropore and contusions of scabbed blood.

'Kin ye no' *slap* it?' he repeated, grinning a little at my amateurish ignorance.

'Um, you mean can I play slap bass?'

'Aye,' he said, his grin turning to derisive laughter. 'Slap it, pal. Ye *kin* slap it, no?'

I felt at once crestfallen and deeply ashamed. For all the blood and bruises, he had seen right through me. The truth was that I could 'no' slap it.'

According to one popular folk tale, the art of 'slapping it' was invented by Bill Johnson of the Original Creole Ragtime Band who broke his bow in Shreveport, Louisiana in 1911 but carried on banging away with just his hand – and really liked the resulting sound. By snapping the strings of the bass against

The Bottlers in Covent Garden; note the gardening gloves.

the fingerboard and then smacking the wood with the open hand, you can effectively mimic the sound of a snare and bass drum with the added bonus of a loud bass note. It's not pretty, but it is effective.

It's also impossible to do until someone shows you how to do it – and up until this point I hadn't met anyone with that particular skill set. Ever since I first bought the bass I'd been struggling just to play the notes without haemorrhaging to death. And although I'd *seen* people playing slap-bass (I'd been going to rockabilly gigs since the age of fourteen) I'd never had the nerve to ask how it was done.

Until now.

'Can you show me?' I asked, less in hope than fear.

'Kin I *show* ye?' he replied. Then, grabbing the bass out of my bloody hands, he spun it round towards him and proceeded to slap the hell out of it, producing runs, triplets and mind-bending paradiddles with his right hand with an effortless ease that made me shiver with envy. I looked at his hand, and could see nothing but a graceful blur, bouncing back and forth on the strings like one of those Olympic athletes on a trampoline. The sound was astonishing, as if he'd suddenly been joined by a drummer who was even now hiding within the body of the bass. It was like watching a magic trick, and I was utterly mesmerised.

'How do you *do* that?' I asked, genuinely baffled.

'S'easy!' he said, before showing me *exactly* how it was done.

He was lying. It wasn't easy. In fact, it was very hard and *very* painful. I once shut my fingers in a car door, and the anguish was nothing compared to that of attempting to slap that bass for the first time. At one point, I pulled a flap of skin off the end of my middle finger that was so sizeable I thought I might have to go to hospital. In the end, I reattached it with superglue, which turned out to be a very useful 'second skin'. Later on, I briefly lost the feeling in my right hand and had to gaffer tape a fork to my palm so that I could eat. Every night, I would bathe my knuckles in surgical spirit and every morning I'd wake up with a headache caused by inhaling those toxic fumes. I briefly lost the nail on my little finger which fell off almost unnoticed, like Jeff Goldblum falling apart in *The Fly*. For years, I had been breaking strings; now the strings were breaking me.

It was horrible.

But it was worth it.

Gradually my hands hardened up and my slapping technique improved. And once I'd got the technique, *nothing* could stop me. I felt like I'd been inducted into some super-secret society – given the key to a life-changing knowledge which had been passed down from generation to generation, from master to pupil. The next summer, The Bottlers played a residency at the Pleasance as part of the Edinburgh Fringe Festival and the jazz-musician-turned-journo Miles Kington came to review our show. Afterwards, he came up to me and asked me to explain how I made all 'those percussive noises' with my bass, and then he wrote a lovely column in the *Independent* which made me sound like the best slapper in the world – in a good way.

The downside of slapping, of course, is that it takes its toll on the instrument. One evening in the early nineties, after I'd relocated back to London, the Bottlers were playing a gig at The Trolley Stop in Hackney, a venue which had become our second home in the south. Towards the end of the gig there

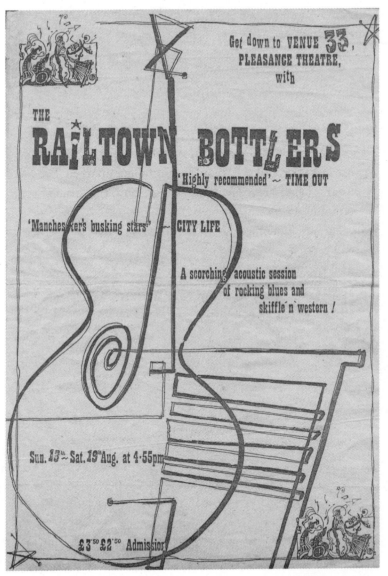

Poster designed by Olly for the Bottlers' shows in Edinburgh.

was an ominous cracking sound from the place where the neck of the bass meets the body and, a few thumps later, my instrument (which was named Eileen) exploded. The weighty wooden headstock flew out into the crowd and struck a guy with a particularly splendid quiff squarely in the middle of the forehead. It hit him hard enough to draw blood that was still trickling down his forehead into his eyes when he came to speak to me after the gig. I thought he was going to hit me; instead, he hugged me.

'That was *amazing*!' he groaned, as his blood seeped onto my shoulder. 'I have *never* seen that happen before! Never!'

I looked at his forehead which had a nasty headstock-shaped gash.

'You should get that stitched,' I said. 'It's going to leave a scar.'

'I bloody well hope so!' he roared, before embracing me again and heading towards the bar to show off his war wound.

For sentimental reasons I kept the broken neck of the bass which smacked that poor guy on the head. I still have it in my office where it sits next to the neck of the Delta guitar I built as a child. Since then, I've trashed another two double basses, one of which was actually built out of a wardrobe by a jazz musician in Manchester named Les, who had made it his mission to create an instrument which I could not break. Inevitably, I turned it into firewood. For my thirtieth birthday, I drove out to Thwaites music store in Watford where I bought a lovely old fifties ply-job which I rigged with an all-but-indestructible Selmer steel bridge. It did grand service before finally giving up the ghost just before I turned fifty. At which point, Thwaites set about building me an entirely new instrument which is my current weapon of choice. I fully expect it to fall apart by the time I turn seventy.

Over the next few years, The Railtown Bottlers became a fixture at street festivals and busking pitches up and down the country. In Glasgow, we ended up playing under some historic arches as part of their 'City of Culture' celebrations. That same year we played a late night slot at the Sidmouth Folk Festival, where we were booked to follow two bands specialising in Appalachian clog music. The crowd that night were particularly hardcore, consisting entirely of clogging devotees – real ale types, many of whom carried their own pewter tankards, with a hard crust of yeast, tied to their belts with pieces of string. They had come here to drink and to clog and, as far as they were concerned, nothing else would hit the spot. Before we took to the stage, the MC said, 'And now for something a little bit different', an announcement which was met with barely suppressed murmurs of disapproval. During the gig, I was pretty certain I could see some members of the crowd building a sacrificial pyre at the back of the hall.

This kind of musical tribalism was a big part of the folk and blues scene and continues to be so. On our travels up and down the country, the Bottlers met up with other street skiffle acts like the brilliant Railroad Bill, with whom we shared tips on how to play the kazoo and how to work a busking crowd. A year after our first appearance in Covent Garden for the International Street Entertainers of the Year competition, we had returned to the fray and this time we won, earning ourselves a place onstage at the London Palladium. Back then, there was a band called the Gutter Brothers who did a skiffle version of Prince's 'Kiss' with a tea chest bass, but who still called their music rhythm and blues. Matt always preferred the term 'Western Swing', which he thought more accurately described the kind of sound the Bottlers were making, while

*The Bottlers busking on the streets of Sidmouth
before our festival showdown.*

listings magazines regularly described us as 'hillbilly' or 'blue-grass' (we had briefly been named The Hoedown Bottlers). Years later, after I'd done that piece for *The Culture Show* on the joys of skiffle, Dan from Railroad Bill got in touch to say, 'Of course, it's not quite skiffle', and to point out that 'the real thing is on our site'. And it was. If you go to skiffle.co.uk you can still see Railroad Bill ('Lonnie Donegan on speed') leaping around with tea chest, washboard, saw, ukulele, kazoo and (in one instance) a ripping roll of Sellotape. They're really good. And they're really skiffle.

But for me, it was always more about attitude than the instruments. Having shambled my way through any number of musical genres, I felt at home with something which celebrated the triumph of amateurish enthusiasm over technical skill. Here at last was a musical form in which my total lack of proficiency was an asset rather than a hindrance – a type of music in which hitting an instrument rather than playing it was seen as a plus. And, of course, declaring ourselves to be a skiffle band was also seen as a badge of honour, what you'd now call a USP.

Indeed, following our success in the International Street Entertainers competition, we wound up talking and playing skiffle on the TV Show *This Morning with Richard and Judy*, an appearance which led to a string of TV bookings on shows like *First Exposure*, *Motormouth* and *The Wide Awake Club*. The last of these was a particularly baffling kids TV show, broadcast live from the Granada Studios in Manchester. We'd done a gig in London the night before and driven up the M6 for an early start and, when we arrived, we all looked so knackered that the producer insisted we wear dark glasses so as not to scare the children. I have never seen that performance – not even when we *performed* it, since the dark glasses were so dark that I literally couldn't see anything at all. Thankfully, no one has uploaded that particular debacle to YouTube, unlike *Motormouth* in which you can still find me dressed from head to foot in black leather, playing a tea chest bass while Olly and Matt show presenter Andy Crane how to make a musical instrument by sticking a trumpet mouthpiece up the spout of a watering can. We also spent an exciting half-hour teaching Timmy Mallet how to be 'utterly skiffle' on his long-running kids TV show, *Utterly Brilliant*.

We were not picky.

By this time, we had acquired a drummer in the shape of Steve Hiscock, whom you will remember from the glory days of

Hopeless, Russians Eat Bambi and Fatspeak. Steve had joined the Bottlers on condition that he did not have to bring with him a drum kit. Instead, he preferred to make do with a single drum, which was affectionately referred to as 'the biscuit tin' since that was exactly what it sounded like. In keeping with our skiffle ethos, we had adopted a strict rule: 'If you can't carry it, you can't play it.' This was a rule that we had learned first-hand from Jonathan Richman, whose Modern Lovers had had hits with 'Roadrunner' and 'Egyptian Reggae' back in the late seventies, and whom I regarded as something of a legend.

One Saturday afternoon, we were busking in Manchester and I'd looked out into the crowd to see somebody who looked *exactly* like Jonathan Richman. At the end of the set, he wandered over to talk to us, at which point it became apparent that the reason he looked so much like Jonathan Richman was that he *was*, in fact, Jonathan Richman. It turned out that he was doing a gig in Manchester that night and he was just killing time before the soundcheck.

'I really like your music,' he said, sounding *exactly* like Jonathan Richman. Because that's who he was.

'Thanks,' I said. 'And I really like *your* music!'

'Cool,' he said, before adding casually, 'Do you wanna play with me?'

Bearing in mind that Richman once recorded a song called 'I Have Come Out to Play', I thought he was being cute and that he was asking (in an affectedly childish way) if we'd like to hang out with him. But no, he meant 'play' in the musical sense – that night, at his gig.

'We don't have a support group,' he explained, 'and you guys are great because you have so little *stuff*. I just play with two guys now; one has a guitar, the other has a floor tom. And

Bottlers promo featuring a genuine steam train!

we have a rule "If you can't carry it . . ."'

'You can't play it!' I butted in. 'Yup, that's us!'

'OK,' he said. 'Well, come to the venue around 8. You don't need a soundcheck, right?'

'Nope!' I assured him, before Matt could jump in and say that a soundcheck would actually be quite useful.

'Cool. See you there.'

And that was that.

That evening we rolled up to the venue, where Jonathan Richman ushered us on to the stage, and we supported one of my rock 'n' roll idols. The gig went smoothly – so smoothly, in fact, that at the end I swapped shirts with Jonathan and I still have his pink pinstriped button-down to prove it.

Later on, in the downstairs disco, Jonathan asked if we'd like to support him at the Town and Country in Kentish Town, a venue I'd been to loads of times before, but never dreamed of playing. We jumped at the chance, following him to London where we shared a stage with The Modern Lovers, the African palm wine guitarist S.E. Rogie and Frank Sidebottom's Oh Blimey Big Band. I didn't know it at the time, but apparently the keyboard player of Frank's band was Jon Ronson, who had inherited the role from Mark Radcliffe – both of whom I would get to know in a non-musical capacity in the coming years.

Also at that gig was the Radio 1 DJ Andy Kershaw. He'd seen the Bottlers' set and thought we were shit – an opinion he seemed only too happy to share with us. Propping up the bar with Matt, I promised him that we'd prove Kershaw wrong – that we'd have our moment in the sun and he'd have to eat his words. As it turned out, the Bottlers *would* go on to achieve a bizarre level of success that none of us could ever have imagined, thanks in no small part to the enthusiastic support of our greatest champion, radio legend Danny Baker.

But all that was in the future.

First, we had to face the *Royal Iris* . . .

6
FERRY CROSS THE MERSEY

Looking back, I'm still not entirely sure how the debacle involving a skiffle band, a Mersey ferry, a group of irate pensioners and a Country and Western dancing drag act happened. Indeed, I am inclined on occasion to imagine that I have simply made the whole thing up – a view supported by at least one member of the Bottlers who assures me that what I'm about to tell you is a collection of exaggerations, half-truths, and outright inventions. But that same band member also concedes that if each of us were to write their own version of the Bottlers story, you'd wind up with five completely different (and completely contradictory) books. And since this is *my* book, it's *my* version that you're going to get. This is how *I* remember it – take it or leave it. As the disclaimer to the fictionalised film version of Jon Ronson's factual book *The Men Who Stare at Goats* boldly states: 'More of this is true than you would believe . . .'

It began with a boat – a twin-screw, diesel-electric named *Royal Iris*. Designed by W.H. Fry, and built on the Clyde back in 1951, she was once a grand vessel, replete with a tearoom, a cocktail bar, a stage and a dance hall. Back in the late fifties and early sixties, the *Royal Iris* had become a ship of dreams, playing host to a number of top pop acts as it cruised up and down the Mersey. The Beatles, Acker Bilk, and Gerry and the Pacemakers were just some of the legendary figures to have cut a rug on the *Royal Iris* at the height of its fame. Paul McCartney name-checked the vessel in his autobiographical song 'That Was Me' from his oddly forgettable 2007 album *Memory Almost Full*. Indeed, it was probably on this very boat that war-hero-turned-showbiz-impresario Leggy Mountbatten first noticed the particularly tight trousers of the so-called 'pre-Fab Four' back in the early sixties.

Twenty years later, much of the glamour had faded, but the *Royal Iris* was still doing faithful service as a 'pleasure cruiser', pootling up and down the Mersey, providing entertainment for passengers who enjoyed a hint of seasickness with their caba-ret and chips. A few short years later, the ship would start to come apart and, the last time anyone looked, the once-majestic vessel was resting on a mud bank in the Thames, a hole in her lower side. But for a while, she had a bizarre nostalgic appeal – just like many of the acts who once trod her boards with a youthful spring in their step, and who now drew hair-thinned crowds, playing oldies but goldies on the chicken-in-a-basket circuit.

Given her prestigious heritage, it's not entirely surprising that The Railtown Bottlers were keen to play the *Royal Iris*. After all, if it was good enough for Paul McCartney, then it was certainly good enough for 'four teds and a woman with a washboard' (as my good friend and colleague Nigel Floyd once cruelly but accurately described our band).

If memory serves (and, as I have duly noted, it often doesn't) we'd got the gig from a promoter who had done a lot to help the Bottlers, and whom we'd been badgering for more work. In this particular case, the booking was actually part of a comedy festival into which we had somehow been awkwardly shoe-horned. We drove over from Manchester in the morning and we'd been playing street sets in Liverpool during the day. This was the way it usually worked; an indoor gig in the evening preceded by a day's vigorous busking, which would usually be the more profitable enterprise. Six or seven sets could bag you over a hundred quid if you worked them properly, which was twenty quid each cash in hand; a nice little earner. The trick was to play short sets of no more than five songs and to have a keen-eyed bottler working the crowd, making sure that nobody was under any illusion that we were doing this for fun or for free. Over the years, we'd studied enough street entertainers to know that it was a cut-throat business, and if you were going to lie on your back on the pavement while pre-cariously balancing a double bass over your head, then, damn it, you were going to get paid for it.

Many of the acts we watched also used well-rehearsed patter to effectively blackmail audiences into emptying their pockets, ranging from the genially innocuous ('Take your contribution, *fold it carefully . . .*') to the weirdly embittered ('and remember children, if your parents won't give you anything to put in the hat, it's because they don't love you'). As for the Bottlers, we just figured that the sight of Olly running up the side of my bull-fiddle while playing the clarinet was probably enough to do the trick, relying more on musical acrobatics than thinly veiled threats to part our audience from their spare change. It seemed to work.

Anyway, after a hard day's busk, we knew we had to be pulling up alongside the *Royal Iris* 'at seven o'clock sharp'. I can't remember which mode of transport we used to get there.

The Royal Iris, in all her majesty.

At one point we prided ourselves on being 'the band that fits snugly into the back of a Lada', in honour of Al's mustard-yellow banger which (like the band members) pulled inexorably to the left. Sometimes, a few of us would squeeze into Matt's white Beetle while the others were left to take the bus or the train. Later on, we grouped together and bought a knackered old VW camper van, with rusty paintwork and unstable sliding side doors, and I have the suspicion that it may have been in this jalopy that we had travelled to Liverpool on that fateful day. We didn't have that camper van for long – one day, the engine caught fire on a motorway slip road, after which it lost much of its previously quaint charm.

At almost exactly 7 p.m., we rolled up to the dock at which the *Royal Iris* was moored, and started wearily unloading the equipment from whichever vehicle it was. We'd got most of the kit onto the pavement when someone wearing an important-looking uniform came hurrying up the gangway with an urgent look in their eyes.

'You're late!' he said. 'Come on, come on! Chop chop!'

We all stood around looking unimpressed, checking our watches. It was 7.03 p.m., almost exactly the time we were meant to be there. We weren't 'late'. We were, in fact, impressively punctual.

'We're not late,' said Matt, taking command of the situation. 'It's almost exactly seven o'clock.'

'Yes, yes,' said the man, whose uniform was revealed in the half-light to be that of a steward, or perhaps a petty officer. 'Seven o'clock *on board*, ready to sail. We were about to leave without you. Come on, double quick, let's go, let's go.'

And with that he turned and scurried back down the gangway at a pace which we were presumably intended to match. We didn't. Instead we all stood on the dockside, looking at each other, nonplussed. After a while, Matt shrugged and picked up his guitar while the rest of us gathered our various bits of kit, and trudged after him. Down the gangway. Down, down into the *Royal Iris* . . .

The vessel itself was surprisingly spacious, with more stairs than one might expect, or hope for. Believe me, when you're carrying a double bass, you tend to notice stairs; how many there are, how narrow they are, how steeply they climb or descend. The reason is simple – getting in and out of a Lada, a VW camper van, a taxi or even a portaloo with a bull-fiddle is simple compared to carrying it up or down a flight of stairs. Whichever way you hold it, it's wrong. Try lugging it on your back, and the headstock (which you can't see – because it's on your back) will systematically catch and smash any lights, signage, ventilation shafts or low-hanging wiring before hooking itself onto a door frame and pulling you over backwards, causing you to lose your footing and fall heavily onto your coccyx. Carry it in front of you and it will effectively block out any view of approaching obstacles, ensuring that you either crash into a wall, barge into a door, fall forward onto the bass (which will then crack, rendering it unplayable) or topple backwards downstairs, *followed* by the bass which will then fall on top of you. And crack.

In essence, double bassists are the musical equivalent of Daleks; imposingly powerful at first glance, yet utterly thwarted by any task involving steps or ladders.

After tackling several levels of fantastically inaccessible bars and restaurants, we found our way to the grand art deco ballroom area, wherein we were presumably booked to play later on. It was an imposing arena – large, with sturdy sprung wooden floors, a stage at one end, a cluster of tables at the other and vast acres of empty space between. Presumably, this would become packed with skiffle-hungry devotees in the hours before we made our entrance. For the moment, there were just a bunch of elderly passengers looking somewhat lost as they huddled in the distance, gathered around those lonely tables at the very far end of the room. One of them looked at me and my battered double bass suspiciously. I smiled at him. He scowled at me, and turned his attention back towards a plate of sandwiches.

'Wait till the youngsters arrive,' I thought to myself. 'This whole place will become like a waterborne version of the Cavern Club. Better watch out then, grandad!'

In fact, the *Royal Iris* really *was* 'a waterborne version of the Cavern Club', and had been so for decades. Since 1957, its regular 'Riverboat Shuffles' had been promoted as 'The Cavern

Presents' events, a banner which was still fondly remembered when the Bottlers rocked up that rainy Saturday night. So, in a way, we were supporting The Beatles. A couple of decades down the bill admittedly, but 'supporting' nonetheless.

Sort of . . .

I held onto this quasi-historical thought as I trudged out of the ballroom and back up to the main deck, to await the arrival of all the other enthusiastic punters who would soon be dancing and twirling to our good-time skiffle vibes. Arriving on the upper deck, I squinted through the drizzle at the glittering lights, shimmering on the bank which receded before me like the green light at the end of Daisy's dock in *The Great Gatsby*. I reached out a hand, imagining myself to be Robert Redford in an improbable Rubettes cap. The dark waters swirled around the hull of the boat, which chugged gently out into the murky abyss, the landmarks growing smaller as I stared. I felt a wave of overwhelming melancholy, glancing back towards the Liver Building, its birds arching their wings against the night sky.

It was at exactly that moment that I was struck by a worrying thought; if we were already cruising down the Mersey, how were all the excited punters queuing up to see the Bottlers going to get on board? Maybe we were going to make a crowd-gathering stop somewhere further down the river? Or perhaps there were rigid-sided inflatables waiting, even now, to whoosh expectant fans into the waters, ready to board the *Royal Iris* in anticipation of a night's rocking and rolling entertainment. There could even be an SAS-style helicopter drop, which would send eager skiffle enthusiasts tumbling onto the ship's upper deck, rushing down into the ballroom for a heady night's worth of backbeat entertainment.

As I gazed out in the Stygian gloom, I started to realise that none of these possibilities were actually possibilities. Indeed, they seemed more like the paranoid fever dreams of a slightly damp bassist desperately attempting to avoid the awful truth: nobody else was coming. Like Martin Sheen and a ridiculously young Laurence Fishburne in *Apocalypse Now*, we were travelling upriver without a paddle, and *no one* was getting on or off the boat. We were moving inexorably towards the heart of darkness and, if anyone was joining us on this voyage into the ninth circle of hell, they were on the boat already. The ferryman had been paid, the die had been cast – we were all just passengers on this pleasure cruise across the River Styx. All aboard!

A strange calm descended upon me as I began to appreciate the level of our isolation, followed swiftly by a note of idiotic optimism. Surely those oldies couldn't be the only passengers aboard this mighty vessel? There *must* be another as-yet-undiscovered level within which vast swathes of hardcore young skiffle fans were waiting to be unleashed? As a child, travelling from Liverpool to the Isle of Man on the *Ben-my-Chree*, I had fantasised about abseiling down the side of the boat and bursting in through one of the lower portals, discovering new life and new civilisations thriving just above the water level. In fact, James Cameron put a version of my youthful dreams on screen in *Titanic*, in which Kate Winslet's posho Rose ventured 'below decks' and found an entire colony of comical stereotypes drinking Guinness and dancing a merry jig in a manner that was not in the least bit patronising. Really. If only I could find my way down to the *Brigadoon*-style magic-land that lurked somewhere in the bowels of the *Iris*, I could rally support for our musical cause and snatch glorious victory from the jaws of ignominious defeat.

Or something.

Acting more on impulse than sense, I ran to the stairwell and hurtled down the decks – zipping past the ballroom, scampering around the toilets, ignoring the Muster Station signposts (incidentally, what the hell *is* a Muster Station? I'm asking for a friend). Down, down, down I went, deep into the hidden sectors of the ship to which, like side six of *Sandinista!*, only the very brave dare to go. Onwards and onwards I spiralled, a latter-day Orpheus in the underworld, spurred on by choirs of angels and washboards of fire.

I came upon more toilets.

And a place for storing baggage.

Hmm.

This was going to be harder than I thought.

I headed back upstairs, up towards the glittering lights of the ballroom, the heady glow of reverie and entertainment, of fish and chips served amid an ambience of poptastic excitement. Perhaps the good-time revellers had passed me on the stairwell and were even now ensconced in the warm throng of this historical dance hall; locked and loaded, suited and booted, ready to rock.

I poked my head around the door, hoping against hope.

Someone eating an egg-and-cress sandwich looked up from their feasting and glared at me menacingly. Have you ever seen that Belgian film *Calvaire*? There's a scene in it in which an innocent abroad wanders into a hostelry where men with antlered headgear do strange wombly dances and behave in a manner which suggests that they are about to flay you alive. I hadn't seen the film either at that point (it didn't come out for another fifteen years), but peering into the ballroom of the

Royal Iris that evening, I experienced a sensation of creeping dread that would come back to haunt me in a preview theatre many years hence.

The truth was too terrible to contemplate, yet too real to ignore.

This was our audience.

All of it.

Bugger.

I went back up to find the other members of the band. It turned out they'd reached the same conclusion and were all now lurking rather glumly on the upper deck.

A light drizzle started to fall.

'I suppose we'd better go and set up,' said Steve, trying to keep the air of despair out of his voice, and failing.

We all looked at each other, in silence, and shrugged. There really was nothing to say. Together, we all trudged down towards the ballroom.

At some point, during the setting up of the instruments, an explanation for what had happened began to emerge. Apparently, the audience consisted of people who had signed up for a Country and Western cruise up and down the Mersey, with sandwiches and bingo thrown in to augment the excitement. In the absence of an available C&W band, it had been decided that skiffle was close enough. And thus the Bottlers had been booked to entertain a crowd who had paid good money to get drunk and seasick while shouting 'House!' and singing along to 'Rawhide'.

Now, to the untrained ear, skiffle and C&W may seem to be similar forms of music. Both traditionally involve an upright bass. Both have a history of being sung in comedy American accents (check out Lonnie Donegan's spoken word breaks for proof). And both walk a tightrope between reverence and ridicule, proving equally divisive among the cognoscenti and the casual listener. But whereas it is technically possible to play almost any C&W song in a skiffle style, the reverse is not the case. As *The Blues Brothers* taught us, proper C&W fans like 'both types' of music; Country *and* Western. And for many (if not most) of them, anything else just isn't cricket.

That thought was clearly forming in the mind of a large section of our audience as we went about soundchecking the washboard. There is no instrument in the world that says skiffle more clearly than a washboard, and the sight of it provoked an almost immediate ripple of disapproval among the Country-hungry crowd. As far as they were concerned, we might as well have been The Jesus and Mary Chain, eager to try out some of their more experimental new material.

This was not going to end well for any of us.

And then we met the dancers . . .

There were two of them (I think their drag stage names were Tammy and Dolly), and when we met them in the area behind the bar that passed for a dressing room, they were getting changed into their brightly coloured costumes. Both were attired from head to toe in toxic pink, except for their naked (and enviably lithe) stomach areas which glowed with deep brown tans between the tops of their waistbands and the bottoms of their gingham-tinged shirts. On their heads they wore black hats which I mistook for sombreros, but were actually Stetsons, set at a jaunty angle, and tied around the neck with terrifically stylish leather thongs. On their feet were the kind of shoes that suggested that they had come here to dance, dance, dance themselves dizzy. They were both almost unnaturally beautiful – tall, slender and proud.

'They are going to get killed,' I thought, as visions of Edward Woodward in a burning wicker man leapt unbidden into my mind. Still, on the positive side, at least they looked even more out of place than we did. Surely they would deflect *some* of the inevitable seething anger which was bound to greet us as we made our way to the stage? Perhaps we might get away with this after all?

'Alright?' I said politely as one of the dancers smoothly adjusted his costume.

'Alright!' he replied enthusiastically, extending a hand of friendship which came with an alarmingly powerful grip.

'We're the Bottlers,' I said, gesturing towards the array of jeans and cowboy shirts now shuffling around in the middle distance, plugging and unplugging amplifiers.

'We're the dancers,' he replied, as breezily cheerful as before. 'We do line-dancing.'

Ah, so *that* was why they were here; line-dancing made sense. Sort of.

'Quite a crowd!' he said in a tone so upbeat that I immediately mistook it for sarcasm, before realising that he was, in fact, entirely serious.

'Pardon?'

'Quite a crowd!' he repeated, with not even the slightest hint of cynicism.

'Where?' I asked, suddenly wondering whether there was indeed a hidden deck full of hip revellers upon whom I had failed to chance during my search of the ship.

'There,' said Tammy-or-Dolly, gesturing vaguely towards the ballroom which by now had taken on the atmosphere of the Overlook hotel – specifically the scene from Kubrick's alternate cut of *The Shining*, in which Wendy stumbles upon a

*Never knowingly understated – me in low-key
form in a skiffling Bottlers promo pic.*

gaggle of cobwebbed skeletons sitting at tables, awaiting the
end of the world.

'Oh,' I said, deflated. 'Right. Yes. Of course.'

I went back to fiddling with some bass strings and trying to
look busy.

'Shall we go on then?' asked Matt.

'Probably,' I replied.

And, on we went . . .

Things got off to a ropey start. As we walked out into the hall, the masses at the other end of the room stopped munching egg sandwiches and comparing bingo scores and turned in stony silence towards us. It felt like a showdown at the OK Corral. If someone had been playing a piano in the back, they would have stopped on cue.

Matt strode boldly towards the microphone, smiled and said, 'Good evening! We are The Railtown Bottlers!'

Silence. Then . . .

'Who?'

The lone voice from the back of the room was joined by a chorus of others.

'The Royal Town Whattlers? Where did you come from? Keep it down, sunshine, we're trying to talk back here . . .'

Matt continued undeterred. 'We're The Railtown Bottlers, and we're here from Manchester . . .'

'Manchester?!'

'. . . to entertain you.'

And like the well-oiled machine that we were, we launched straight into 'Get Right Back', a reliably crowd-pleasing opener with a slaptastic bass intro which usually grabbed the audience's attention. Usually. Sadly, on this occasion, all it seemed to do was antagonise them. For one thing, we were screwing up their enjoyment of the bingo which was still very much in full swing, and now nobody could hear if their number came up. Worse still, the sound that was drowning out their numerical enjoyment was neither Country *nor* Western. It was as if a musical gauntlet had been thrown down and a fighting response was called for.

At the end of the first number, in the space where a polite smattering of applause might have been expected, there was only a momentary silence, broken almost immediately by the dulcet announcement:

'Knock at the door, twenty-four!'

Another brief silence.

'House!'

More silence. Then polite applause. Although sadly, not for us.

We launched into our second number, once again drowning out the gaiety of the bingo with our irksome skiffle racket. Some of the old codgers went back to looking at their game cards and pretending they hadn't noticed we were there. Others scowled angrily at us across the empty ballroom. More sandwiches were consumed, washed down with pale ale and Cinzano. Every time we finished another song, the arcane number-calling would leap briefly back into life, bringing a fleeting moment of joy upon which we would promptly stamp as we embarked upon yet another utterly uncalled-for musical number.

'In a state . . . twenty-eight!'

'Man alive . . . number five!'

'Two little ducks . . . quack quack . . .'

CRASH!

And off we went again, contractually obliged to carry on regardless.

As I peered out from behind the comparative safety of my double bass, I began to feel sorry for our audience. Over the years I'd played plenty of gigs during which the unfortunate crowd fully deserved my sympathy, but my motto had always been: 'I suffered for my art, now it's your turn.' Many a night at The Moonlight Club in West Hampstead had been spent testing the audience's patience with the sounds of stupidly loud guitars playing screechingly earnest rock music designed to give the listener tinnitus. Like Elvis Costello, the only two things I understood back then were guilt and revenge, and I was hell-bent on making everyone else feel the same. But the Bottlers were different. Like Brag, their primary aim was to entertain rather than infuriate or upset the audience – still something of a novelty for me. Indeed, during the time of our whirlwind ascent to becoming the premiere skiffle busking band in the north-west metropolitan area (a small pond, admittedly), I had grown to love the sensation of actually making people happy with my music. And so it was with genuine disappointment that I realised just how miserable we were now making our audience feel. Worse than miserable, in fact – from the looks on their faces, they had gone past unhappiness and were sailing merrily into the murky waters of anger and recrimination.

And that was when things turned nasty.

Somewhere in the middle of our fifth or sixth number, one particularly outraged patron decided that he'd finally had enough. Rising unsteadily to his feet, he fixed us with a glare more steely than that employed by the Ancient Mariner to stoppeth one of three. He raised his hand, and pointed an accusing finger towards the band, indicating clearly to the assembled masses that he wanted a word. They seemed to be on his side, looking up to his apocalyptic gesture and then across the room to the focus of his ire. I think he assumed that we would simply stop playing, halted in our tracks by his quasi-biblical stance, stunned into silence by his Moses-like presence. I glanced behind him, fully expecting to see two massive tablets of stone perched neatly atop his table. Instead, I saw only a Ventolin inhaler, a bingo card and several empty cans of Stella. Squinting across the ballroom, I realised that he was speaking; his lips were moving although since I was standing in front of a couple of 4 x 12 speaker cabs all I could hear was '*Boom-Dacka-Boom-Dacka-Boom-Boom-Bang*' – which is basically what every skiffle song sounds like when amplified through a fudgy house PA system. If this prophet of doom was going to make himself heard, he was going to have to part the waves of the ballroom floor and cross it like the Red Sea. Which he proceeded to do, wielding his cane like a staff, his face full of thunder.

As I may have explained earlier, the ballroom floor was not small. On the contrary, it was large enough to accommodate several hundred revellers, all partying like it was 1959. The fact that it was currently empty didn't make it any smaller – indeed, the utter absence of a crowd made the space seem even more vast; an ocean of emptiness and regret. And it was across this miserable abyss that our intrepid mariner now began his lonely voyage, teetering and listing as the *Royal Iris* rolled beneath him, the floor rising and falling with the waves of the Mersey. His step was slow and unsteady. At one point he appeared to lose his nerve, glancing back over his shoulder, presumably expecting to be turned into a pillar of salt. But behind him, his seated comrades urged him on, clearly keen that he should complete his quest and slay the skiffle dragon which was still spoiling their bingo. Emboldened, he renewed his mission, marching onward, onward, ever onward . . .

When he first rose to his feet, we were in the middle of the Lead Belly standard 'Rock Island Line'. As part of our street set, this twelve-bar favourite always proved a popular hit, involving audience participation in the form of comical animal noises amusingly suggested by the singalong lyrics. ('We got cows, we got sheep, we got pigs . . . we got aaaallll livestock.')

Unsurprisingly, it was dying a death on the *Royal Iris* and we'd opted to leave out all the joining-in bits on the assumption that the only people likely to be joining in were the band. That little bit of on-the-hoof editing had probably trimmed about forty or fifty seconds from the song's length, but it was still a good three and a half minutes long when we performed it that night, during which time our adversary advanced only some of the way across the floor towards us. Indeed, between the time that he left his seat and the moment when he finally came face to face with the band, we finished 'Rock Island Line', started *and* finished a mid-tempo number called 'Fooled by a Memory', and had just begun cranking things up again with 'Love Train'. (No, not *that* 'Love Train'; *another* 'Love Train' – a *skiffle* 'Love Train'. Totally different.)

Looking back on it now, I realise that if we'd had our wits about us, we could probably have played the whole of 'Stair-way to Heaven' as this gentleman made his way across the dance-floor, providing a splendidly sardonic Tolkien-esque accompaniment to his Hobbity quest. Sadly, our wits had long since gone over the side of the boat, along with our high spirits and winning brand of perky *joie de vivre* with which we regularly won over even the most recalcitrant audiences. But not today.

So he hobbled and shuffled and hobbled some more as we churned out the old favourites. And then, there he was, stand-ing right in front of me, like the ghost of Joe Hill. Or rather, standing right in front of Matt, whom he had decided was the leader of the group: the guitarist, the singer – the boss. I felt a wave of relief that my inability to play a guitar without breaking it had long since relegated me to bass duties, giving me something large to hide behind. I looked over to my left and saw Matt bravely carrying on with the important business of singing, even as his opponent squared up to him to deliver his message.

Being, as he was, in very close proximity to both Matt and the microphone into which he was singing, this message was perfectly picked up by the PA system and broadcast loudly to the entire room, and very probably the entire boat. His words were crisp and concise, and three decades later I can still hear them ringing in my ears as loud as they did all those years ago. They have stayed with me ever since, and I don't expect them to leave me anytime soon.

Here is what he said:

'All right, you've had your fun. Now fuck off.'

Would that it were so simple. Much as we all very much wanted to fuck off, the fact that we were on a boat in the middle of the Mersey made that task rather difficult. Moreover, we had been signed up to play for an hour and, if we stopped short of the agreed time, there was every possibility that we wouldn't get paid. The fee was no king's ransom, but it would cover petrol, beer and fish and chips for the band, with a fiver left over to fritter away in the decadent manner of our choosing. And, considering how little fun and how much aggravation this booking had thus far provided, I for one was not keen on going home empty-handed. No, like it or lump it, we were there for the duration and we had every intention of fulfilling our contractual obligations before retiring to the upstairs deck with something strong to numb the pain of all that had gone before.

So, despite our friend's helpful suggestions to the contrary, we just kept playing. Until something very bad indeed happened.

From where I was standing, this particular very bad thing didn't actually look that bad at all, merely a little unfortunate. But from the viewpoint of the crowd at the other end of the ballroom, who could see only the back of their brave comrade, it looked utterly outrageous.

Picture this:

As our harshest critic requested in no uncertain terms that we should pack up and leave, he leaned in towards the microphone, grabbing the stand as he did so. As anyone who has ever used a microphone stand will know all too well, they are not built to sustain the weight of a person or persons. Despite rock stars' perpetual habit of photogenically hanging onto their microphone stands, usually as they draw deeply upon a herbal cigarette, said stands offer little or no support for anyone who is unable to remain erect of their own accord. It may look like Mick Jagger, Johnny Rotten or Ian McCulloch are being physically propped up by the PA system, but this is just a ruse to convince the audience that they are utterly wasted and altogether too cool to stand unassisted. But this is just an *act* – if you lean on a microphone stand and require it to support your weight, the chances are that you will fall over.

This is doubly true if you are standing in a waterborne vessel which, at that precise moment, starts to execute a sharp 180-degree turn, causing the floor to move beneath your feet.

Which is exactly what happened. As the boat turned, this gentleman lost his footing and grabbed the stand in an attempt to steady himself. The stand immediately started to fall over, so Matt briefly stopped playing and reached out to steady it – and the person hanging on to it. But by then, it was too late. Apparently amazed that the stand wouldn't hold him up after all, our heckler let go and proceeded to fall backwards. With theatrical gusto, he did a reverse swan dive onto the dance-floor, where he momentarily lay spread-eagled, gazing up at the ceiling.

The band stopped playing.

The room went silent.

We looked down at the man on the floor.

We looked up at the crowd of pensioners at the far end of the room, all of whom were looking down at him, up at us, and then down at him again.

From where they were standing, all they had seen was their brother-in-arms walk towards Matt who then appeared to have reached out and pushed him to the floor. They couldn't see the microphone stand and didn't know that Matt had been trying to hold it (and him) up. All they knew was that some-one had bravely told us to fuck off and we had responded by beating them up.

Now, there would be blood.

En masse, the group rose to their feet, with none of the uncertainty of their fallen friend who, for the record, seemed utterly unscathed by the ordeal as he too rose nimbly from the floor. He grinned at us through crooked teeth and let out a maniacal cackle. He didn't seem frail anymore. Suddenly, he appeared dangerously agile and a little unhinged. Had it all been an act? I looked back towards the sea of faces that was now advancing across the dancefloor. They looked like extras from George Romero's *Dawn of the Dead* – slow but unstop-pable, and hungry for blood. As they drew closer, it became clear that they weren't perhaps as old as they had looked from a distance, merely ravaged and world-weary. Their feet made a weird plodding sound on the sprung dancefloor which began to vibrate in time with their advance.

Boom, boom, boom.

The not-so-fallen soldier fixed us with a mad-eyed stare, his eyes swivelling left and right as his lips drew back over nicotine-stained incisors.

Boom, boom, boom.

The army of the undead moved closer and closer, the gap between us narrowing by the second.

Dear Lord, I thought, we have somehow stumbled into a real-life remake of that creaky 1974 Spanish horror film *El Buque Maldito* – the one where the young glamorous swim-suit models discover a ghostly galleon only to be set upon and devoured by reanimated mummies.

Boom, boom, boom.

I thought of the last line from Daphne du Maurier's short story 'Don't Look Now'; of John, having been stabbed by a psychotic dwarf, thinking to himself, 'What a bloody silly way to die, what a bloody silly way to die . . .'

Boom, boom, boom.

And then, as if from nowhere, the sound of a twangly guitar came sweeping across the room, joined by a familiar voice, full of pain and defiance.

'*Sometimes it's hard to be a woman . . .*'

I looked over at Matt. He wasn't playing. Or singing. Nor were the rest of the band. The only woman in the group, Al, was still holding her washboard in front of her like a shield, ready to repel the marauding hoards.

From the corner of my eye, I saw something pink and spangly, like a giant flamingo awakening from sleep. (There's a myth that if you watch *The Wizard of Oz* closely enough, you can see a disgruntled stagehand hanging themselves in the background of a scene as Dorothy and the Scarecrow trip their way down the yellow brick road. It's not true; what you can see is actually a very large bird stretching its wings amid the scenic trees, but from a distance it looks like something altogether more sinister, more deadly. But I digress . . .)

I looked back at the crowd, who had stopped in their tracks, mesmerised by the Country and Western sounds that were now drifting over the PA system, soothing the beast within. I heard that distinctive voice telling me to be proud of someone if I loved them, even if they were, after all, just a man. My head began to swim.

Da-na-Na-na-Na-na . . .

After which all I remember is an explosion of colour as the dancers, Tammy and Dolly, burst like a glorious sunrise onto the ballroom floor, spinning and twirling and stamping in an orgasmic rush of crowd-pleasing joy.

'All together now; "*Stand by your man* . . ."'

And, in an instant, we were saved. The baying crowd turned to blissful revellers as the dancers weaved their way through the throng, breathing new life into these old souls all of whom started dancing and singing and swaying ecstatically to the music. All they needed was some proper C&W and two young men dressed in exotic cabaret costumes. And suddenly they were happy.

I stared, dumbfounded – amazed at the transformation which had occurred, touched by the sounds of Tammy Wynette, dazzled by the brash burst of colour with which our dancing partners had effectively saved our lives.

Several hours later, as the *Royal Iris* docked somewhere up by the ventilation towers which loom out over the Mersey, I sat on the deck, nursing a can of Stella, watching our former adversary shuffle his way down the gangplank, satisfied from a bloody good night out.

'Bye!' I shouted as he made his unsteady way off the boat. He turned and looked up at me, squinting into the darkness.

'Who's that?' he yelled, leaning back a little to get a better look and almost falling over in the process. I hoped he wasn't about to drive.

'It's me,' I shouted back. 'From the band.'

He stared down, and shook his head, confused.

'The band?' he shouted back. 'What band?'

'You know, the band. From the boat. From earlier on. The band.'

He appeared to have no memory of any such band, and turned to walk away. Then, after a few more shuffling steps, he paused, and turned back to look again.

'The band?' he said, still trying to remember.

'Yes, the band. You remember?'

'Oh yes!' he roared, half coughing, half laughing. 'You were RUBBISH!'

'Yes, we were,' I replied. 'Sorry.'

'RUBBISH!' he shouted again. 'Utter RUBBISH!' And with that he stumbled off into the night.

I never saw him again, and I doubt very much that he is still with us. After all this was the best part of thirty years ago and he didn't seem to be taking the kind of care with his health usually required of those who hit a century. But wherever he is, he lives on eternally in my mind, his words following me down through the years. If I learned one thing from the *Royal Iris* debacle (other than the fact that one should never underestimate the power of Country and Western music and extravagantly clad line dancers) it's that life is brief and should be enjoyed in the moment, because – as the Manx poet T.E. Brown famously wrote – 'when you look back, it's all like a puff; Happy and over and short enough'.

Or, as our friend from the *Royal Iris* put it:

'You've had your fun. Now fuck off.'

MONEY FOR NOTHING

For those with no interest in football or fighting, and in the absence of either a driving licence or a car, legend has it that being in a band is a tried and tested way of finding a partner. Or perhaps, *many* partners.

This has not been my experience.

Hard as it may be to believe, being in bands like The Basics, Fifth Incident and Hopeless did not prove to be a powerful aphrodisiac. Similarly, the release of the Mighty Jungle Beasts EP did not turn me into a highly desirable pop pin-up; nor did the career of Russians Eat Bambi place me upon the list of Manchester's Most Desirable Men. Indeed, despite the fact that I had been in bands since the age of twelve and had built my own electric guitar from scratch as a teenager (stop me if you've heard this one), girls remained largely immune to my charms, clearly preferring to admire me from a distance.

There is, however, one notable exception to this rule: Linda.

Linda and I first met in the mid to late eighties when I was doing a PhD at Manchester University snappily entitled 'The Radical, Ethical and Political Implications of Modern English and American Horror Fiction'. This was just before the Bottlers formed, so probably around the same time as I was delighting the people of Hull with my Henry One Hundred persona. I'd pretty much stopped playing with Russians by this time, and they were doing much better without me. As far as I remember, Charlie Baker had taken over on lead vocals (he was always a far better singer than I) while John Pardue was playing guitar. They had made a demo in The Kitchen with this new line-up which sounded way better than anything I had ever recorded with them. Twas ever thus.

Linda had just finished her own PhD at Sussex and had landed something called the Lees Fellowship, her entry-level job on the academic ladder in the English department at Manchester. The first time I saw Linda was at a department drinks reception which I'd attended with Kevin from Hopeless, both of us hoping for free snacks. I fell in love with her immediately: I thought she was the smartest, sharpest, most beautiful woman I had ever seen and I knew in that moment that I would be unhappy for the rest of my life if we didn't get married. The problem was that Linda didn't like me very much. She thought I was something of an academic lightweight (which I was and still am) and the paper I delivered in the Manchester University English Department that afternoon did very little to change her mind. She was friendly and polite and asked a question about my thesis being 'haunted by Freud', which made me think I was smart. But she remained essentially unsmitten. Also, she had other things going on in her life (as did I) so she saw no reason to complicate things further with some bloke who thought a horror novel from 1971 was the pinnacle of literature.

Our first date was, apparently, not a date. Despite the fact that she didn't seem to like me, I rashly asked Linda if she fancied coming to Cornerhouse to see *Near Dark*, the Kathryn Bigelow vampire western which had been getting rave reviews from the critics. She agreed to come because she wanted to see the film, not because she wanted to see the film *with me*. When we said goodnight at the end of the evening, she shook my hand in businesslike fashion, making clear that the evening's entertainment was over.

This situation continued for several years. Every now and then I would get in contact with her to see if she wanted to meet up. Most of the time, she didn't. In the end, we both moved away from Manchester. Linda got a job teaching at Exeter University some time in 1988, and then moved on to Liverpool. Meanwhile I went back to London to work as a freelance journalist. As the Bottlers' success increased, I made sure that Linda was aware of my rock 'n' roll triumphs. But she never seemed very impressed. Or interested.

Then one day, out of the blue, I got a phone call that made my heart skip a beat. It was Linda, who had *never* attempted to contact me before. I was elated: had she finally realised that I was the one? Sadly not. It soon became apparent that the reason she was calling was to ask if she could borrow my Amstrad. Back in those days, an Amstrad home computer was considered a flashy piece of technology. I had bought my first Amstrad green screen with the grant cheque for my PhD and it had effectively revolutionised my life. Nowadays, everyone has a laptop – indeed, I'm writing this book on one now. On a train! But in the late eighties, a 'word processor' was still a thing of wonder and somehow Linda had remembered that both she and I had written our theses using a similar version of Locoscript – an early word-processing format. Now, Linda had broken up with her long-term boyfriend (hooray!) and somehow he had gained possession of the green screen. So, she was contacting me to see if I could lend her mine.

After a moment of elation that she had called me, my dreams were shattered when I realised the true purpose of her call. Still, not one to be easily dissuaded, I agreed to lend her the equipment if she met me for a drink. She agreed. We met. We shook hands. That was that.

Other boyfriends and girlfriends came and went. Somehow I managed to cobble together the beginnings of a career as a film critic. Having started writing for *City Life* magazine while in Manchester, I'd blagged my way into a job at London's *Time Out* (see *It's Only a Movie* for all the thrilling details) and had started filing for papers like the *New Musical Express* and *Monthly Film Bulletin*. Through a mixture of pushiness and exaggeration, I'd also landed a couple of radio gigs, first on LBC and then on the newly formed BBC Radio 5. The next time I spoke to Linda, I told her that I was now a fabulously successful writer and broadcaster, hoping that might do the trick.

She remained unimpressed.

Yet more time went by. The Bottlers continued to play gigs up and down the country – generally more up than down. I juggled their largely northern-based schedule with my day job as a proper London film critic. Then, one Friday night in 1990, we had a Manchester gig booked upstairs at the Southern Hotel pub in Chorlton. We'd played there a number of times, alternating sets with comedians, many of whom went on to have stellar careers. Steve Coogan was a mainstay of the circuit back then, and we'd shared a stage with him on a few occasions. At one gig, we played with someone billed as Sea Monster who went on to be better known as Jo Brand.

These gigs were always packed and riotous, and the Bottlers were essentially on home turf. We always went down well, and the audience usually got completely hammered. Knowing that Linda was now living in Liverpool, and finding myself conveniently unattached (a not uncommon state of affairs), I figured I'd give it one last try and invite her to come and see the band. After all, everything else had failed – perhaps the spectacle of me beating up a double bass onstage while dressed as a young Gene Vincent would finally be the incentive she needed to fall head over heels in love with me.

I rang her up, reminded her who I was and invited her to come to the gig.

She declined.

I persisted.

'I can't get home afterwards,' she explained. 'The last train to Liverpool leaves Manchester too early and I'd miss most of the set.'

Luckily, I had anticipated this stumbling block, and had a pre-prepared solution.

'That's OK,' I said, 'I can drive you back to Liverpool.' This was technically true. At this point I was driving a beaten-up old gold Ford Escort that my brother had sold me on the cheap and that once caught fire on the M6. It was no Greased Lightning, but it would do the job. But Linda was having none of it.

'You can't drive me back to Liverpool,' she insisted. 'It'll take an hour there and an hour back. I'll just give it a miss.'

Bugger.

Then, an idea struck me.

'It's alright, I've got a friend in Liverpool,' I said. 'I can drop you off and then go and see him. It'll be no trouble at all.'

There was a lengthy silence during which Linda seemed to

be swithering about whether to believe this phoney-baloney story. I was convinced she was going to say no. Again.

'OK,' she replied.

'*Really?!*' I exclaimed, before attempting to settle myself and make it all sound fantastically casual. 'Er, cool; it'll be fun. Be good to see you there. Or not, whatever . . .'

'Sure,' she said, and hung up.

I was so excited I went straight out and got my hair cut. For the next few days, I did everything I could to ensure that I looked as rocking as possible, convinced that it was now or never. If she didn't fancy me after seeing me play with the Bottlers, with a room full of pissed people singing along to all our favourite songs, then *nothing* was going to win her over.

The evening of the gig arrived. We soundchecked early, after which I spent a couple of hours trying to perfect an air of insouciance. I was sorely in need of a spirit-stiffening drink, but since I'd already promised to be the designated driver it was nothing but fizzy pop all night – something which made me uncontrollably bilious. As the night wore on, I started to wonder if Linda would be a no-show. Perhaps she'd thought it through and realised that this wasn't such a great idea after all. But then, just a few moments before we were due to go onstage, she walked into the room and my heart skipped again.

I think we played well that night, although most of my attention was taken up by trying to see if Linda looked like she was enjoying it, without looking like I was trying to see if Linda looked like she was enjoying it. If you see what I mean. The bar certainly did good business, so the club management were happy. At the end of the gig, I bounded over to Linda and spent a good fifteen minutes trying to get her to tell me how great I looked onstage. (As Charlie Baker once said: 'You don't fish for compliments, you *trawl* for them.') Eventually, she succumbed and admitted that the double bass was indeed an extremely cool instrument. After which, I drove her home to Liverpool . . .

Almost exactly a year later, Linda and I got married. I was living in London and she still had her job in Liverpool, so we tied the knot at Birkenhead town hall. It was a bleak and blustery December day and the photographs taken outside the town hall made us look like we'd just won a major court battle. Linda was wearing a fabulous dress in which she resembled a movie star from the 1950s. I was wearing a suit from the Polecats' tailor, Jack Geach in Harrow, which made me look like a waiter. Seriously, when we arrived at our wedding reception at the Adelphi hotel, someone asked me for, 'Two lagers and a Babycham on table four, quick as you can.'

For the evening, we'd booked the upstairs room at the Philharmonic pub, a Liverpool icon. Ever the cheapskate, I'd decided to book the Bottlers to play my own wedding because, hey, a gig's a gig. Unfortunately, the band had travelled from Manchester to Liverpool in a van which they had parked round the back of the Adelphi; somewhere between the dessert and the speeches it got royally burgled. The thieves stole Olly's saxophone and Matt's guitars, one of which was that vintage Martin which had once been played by B.B. King. Like the homemade Delta which got nicked from my flat in Hulme, the thieves doubtless had little idea of its value (actual or sentimental) and probably sold it for firewood.

The break-in provided an interesting afternoon hiatus

With Linda, outside Birkenhead town hall,
where we got married.

during which we all traipsed down to the local nick to fill
in police reports. So, along with marrying a glamorous film
critic and aspiring rock star, Linda got the added excitement of
wearing her wedding dress to the police station. Pictures of this
event are included in our wedding album, adding to the air of
celebration and delight.

Bereft of instruments, the Bottlers called in a bunch of
favours to ensure that the evening gig was fully equipped.
Somehow my good friend Paul Simpson managed to produce
a lovely Fender Strat at very short notice and the gig went

ahead as planned. For the wedding dance, Charlie took over duties on the double bass while the band played an old Buddy Holly number and Linda and I twirled around the dancefloor. Later, Simon Booth strapped on his black Aria as the Bottlers took a running jump at a succession of blues standards. It was a brilliant evening.

Linda and I recently celebrated our twenty-sixth wedding anniversary. Whenever I ask her (as I often do) what it was that finally persuaded her that I was indeed the man of her dreams, she always shrugs and gives me the same answer: 'It was the double bass.'

The more I think about it, the happier I am that I turned out to be such a rubbish guitarist. As a kid, I'd never really thought of being a bassist as something to which to aspire. When I saw bands like Slade or The Rubettes on *Top of the Pops*, my attention was always on the guitarist or the singer, the two people who traditionally vied for the spotlight. Sometimes they would be the same person, thus doubling the chances of becoming the centre of attention. In the house where I grew up in Finchley, there was a wardrobe with a mirror on the inside of the door, and when everyone else was out I'd practise rock star poses in front of it, imagining how it felt to front a really successful band. Back then, I thought that owning and playing an electric guitar would open the door to my dreams. Later, I'd invested every penny I had in overpriced guitar amps and effects pedals, convinced that these would make me famous. At school I'd organised entire weeks of music concerts just so I could get the chance to play my Westbury Deluxe in front of an audience. In Manchester I'd charged around stages with someone else's black Stratocaster, convinced that it held the key to eternal happiness. And as Henry One Hundred, I'd faced down hostile crowds armed with nothing more than a cherry-red Epiphone semi-acoustic.

It sounds pitiful, but the fact is that, for a great portion of my life, I believed that an electric guitar could win me the adulation I so sorely craved. When it finally transpired that I was simply *never* going to be a heroic axe-wielder after all, my disappointment was crushing.

And yet, as it turned out, my incompetence was entirely providential. If I'd ever been any good at the guitar, I would never have wound up playing the double bass. If I'd studied music (French horn lessons aside) or learned to play with a little more finesse and a little less aggression, I'd still be twiddling around somewhere above the twelfth fret to this day. The fact that I never rose above the level of cack-handed chord-basher led me to abandon the guitar in favour of an instrument which was tailor-made for someone for whom enthusiasm had always outstripped technique.

And, as it turned out, playing that instrument made the girl of my dreams agree to marry me.

For that I will always be the world's most militant and most grateful bassist.

How does it feel?

It feels wonderful.

7

KINDA LIVE FROM LONDON

By the early nineties, I was working as the resident film critic on *Danny Baker's Morning Edition* – the breakfast show on BBC Radio 5 (as it was then called). I once described walking into Danny's radio studio as being like walking out onto the deck of a ship in the middle of a Force 10 gale. If you weren't sure of your footing, or willing to stand your ground, the chances were you'd get swept overboard. In his brilliant memoir, *Going Off Alarming*, Danny states that he and I were 'sort of slung together in a spin dryer and blended' and recalls that during our first meeting we had a blazing on-air row about the merits of John Hughes. 'I like to think' wrote Danny, 'that in that moment Mark was freed from his previous role as a robotic reader of fixed dialogue to the magnificent jousting free-form broadcaster he is today.' The compliment is lovely (and, as we have seen, I *crave* compliments), but Danny is also spot-on about how our encounter changed my life. Over the years, any success I've had on radio has been entirely down to people like Danny and Simon Mayo, matchless broadcasters upon whose coat-tails I have proudly ridden. Seriously, if you sit in a radio studio with presenters who love (and understand) the medium as well as they do, then some of that magic will eventually rub off. Believe me, that's how I got here.

One morning, after the radio broadcast, Danny announced, without any fanfare, that he was going to do a Saturday night TV show on BBC One.

'Really?' I said. 'Just like that?'

'Yeah,' he replied. 'It's going to be great! It's going to be a chat show for grown-ups. With guests. And music.'

He paused.

'Do you want to be the house band?'

I was slightly taken aback.

'You mean, the Bottlers?' I asked, not quite taking it in. I knew that Danny had seen us because we had played a party upstairs in the Yorkshire Grey, around the corner from the BBC, where large quantities of alcohol and cheese sandwiches were consumed. As far as I can remember, somebody ended up singing 'Pal of My Cradle Days', while people wept openly into their pints. The Bottlers had valiantly attempted to follow the chords – I think we got one or two of them right. Certainly not much more.

'Yup, the Bottlers,' said Danny. 'Do you want to be the house band? It'll be fun.'

'Er . . . yes!' I replied.

Yes, my skiffle band would very much like to be the house band on a weekly television programme with a super-smart host, broadcast on Saturday night on BBC One, still the biggest TV station in the country.

'Yes, that would indeed be . . . fun!'

'Great,' said Danny. 'Can you write me a theme tune? I need something that I can swagger to.'

'That you can *swagger* to?'

'Yes, *swagger*,' repeated Danny. 'You know, when I walk on. I want to be able to swagger. Can you write something that I can swagger to?'

I thought about this for a moment. All that came into my head was the theme tune from *Starsky and Hutch*, with its wailing *wah-wah* seventies guitars. I was pretty certain the Bottlers couldn't pull that off. But being unable to do something had never stopped me from saying that I *could* do it before. So why should it now?

'Sure,' I said. 'Something like the theme from *Starsky & Hutch*?'

'Exactly!' said Danny. 'Can you knock that up?'

'Sure,' I replied.

And that was that.

That evening I shut myself into the third-floor flat in Mornington Crescent where I was now living with Linda, armed with my Tascam 4-track, my trusty Westbury guitar, a cheap fuzz box and a couple of empty food cartons which would stand in for drums. I had little to go on, except for a chord which Matt had shown me many years before. It was officially known as E7(#9), but was more commonly referred to as 'the Jimi Hendrix' chord. If you heard it, you'd recognise it instantly – it's the dominant chord in 'Purple Haze' and it sounds really distinctive. It is also dead easy to play, which is always a plus. I wrote a little riff that involved shifting the chord shape up and down a single fret, and then moved to A while retaining the distinctive top-note drone, with that semitonal shift. This sounded remarkably rocking, and I was so pleased that I decided to reward myself with a bath. Surely my work here was almost done.

By the time I'd finished my bath, I realised that I had only actually come up with two chords (four, if you counted the semi-tonal shifts). I really needed a third chord (or fifth) if this was to be a 'theme tune' as such. There was nowhere to go but to B, but doing so in a block chord sounded decidedly . . . unswaggery. Instead, I decided to try and play the riff from 'Peter Gunn' (the twangly theme that recurs throughout *The Blues Brothers*) but with the notes all mangled up so it sounded different. This wasn't hard since my cack-handed playing pretty much mangled everything. I had a couple of runs at it, recording the results, and then chose the one with the best random mistakes. Then I added a walking bass, hit some food containers with a wooden spoon for percussion and stuck a bunch of fuzzy distortion over the whole thing. It sounded fine.

But it still lacked swagger.

Rather than re-recording it (which would have involved stopping for another bath), I just slowed the tape down until it seemed more growly. Then I made a comb-and-paper kazoo and tooted a two-note brass riff over the top of the recording, re-recorded it all onto a cassette, then went out to the car to listen to it on the stereo (*everything* sounds better in the car – just ask Kid Jensen; or Simon Blair). Amazingly, it worked. It had oomph. It had swagger. Most importantly, it didn't sound like somebody hitting food containers with a wooden spoon while playing comb-and-paper kazoo and doing a bad Jimi Hendrix impression on a slowed-down Westbury guitar.

'I might just get away with this,' I thought.

And I did.

The next morning, I presented the cassette to Danny. He listened to it once, and then played it again and tried walking to it.

It definitely had swagger. And Danny had swagger. Together, they *swaggered*.

'Great,' he said.

And that was that.

Sometime later, I got a Performing Rights Society royalty cheque for that theme tune; an amount of money that simply took my breath away. I was astonished. Apparently, I had made a smart move in opting to retain *all* the publishing rights to the piece, which meant that I would get residuals every time it got played. This had never even occurred to me before, but it turns out that penning the theme tune for a fairly major BBC One show is a big deal. Who knew? I remember showing the cheque to Linda who was equally gob-smacked, and who insisted that I buy something significant with the money which would remind me of this moment forever, rather than simply frittering it away. So the next day I went up to Hanks guitar store in London (a legendary axe emporium on Denmark Street) and bought something I had always wanted – a Gretsch White Falcon, with a huge gold Bigsby whammy bar and a case that looked like it had ridden on umpteen freight trains before winding up in my eager grasp.

I loved that guitar, although being a big semi-acoustic with a floating bridge it was an absolute bugger to keep in tune. I remembered reading an interview with Paul Weller who said he'd stopped using those iconic Rickenbacker guitars in the studio because their tuning was so wobbly, and I started to understand what he had meant. If the temperature changed, the Falcon went out of tune. If you used the whammy bar, it went out of tune. If you looked at it in a funny way, it went out of tune. But I loved it anyway, largely because of its glorious shape – big and stupid and wonderful. Decades later, my great friend Rob Fawcett (aka Rob Harry Dean) took the Gretsch away for a few months, stripped it down, and then spent umpteen hours resetting the bridge, filing the frets, straightening the neck, and generally putting everything in order. The result was extraordinary; it was like having a new instrument – one that actually *stayed in tune*. I'd never really understood what a difference a proper guitar technician could make, and I promptly sent *all* my instruments to get the Doctor Robert health check. If only I'd known earlier.

Meanwhile, back in the out-of-tune nineties, Danny's TV series – named *Danny Baker After All* – was actually happening. Danny had decided that two rules would apply to all the musical guests. Firstly, that they would play live with the Bottlers, without the aid of sequencers or synthesisers or drum machines or backing tapes. Secondly, they would play two songs, one of which had to be a Beatles cover. The other could be whatever they wanted. When I asked Danny why that was what he wanted he replied, 'Because that's what I want.' Which seemed entirely fair.

The rest of the Bottlers were impressively unfazed by all of this, as well they might be. Despite the fact that I am a supremely clumsy player, the other Bottlers were actually fantastically versatile. Olly could play keyboards, clarinet and saxophone and Matt was a brilliant guitarist who also could stand in on bass. Both could arrange music. And sing harmonies. Perfectly. Steve would go on to play in a percussion outfit called Ensemble Bash who were signed to Sony, and he ended up touring the world with all manner of impressively professional musicians. As for Al, there wasn't a player out there who could do what she did with a kitchen appliance – or look as good while doing it!

I, however, was the weak link in the chain. I couldn't read music, I couldn't play competently and I couldn't arrange a piss-up in a brewery.

So, naturally, the BBC decreed that I should be the show's musical director!

Yes, folks, that's *your* licence fee . . .

We did a couple of dry-run programmes to sort out the format, the first of which featured Suggs as our musical guest. He was great. He chose 'I'm Only Sleeping' as his Beatles track and then got us to do close-harmony vocals for his second number, a cover of the old Ink Spots track 'If I Didn't Care'. 'I'm Only Sleeping' sounded brilliant and bouncy, but everything came a little unstuck with the Ink Spots cover. We had a meeting in which it was decided that we all really needed monitors so we could hear what we were doing – something the Bottlers had rarely been able to do onstage. Nowadays monitoring is done with fancy-schmancy in-ear devices that offer perfect fold-back with no feedback. Back then, it was a matter of lugging a bunch of wedge speakers around that would howl into the microphones if you turned them up too loud and which you couldn't hear if you turned them down to stop the feedback. But we persevered and the problem was solved. Sort of.

The second dry-run show featured Chris Difford and Glenn Tilbrook from Squeeze, both of whom are matchless songwriters and equally adept musicians. For their Beatles choice they wanted to play 'Can't Buy Me Love' which suited the Bottlers down to the ground. We did a full-speed version of the song which rattled along like a freight train and brought the house down. But for the second song, Chris and Glenn chose 'Some Fantastic Place', a deceptively complicated

The Bottlers (and Rob Fawcett, left) with Suggs,
backstage at Danny Baker After All.

Squeeze song that scared the living daylights out of me.

Here is a terrible truth; most of the pop songs you love are built around three chords (A, D and E, with variants depending on the key). If they have a middle-eight that number will rise to six, perhaps seven. Let's say ten, tops.

'Some Fantastic Place' has about nine different chords in its *first verse*. And that's just the beginning of it. It doesn't have a middle-eight as such; instead, it has several interlocking 'musical phases' which employ excitingly unexpected key changes, with loads of abrupt sharps and jumpy flats. There's even a *third* act section when the whole thing turns into a gospel number, before returning to the *original* motif in what may or may not be the same key we started in. By that point, I had lost count.

The thing is, the song doesn't *sound* that complicated. Indeed, when Squeeze play it, it sounds celebrational and wistful. It's a *lovely* song. But it has about twenty separate chord changes.

This was fine for Matt and Olly, who took this stuff in their stride. It was great for Steve, who played the song like he'd known it since birth. And it put a smile on Al's face because washboards are in the key of 'brap' and you don't have to worry about playing in C-sharp for half a bar before moving to B-flat.

I, on the other hand, was simply not up to the task. It was above my paygrade. I was lost in a sea of notes. So, to bail me out, Matt played bass and I hid behind a keyboard with the volume turned down to zero so it *looked* as though I was doing something, although in fact I was basically miming. At one point, the sound engineer must have realised that I wasn't adding to the overall noise because suddenly the keyboard on which I was industriously miming leapt into sonic life with ugly results. He pulled the fader back down forthwith and I remained silent for the rest of the song.

Everyone was grateful.

That second pilot went well enough to convince the BBC that we had a seaworthy vessel. And so, one Saturday night in the autumn of 1993, *Danny Baker After All* took to the airwaves.

The first musical guest had been announced in advance as a spectacularly mulleted American soft-rocker who had sold millions of records. For the purposes of this book, I am going to call him Derek. (That's not his name, but that's what I'm going to call him, for reasons that will become clear.) The show was recorded on a Thursday night and we wouldn't get to meet Derek until late Thursday afternoon. This worried me a little, since I thought it was probably a good idea to run through the songs, one of which was Derek's supremely unmemorable new single. But in the star's absence, we agreed to meet his

UK manager instead, at BBC TV Centre in White City, to talk through the details of the gig.

For his Beatles track, Derek apparently wanted 'Come Together'. This put a spring in my step since it's a bass-led number with some lovely swooping lower-end chords and no complicated junctions or changes. When it came to Derek's single, however, things weren't so simple.

'We'll need to put the synths out front,' said Derek's manager, 'so you lot can just pootle around in the background.'

'I can't go for that,' I said, 'no can do. It's all done live. We don't use synths. We play everything live.'

Derek's manager looked at me and laughed.

'On what?' he said derisively.

'On whatever you want,' I replied. 'Bass, keyboards, drums, sax, clarinet, trumpet, vocals . . .'

'We want synths,' said Derek's manager.

'Sorry, you can't have them,' I replied.

Derek's manager looked perplexed.

'Listen . . .' he started to say.

At which point Matt cut in: 'The thing is, people will really want to hear Derek's voice. They don't want a load of synths and electronics. They want to hear him *sing*.'

There was a pause.

'Oh no, they don't!' said Derek's manager.

This surprised me. I wasn't a fan of Derek and his terrible hair, but I'd never heard any suggestion that his blue-eyed soul-singing voice was anything other than sweet. In fact, with his peerless performing pedigree, there was little doubt that the singer could have waltzed through an acoustic set without any electronic accompaniment – with flying colours. And yet, for some reason, his manager was digging his heels in.

I decided to call his bluff.

'OK,' I said, 'here's the choice. Either Derek sings live without the synths or he doesn't do the show.'

That told him.

'Then he's not doing the show,' said his manager, and walked off in a huff.

Bugger.

I honestly hadn't expected him to pull the gig. And now that he had, it was all my fault. We were less than twenty-four hours away from showtime and we had no musical guest. I was screwed. There was only one thing to do.

We called Suggs.

Bette Bright, former singer of Deaf School (and sometime musical compatriot of Henry Priestman), answered the phone.

'Hello,' I said, sounding panicked. 'Is Suggs there? Graham? Is Graham Suggs there?'

Silence.

'Is that Bette? Ms Bright? Mrs Suggs?'

More silence.

'Hello?'

'He's having his tea.'

'Pardon?'

'He's having his tea. Who is this?'

'It's Mark. From the Danny Baker show. You know, the TV show that Suggs, er . . . Graham . . .'

'Suggs,' she said.

'OK, that Suggs did a couple of weeks ago. We said we wanted him to do the show proper when it went live. Well, it's going live. Now. And we really want him to do it. Now.'

Another pause.

'Can I speak to him?'

'He's still having his tea. Call back in half an hour.'

Which I did. This time, Suggs answered the phone.

'How was your tea?' I asked innocently.

'Lovely,' replied Suggs. 'So, what happened? I thought "Derek" [he used his real name, obviously] was doing the first show.'

'Er, yes,' I replied. 'The thing is, he *was* going to do it, but then his manager said he wouldn't let him do it without synthesisers . . .'

'Ha!' The sound of Suggs descending into a laughing-coughing fit fizzled down the phone.

'Yes, well, anyway he's not doing it now. So will you do it instead?'

'When?' said Suggs, supremely unflustered.

'Um . . . *tomorrow*?' I said, with desperation in my voice. 'Please . . .?'

Suggs thought about it for a moment.

'OK,' he said. 'But I don't want to do "If I Didn't Care" again.'

I didn't argue.

'Do you know "Suedehead"?' he asked.

'The Morrissey song?'

'Yeah. Can you play that?'

I ran it through in my head. Four chords tops, with a middle-eight – in the same key. No worries.

'Absolutely!' I assured him.

'Ok, then let's do that. I can't get there before five. What time are we on?'

'Six!'

'Great. That gives us an hour. See you there.'

And it was done.

The next day, at the appointed hour, Suggs wandered into BBC TV Centre, in a dapper pale suit and shades with leopard-print frames that made him look like an extra from *Casablanca*. He was so suave that I almost swooned. The Bottlers welcomed him with open arms, like a long-lost relative. Everything about him oozed confidence and bonhomie. He was (and I do not say this lightly) the smoothest-looking man I had ever seen in my life.

An hour or so later, we took to the stage. The show started. We opened up with the theme tune that I'd ripped off *Starsky & Hutch* and 'Peter Gunn' and the crowd (all diehard Danny fans) went mad.

'Kinda live from London . . .' said Lori, the American announcer, actually a caller that Danny had befriended from his radio show.

'It's *Danny Baker After All*!'

As we played the theme tune, Danny walked onstage, and boy did his swagger seem mighty. He was the king of all that he surveyed and, in that instant, I felt prouder of those silly three chords than I had ever expected to feel. Then, on came Suggs and we ripped through 'I'm Only Sleeping', thrilled to be playing with someone who didn't need electronic aids to sound absolutely ace.

The crowd loved Suggs and they loved Danny – that first show went by in a whirl. We finished with 'Suedehead', which was a delight to play – a big, rousing, silly, petulant song with a lovely, twangly guitar motif that put a tear in my eye. The show finished on a high, and we all went to the bar to drink our bodyweight in alcohol.

We had gotten away with it.

At the bar, I asked Suggs, 'Why "Suedehead"? I mean, it's a great song, but why *that* song?'

And then Suggs told me something I vaguely remembered reading about in the *NME*. Back in the August of 1992, Morrissey had been a late addition to Madness's regular Madstock Festival in Finsbury Park. Ever the contrarian, Morrissey had misjudged the crowd, some of whom expressed their displeasure at his performance through the medium of throwing things – bottles, coins, a carton of orange juice. After nine songs, his pride presumably battered, Morrissey walked off the stage, never to return.

It seemed to me that playing 'Suedehead' on *Danny Baker After All* could be interpreted as an olive branch, a gesture of goodwill. But Suggs insisted that he just liked 'the title and the song' and was 'tickled' by the idea of 'Suggs singing Morrissey'. As for Moz, the increasingly self-pitying whinge-bag probably just saw it as yet another sign that the whole world was against him, and that no one had ever suffered as profoundly, mightily or unjustly as he. I used to be a huge Morrissey fan, until finally – after many, *many* years defending his 'misunderstood sense of humour' – I finally got tired of apologising for a dreary old moo with a chip on his shoulder. The breakpoint came when Morrissey wrote a song encouraging people to stop watching the news and to spend more time listening to him complaining about how misunderstood he was.

As Sean Hughes memorably observed, everyone eventually grows out of their Morrissey phase . . . except Morrissey.

Over the course of the next few months, *Danny Baker After All* would put the Bottlers in some illustrious company. On show two, we played with former Split Enz frontman Tim Finn, who was a total sweetheart. He sang a version of 'Across

Performing with Alison Moyet on Danny Baker After All.

the Universe' that made my heart break a little. Then there was the fabulous Alison Moyet, who told brilliantly bawdy jokes between beautifully melodic takes of 'Norwegian Wood'; and Lloyd Cole, a super-cool presence who demonstrated an unexpectedly thorough interest in golf which was apparently his preferred pastime. A highlight was playing with Nick Heyward, who turned up with a gorgeous Gretsch Country Gentleman which he strummed on a particularly rocking version of 'Doctor Robert'. To this day, I can clearly recall standing behind him onstage, playing the double bass and marvelling at the size of his biceps, which resembled (to quote Douglas Adams once more) two Volkswagens parking.

One Thursday, we were playing a warm-up set before the show recording started. Olly had started playing 'Tonight the Bottle Let Me Down', and we'd all joined in as if we were busking on a street corner. In the middle of the song, I noticed some rather lovely high harmonies, and turned around to find that Nashville legend Nanci Griffith had wandered onto the stage to join in. I remember standing there in front of the studio audience thinking, 'Oh my God, Nanci Griffith is singing backing vocals in my band! This must be what it feels like to be really, *really* famous!' The next week, we played with Aimee Mann, who would go on to provide the spine-tingling music for one of my favourite movies of the nineties, Paul Thomas Anderson's magnificent *Magnolia*.

Yet my favourite memory from that strange, whirlwind period was the programme on which Rick Wakeman was a guest. Danny had asked if we could play David Bowie's 'Life on Mars?', and I had assured him that we could, if pushed.

'Great,' said Danny. 'Because I'm going to sing it. With Rick.'

For those not in the know, when not changing the face of prog-rock with Yes or embarking upon another extravagantly caped solo album, Rick Wakeman played session keyboards on a staggering number of sixties and seventies hits, ranging from Edison Lighthouse's 'Love Grows (Where My Rosemary Goes)' to Cat Stevens's multi-million-selling version of 'Morning Has Broken'. Most famously, he played the Mellotron on Bowie's 1969 recording of 'Space Oddity' (for the princely sum of £9) and most of the keyboards on his 1971 album *Hunky Dory*. Knowing this, Danny decided to seize the opportunity to make a lifelong dream come true and sing 'Life on Mars?' with the keyboard wizard who had actually played on the record.

The only problem was that Rick claimed (probably in jest) that he could neither remember the song, nor what he had played on it.

'Are you sure it was me?' he asked mischievously in the rehearsal room, down in the basement of White City.

'Yes, Rick,' I replied, 'I am absolutely *certain* that you played piano on "Life on Mars?" Indeed, one of the reasons I am so certain about it is that I spent a considerable portion of my childhood trying to figure out how to play what it was that *you* played on "Life on Mars?"'

'Ah,' said Rick. 'And did you succeed?'

'Sort of,' I replied. 'Actually, I cheated. I went to that sheet music shop up by Denmark Street and bought a book which had the guitar tabs for the song, which I then spent a couple of years trying to master. On the piano. It was a labour of love. And by the end of it, my parents wished they'd never bought a piano. But I did figure out how to play it.'

'Great,' said Rick. 'Show me.'

'What?'

'Show me how to play "Life on Mars?"'

This seemed nuts.

'You want *me*,' I said slowly, 'to show *you*, how to play "Life on Mars?"'

'Yes please,' said Rick.

'The same "Life on Mars?" for which you wrote the piano part?'

'Yup.'

'The one that I learned from the music which *you* had written?'

'In your own time . . .'

Righto.

'OK, well, we start in F, and then the chord descends in semitones like this . . .'

I started playing the instantly recognisable piano line from the track.

'That's actually rather good,' said Rick.

'Yes, it is, isn't it!' I agreed, my head swirling with the weirdness of it all.

'And then it goes up to this,' I said, shifting to G-minor.

'Hang on,' said Rick. 'That's "My Way".'

Which, of course, it was. As anyone who knows their music history is doubtless aware, 'Life on Mars?' takes its lead from the French tune 'Comme d'habitude' by Claude François, Jacques Revaux and Gilles Thibault, which Paul Anka later refashioned into Frank Sinatra's theme tune.

'I know how to play "My Way"!' said Rick jubilantly.

'Well, in that case, you know how to play "Life on Mars?"' I announced, vacating the piano stool so Rick could take over, which he did, like a pro.

Brilliantly, Rob (guitar wizard Rob, who at that point we had roped in as our engineer-cum-problem-solver) had the foresight to press 'Record' on a handy taping device, so this moment was preserved for posterity. So whenever anyone says, 'Don't try to tell me that you taught Rick Wakeman how to play "Life on Mars?",' I can simply reach for the material evidence.

Doing *Danny Baker After All* really was one of the best experiences of my musical life. As it turned out, the Bottlers lasted only one series. By the time the show got to its second outing, an executive producer had decided that they only wanted the Bottlers to play the intro and outro music and the stings in between the acts. I remember the meeting at which this arrangement was proposed. It was met with stony silence, broken finally by Steve saying, deadpan: 'You mean, like the band on *Pebble Mill at One*?'

More silence.

'Erm . . .' said the BBC exec.

'Because that's what the band on *Pebble Mill at One* do,' said Steve.

'Well, I was thinking more of . . .'

'I don't think that's such a great idea,' said Steve. 'It sounds to me like you don't really want a house band.'

He was right; they didn't. So that was that. But, as ever, it had been fun while it lasted.

With *After All* done and dusted, the Bottlers looked around for new frontiers to conquer. A promoter who had seen us on TV decided that we would be a saleable commodity in America, and offered to send us there on tour. It sounded enticing until it became apparent that he really wanted us to be a British novelty act and suggested that we could travel the States in a double-decker bus wearing bowler hats and Union Jack waistcoats. Unsurprisingly, having already decided that we didn't want to be the house band on *Pebble Mill at One*, we found it fairly easy to turn down this promoter's plans to sell us to the Americans as the gor-blimey sons of Lonnie Donegan. So, we didn't do that either.

Instead, we decided to take *ourselves* to the States. In the days before the internet, this meant lots of long-distance phone calls and correspondence delivered by fax or post. Somehow, Matt managed to figure out a schedule which would take us from festivals up in the Pacific Northwest, down the coast towards LA, ending up in Venice Beach. At each stop, we had a paid gig and accommodation, which meant that effectively we were all getting a free holiday. Linda, who was now pretty much the sixth Bottler, came along to lend moral support. So we packed our bags and left.

A couple of festivals up in the Portland area stick in the mind. At one, I borrowed a double bass from a local rockabilly band whom Matt had contacted in advance. It was a fine-looking instrument – big and black and scary, with white trim round the F holes. Striding out onto the stage in front of a packed crowd with a dirty great PA system (with proper monitors and everything) I felt quite the rock star. The crowd were enthusiastic, largely because the MC had announced us as coming 'All the way from Engerland!!!' where we were apparently 'huge!'. Nowadays, it would take someone five seconds on Twitter to discover that the Bottlers were at best 'moderately well known within certain circles of rarefied musical interest'. But in the mid-nineties, no one was any the wiser; for all they knew, we were a chart-topping sensation across the pond, and it was their own fault that they hadn't been hip enough to have heard of us yet. In fact, I think we did a local radio interview in which we sold them that line, and they bought it. Why wouldn't they?

Anyway, we marched out onto the festival stage, said something sarcastic like, 'Hello, we've come here from the UK to ask for the country back' (a joke we stole from Elvis Costello) and then launched into our first number. Buoyed up by the crowd, and buzzing with jet-lagged energy, I slapped the big black rocking bass with the white trim particularly hard ... and the fingerboard snapped straight off the neck. Things ground to a halt as I attempted to gaffer-tape the fingerboard *back* onto the neck so that we could carry on, but it was a bodge job at best, and the bass continued to fall apart for the rest of the gig. Somewhere out in the crowd I saw the quiff of the man who had lent me his instrument hung low in shame and despondency. I couldn't tell whether he was cross with me for breaking his bass or cross with his instrument for not breaking me. It was probably a bit of both.

There is a lesson in this; never lend me a musical instrument, because one of us will get hurt.

Moving along the coast, we played an outdoor festival in the vicinity of Seattle which was sponsored by something called Pyramid Beer. Before we went on, a representative from Pyramid approached the band with a bagful of T-shirts advertising their doubtless excellent product and asked if one of us would be willing to wear it.

'Do we get free beer?' asked Steve, with typical cut-to-the-chase precision.

'Yes!' said the Pyramid Beer man.

'How *much* free beer?' asked Al.

'How much can you drink?' replied the PBM. This was a foolish question. Clearly, our new friend had no idea that the Bottlers had basically been raised on free beer, and our capacity to drink most others under the table was something of which we were stupidly proud.

'Oh, we can drink *a lot* of free beer,' said Steve, who was once rumoured to have lived for an entire year on a diet of white bread and Stella.

'Well,' said the PBM, 'if you *all* wear the T-shirts, I'll make sure you get *all* the free beer you want.'

Done!

It was, if I remember correctly, a particularly lively gig, fuelled by strong lager and sunshine. The crowd were friendly,

*On stage with the Queen of the Washboard
during the Bottlers' West Coast adventures.*

and many of them appeared to be in an advanced state of re-freshment even before we came on. We started playing, they started dancing, and for an instant I imagined a life of West Coast rock 'n' roll success, playing gigs for adoring fans, and very probably collaborating with various members of the Eagles on their sensitive solo projects.

As it happened, I had briefly flirted with life as an LA musician at the end of the eighties, when Tim Worman (who had done the cover artwork for the Mighty Jungle Beasts EP) moved out to Hollywood to work as a film-and-video artist. Tim and his then-wife Jenny had set up a band called Destroy All Monsters whose video had been played on a couple of Saturday morning kids TV shows in the UK. International superstardom seemed eminently within their reach. Tim had already had a string of Top Forty hits with The Polecats, and the new Destroy All Monsters material mixed old rockabilly riffs with modern techno-pop trappings. Tim wanted me to join the band as an all-purpose instrument-player and electro knob-twiddler, and together we'd bought some weirdly futuristic trigger-pads which could be connected to synthesisers to make an array of agreeably bonkers percussion noises. I went out to Hollywood for a few weeks to get the feel of the place, but despite Tim and Jenny being lovely hosts, I just felt like a very British fish out of water.

So I went back to East Finchley.

Now, just a few years later, here I was, touring a string of US festivals with an apparently successful band and feeling like I owned the place. At some point in the set, Steve thought it would be a good idea to get the crowd to shout the word 'Pyramid!' in order to drum up more supplies of free booze. A little later, encouraged by the alcohol, someone else decided it would be an even better idea to get the crowd to shout 'Bollocks!', a word which had zero meaning to our American cousins.

After that, everything got a bit hazy.

One evening on that tour, we wound up in a karaoke bar where Steve delivered a memorable version of 'Nights in White Satin' which earned him an enthusiastic fanbase among a gaggle of Japanese tourists. Only in Venice Beach did we fail to raise a cheer, presumably because in order to get noticed amid that twenty-four-hour freak show you pretty much have to set your own head on fire. As it was, we just weren't exotic enough to catch anyone's attention. Or their money.

Back in the UK, the Bottlers found themselves more TV work.

Matt got us a gig doing the music for a short-lived Granada
TV comedy series entitled *Mother's Ruin* starring Roy Barra-
clough, Dora Bryan and Kay Adshead. Always a talented
composer, Matt had come up with a catchy barrel-hall tune,
full of comedy 'boing' noises and quirkily irrelevant key
changes, along with a selection of shorter interstitial pieces.
We recorded the theme tune and all the stings one weekend in
Liverpool and the results were surprisingly good. But the show
was a dud, only lasting one series. I never saw it.

By this time, *Morning Edition* had run its course and both
Danny and I had moved on to Radio 1; he to host his own
show, me to join Simon Mayo as film critic on his mid-morning
programme. I still saw Danny in the corridors of the BBC and
we swore that we'd work together again, although since then
our lives and careers have gone in different directions. Danny
continued to be a broadcasting force of nature, turning his
hand to writing books, performing one-man stage shows and
even creating a very successful autobiographical TV series
Cradle to Grave for which Chris Difford and Glenn Tilbrook
provided the music, bringing everything full circle.

Just one other moment from this period stays with me. In
1994, as part of his *TV Heroes* series, Danny filmed a short
tribute to former *Old Grey Whistle Test* host 'Whispering' Bob
Harris. It was a ten-minute piece, written and presented by
Danny with typical wit, insight and affection.

In the middle of the segment, Danny wanted to do a visual
gag which would reproduce a regular *Whistle Test* trope – the
moment when whichever seventies rockers were playing the
show that week would finish their latest magnum opus, and
the camera would pan to find Bob sitting in his chair, listening
with beardy intensity. Danny wanted to put himself in Bob's

Bubble perms and loon pants on TV Heroes.

chair, in front of the band. But the computer graphics needed to pull off that trick hadn't yet reached the BBC. Instead, he called in the Bottlers.

If you watch the piece, which is (of course) on YouTube, and go to somewhere around the six-and-a-half-minute mark, you'll find a montage of hairy hippies playing the last chords of their songs, with Bob's face hoving into view as the final notes fade away. There are four bands. Three of them are vaguely recognisable. The fourth are utterly generic, and consist of a long-haired Herbert on guitar, a woman in platform boots on bass and a man with a bubble-perm and a silver blouson shirt hanging onto a mic stand while a yellow-topped drummer pounds the toms. And over to Danny . . .

That band is the Bottlers, and the man with the bubble perm is me.

We put on wigs and loon pants, we played three chords and left.

As we were leaving, the person in charge of keeping track of all the music played on the show asked me the name of the song we'd just played.

'It wasn't a song,' I said. 'It was just three chords.' Those three chords were D, A and E, chosen because Al (who couldn't play the bass) was playing the bass and those were the open lower three strings of the instrument.

'But I need to log it as something for the PRS,' said the helpful production assistant. 'Who wrote the chords?'

I paused.

'Well, I suppose I did,' I said.

'Great. And what are they called?'

'What are they *called*? They are called D, A and E,' I said.

'No, I mean, what's the title of the song?'

I looked at him as if he was mad.

'It's not a *song* . . .' I said. 'It's just three chords put together as a joke. It doesn't have a name.'

'It's just that without a song name . . .'

'It's *not* a song!'

'. . . I can't fill in the PRS form . . .'

'You can't fill in a PRS form for three chords!'

'. . . and I need to fill in the PRS form . . .'

'Why are we even talking about PRS forms?'

'. . . so you can get paid.'

Ah!

'It *is* a song!' I said. 'It's *definitely* a song. That I wrote. A song that I wrote with three chords. That I chose. For the song that I wrote.'

'Great!' he said. 'And what's it *called* . . .?'

'It's called . . .'

I fumbled for a title.

'It's called . . .'

Nothing.

'It's called . . .'

Steve jumped in. 'It's called "I've Got a Zeppelin in My Trousers".'

'*What?!*'

'It's called 'I've Got a Zeppelin in My Trousers",' Steve repeated.

'Yes,' I agreed. 'Exactly. It's called "I've Got a Zeppelin in My Trousers". That's the name of the song. That I wrote. Write that down on the PRS form.'

'Seriously?'

'Yes! Absolutely!'

And so he did.

Several months later, I was opening the mail and I noticed an envelope from PRS. If you're on their books, they send out quarterly statements for all the money owing to you from compositions you have written that have been performed in public, whether live or on the radio or TV. Nowadays the money is transferred electronically to your bank account, but back then it arrived in the form of a cheque, with an accompanying payslip detailing exactly what the money was for.

I opened the envelope and pulled out a cheque for £4.57 – not a princely sum, but unexpected nonetheless. I opened the advice slip which was a printed form, on which the length of each line of text was restricted to a limited number of characters.

It read simply:

DANNYBAKER'STVHE
COMPOSER: MARKKE
'IVEGOTAZEPPELININ
TOTAL: £4.57 ATTACH

I banked the cheque, and used the money to buy Linda some flowers and a Led Zeppelin CD.

As she said, you can't just fritter that kind of money away – you have to use it to buy something that *means* something.

Which it most definitely did.

8

TUNES OF PROVEN MERIT

As the nineties drifted towards the noughties, the Bottlers went their separate ways. We never split up as such, we just gradually moved apart, with gigs becoming more and more infrequent, and recording sessions left unfinished. We all stayed friends and today we continue to view each other as a kind of extended family. Every now and then we get together to relive past glories, reforming for one-off gigs at significant birthdays and anniversaries. A lot has changed over the years, but what's notable is just how much remains the same. A few of us are now parents (Linda and I have a teenage daughter and son, Georgia and Gabriel) but when the Bottlers get together we still behave like big kids. A couple of years ago, we played together in Manchester and I was delighted to discover that Olly was still sprightly enough to run up the side of my double bass while playing the clarinet. Last summer, we reunited again in Cornwall where Linda and I were belatedly celebrating our twenty-fifth wedding anniversary. The Bottlers got up and played a bunch of songs and I burst into tears, overwhelmed by the emotion of it all.

By the turn of the century, Linda and I were living in the

New Forest. She was lecturing at Southampton University and I was commuting up to London three days a week to do my regular film reviews. Having appeared on Radio 1 with Simon Mayo for much of the nineties, we had reunited in the noughties on what was now called Radio 5Live. I had also started filing for the *Observer* newspaper, learning all I could from the great Philip French, into whose shoes I would step as chief film critic in 2013.

One evening, Linda and I went to Lymington to see Mike and Mary Hammond. Mary (who is now a professor) had studied English at Southampton University, where Linda was lecturing, and Mike was teaching film at Southampton Institute. Mike and Linda had crossed paths a few times, and kept suggesting that we should all get together. We ate vegetarian chilli and drank Mexican beer, which are two things I enjoy doing enormously. After dinner, talk between Linda and Mary turned to matters academic, so I suggested to Mike that we retire to the living room, where I had noticed an old upright piano that seemed in need of playing.

Mike and I had, in fact, met before; I had stood in for Kim Newman at a film conference in Glasgow several years earlier, and Mike had been there too. Apparently we'd got on well and had ended up propping up the bar and talking about Cloris Leachman who was the conference's eccentric guest of honour. Neither of us could remember much about that meeting, other than those three salient facts: the location, the bar and Cloris Leachman. I think that snapshot speaks volumes.

Anyway, it turned out that Mike – who was from Alabama via Los Angeles – was a musician. He may have become a film studies academic, but in a previous life he'd rocked the Whiskey A-Go-Go on Sunset with a band called The Whizz Kidds.

The Whizz Kidds had been courted by Capitol and had made a record produced by Flo & Eddie, founder members of 'Happy Together' hit-makers The Turtles. Mike had played bass and keyboards and still had a vintage Gibson Thunderbird Bass lying in its original case under his bed. He had also apparently once spent some time at an LA bar drinking with Rene Russo.

I was impressed.

Mike and I opened a bottle of whiskey, sat down at his old piano and started seeing how many tunes from classic Americana we both knew. The answer was 'a lot'. Like me, Mike was more interested in music made back in the middle of the century and we began playing things like 'Going to Kansas City', 'Worried Man Blues' and 'Railroad Bill' – you know the drill, all bangers, no clangers. Through the haze of alcohol, we decided that we sounded brilliant and I suggested (or perhaps insisted) that we form a band.

'Just the two of us?' asked Mike, uncertain.

'Sure,' I said, not really thinking it through. 'Who else do we need?'

'Well, I know a harmonica player,' said Mike.

'Sounds great,' I replied. 'Just one question: does he have a mullet?'

I had seen someone on television playing harmonica with a spectacular Bono-style mullet and it was an image I would not forget in a hurry.

'Oh, good Lord no!' said Mike. 'He has totally rocking hair. Looks a bit like Nick Lowe. Immaculately dressed. Would *not* be seen in anything that looked like it was designed after 1953.'

'He's in,' I replied.

His name was Pete Stanfield. When Mike had moved from the States to the UK, he had played with Pete in the still-remembered Norwich band Morty McVicar. A scholar of singing cowboys and authentic blues, Pete was a huge fan of the late lamented Lee Brilleaux and his playing style sounded like a cross between Dr Feelgood and The Velvet Underground. Sometimes he didn't play notes – he just made strange unearthly noises; swooping, bending and growling. He could make a harmonica produce a majestic wall of sound, as if he'd swallowed an orchestra which he was in the process of violently regurgitating. And he did, indeed, look brilliant.

There was just one problem with the plan: Mike and I were both bassists and after my experiences with Russians Eat Bambi, I knew that was one bassist too many.

'Can you play guitar?' I asked Mike.

'Sure,' he replied, 'although I don't actually *have* a guitar.'

'That's OK, I've got a Gretsch White Falcon!'

'Really?'

'Yes, a real one! With a dirty great gold Bigsby whammy bar! And an amp. Well, a couple of amps actually. You can play that.'

'Done.'

The next weekend, Mike, Pete and I got together in mine and Linda's kitchen to rehearse our set. At first, Mike and Pete thought that we should play together for a while, do a few months of rehearsals, maybe make a few recordings, see how things went. I thought this all sounded unnecessarily cumbersome.

'We should just book a gig,' I declared.

'But we haven't played together yet.'

'I know, but look at us – we *look* great! All you need to play a gig is eight songs – how hard can it be to knock eight songs together? Tell you what, it's 11 a.m. now. If we can't play eight songs by four o'clock, we should just give up. Otherwise, we book a gig. OK?'

This sounded eminently reasonable, and thanks to Pete's encyclopaedic knowledge of old cowboy tunes, we had a set list amounting to ten songs (enough for two encores!) before teatime. Pete knew of some film faculty event coming up in Southampton (where he, too, was an academic) in a couple of weeks' time where entertainment was required, and he agreed to try and land us the gig.

'We need a name,' he said.

This was easy. For a few years, I'd been driving an old 1956 Dodge Coronet which I'd bought off someone who imported it from Arizona in the early nineties. It was an oil-burning pig of a car, with sweeping tail fins, and vast amounts of chrome. During one of its many rebuilds I had attached a small bust of Elvis to the back shelf which I had also tastefully upholstered in leopard print. I still have that car, and there are few things I love more than the sound of its 5.8 litre V8 engine purring into life. The car fitted the band, and we'd been toying with songs by the Louvin Brothers, so we decided to call ourselves The Dodge Brothers.

The first Dodge Brothers gig went surprisingly well. Everyone was plastered, the lights were turned down low, and the PA system was fantastically muddy, so it didn't really matter how we looked or sounded. All that mattered was that we played the gig and we didn't get thrown out.

Now, The Dodge Brothers were officially a band.

Emboldened, we secured a residency at a pub in Lymington called the Thomas Tripp, where, even as a three-piece, we often outnumbered the audience. We played on Thursday nights, starting at around 8.30 p.m., and pretty much learning new songs onstage. We knocked together close-harmony versions of ballads like 'Fair and Tender Ladies' and drinking songs like 'Wine Spo-Dee-O-Dee' and 'Drunkard's Special'. At some point we started playing a version of an old Dock Boggs song called 'False Hearted Lover' which we expanded into a twelve-minute epic reminiscent of The Velvet Undergound's 'Heroin'. Or at least, that's how it sounded to us – I suspect that to the audience it was more like listening to a soundcheck with choruses.

One sunny afternoon, we drove the Dodge up to a clearing in the New Forest and took a bunch of big-sky black-and-white photographs which looked more like Nevada than Hampshire. Somehow, we got ourselves a regular gig at the newly built Harbour Lights cinema in Southampton, a beautiful place designed to look like the prow of a ship, the reflection of which glittered majestically off the waters of the Solent. We found a sympathetic recording studio in Poole and recorded ten or eleven songs, including 'Good Night Irene', with which we would invariably close our sets.

It was all going swimmingly. Then Pete got a new job and moved to Portsmouth and it all started to fall apart. Gigs were more difficult, and consequently more infrequent. I could see this going the way of the Bottlers, but I was enjoying The Dodge Brothers too much to let it slide. So I had an idea.

'I'll play harmonica,' I told Mike.

'But you can't play harmonica,' replied Mike. 'Can you . . .?'

As it happened, for my fortieth birthday, my close friend Nick Freand Jones (who directed and produced my first TV documentary, *The Fear of God*, and with whom I have worked

The New Forest pretending to be Nevada;
Pete to the left, Mike to the right.

ever since) had bought me a couple of harmonicas and a book called something like *How to Play Blues Harp*. (It was thanks to Nick's gift that I'd end up playing 'Midnight Cowboy' with the BBC Philharmonic Orchestra several years later.) I loved those harmonicas and had been pootling away on them up in the attic, desperately trying to make the same kind of noises that Pete made. I wasn't much good, but that had never stopped me in the past.

'How hard can it be?' I asked. After all, Pete had made it look absolutely effortless.

'But you'll have to stop playing bass,' said Mike. 'You've only got two hands. You can't play them both at once.'

I'd thought about this too. For Christmas, Linda had given me 'a hooky thing' – one of those strange contraptions that Bob Dylan (and, as previously noted, Les Paul) used to play guitar and harmonica at the same time. Apparently, she'd gone on the Hobgoblin website and, not knowing what it was called, looked up 'harmonica hooky thing' and it came up. So that's what we've called it ever since. I still don't know what it's actually called.

'I've got one of those hooky things,' I told Mike.

'What "hooky things"?' he asked.

'You know, those hooky things that Bob Dylan used. The thing that hooks round your neck so you can play harmonica while playing the guitar.'

'But you don't play the guitar,' said Mike. 'You play the bass. Does anyone play bass *and* harmonica at the same time?'

'I'm sure someone does. Karen Carpenter used to sing and play drums at the same time. Rob Gray up in Manchester used to play guitar, harmonica and bass drum all at once. Seriously, how hard can it be?'

'Um, OK,' said Mike.

Harmonicas, as I mentioned earlier, are wonderful instruments because, when played 'across', it is actually impossible to play a wrong note. As a result, it's really very easy to be passable at playing blues harmonica. Being *good* at playing blues harmonica (like Pete was) takes a lot more practise, and is a lot more complicated. But I didn't want to be good; I just wanted to get away with it. Which really is the story of my life.

The problem is that playing harmonica (at a merely passable level) while also playing double bass is a bit like doing that thing of patting your head and rubbing your stomach at the same time. It's completely counterintuitive and you keep trying to suck the bass while slapping the gob-iron. At first, I found it impossible. Weirdly, after a couple of stiff whiskeys, it became a lot easier. The trick was to try not to think about what you were doing – and when it comes to *not* thinking about what you're doing, few things are more effective than alcohol.

I called Mike to tell him that I could now play harmonica and double bass at the same time. He seemed sceptical, but agreed to let me chance it at the Thomas Tripp that Thursday. By that time, we'd accidentally acquired an engineer in the shape of Aly Hirji who I'd first met when he came over to fix our home computer. Aly had been playing in bands for years and at one point sported an explosive Robert Smith haircut which he had since thankfully reined in. We had talked about music and instruments and I'd discovered that he knew a lot about the workings of guitars, amplifiers and PA systems. The Dodge Brothers had never really worried about their sound as such – we'd been hiring a PA from Fret Music in Shirley which they agreed to sell to us after a while, and we just set it up and operated it ourselves from onstage. Aly had come to see us at the Tripp and suggested that we might sound better if our mix was done by someone who could actually *hear* the band, so we invited him to take control of the PA system. He was right – we did indeed sound better. But now, as a two-piece, we also found ourselves somewhat restricted. There were some songs that we simply couldn't play because we didn't have enough hands between us. So we asked Aly to bring along a guitar and join us for a few numbers. And the next thing we knew, The Dodge Brothers were a three-piece again.

When Aly joined the band, things became rather more melodic, allowing us to play the kind of tunes we'd never have attempted before. We had a rule that if someone gave you an instrument, you had to play it at the next gig – even if the next gig was tomorrow. We had already clubbed together and bought Mike a banjo; he'd learned to play songs like 'Little

Maggie' which opened up a whole new arena of bluegrass possibilities. Linda gave me an accordion on which I'd figured out how to play 'Fair and Tender Ladies' while Aly played the double bass. Then, for his next big birthday, we all bought Aly a mandolin which he was forced to learn in time for the next Thomas Tripp date. And so on. It was an education.

Meanwhile, things were also growing in the rhythm department. When Mike and I first started playing together, Mike's son Alex was just a kid with a fierce interest in matters military. As a teenager, he'd learned the drums and started playing with a punk band called Forty Foot Fall. While we were pootling around in a studio one weekend, we decided that it would be good to have him put some drums on a track called 'Sugar Baby', but we made sure that Al (who was not to be confused with the Bottlers' washboard player, Al) obeyed the Jonathan Richman 'can't carry it, can't play it' rule. Al was game and turned up with a snare and a floor tom on which he did some suitably low-key percussion. Gradually, he became a fixture and the Dodges became a four-piece. As I like to tell audiences: 'We were too cheap to hire a drummer; so we grew one instead.'

One day, in April of 2007, someone suggested that I should do a piece about skiffle for *The Culture Show*. We were coming up to the fiftieth anniversary of the date when Paul McCartney famously met John Lennon at a church fete where the latter's skiffle group, The Quarrymen, were playing. Since it was well known that I was a diehard skiffle devotee, the BBC thought it would be good to do a piece about how this homemade music had given birth to the British rock 'n' roll scene. Our director wanted to film The Dodge Brothers playing a skiffle version of 'Careless Love' with a washboard and tea chest bass. The latter was no problem – after all, I'd already demonstrated the mechanics of the instrument to Timmy Mallet, and it was an act I was happy to repeat. As for the washboard, that was a slightly different matter.

I rang Mike.

'Does Al have a washboard?'

'Not that I know of.'

'OK. If we got one for him, could he learn to play it?'

'Sure. How soon?'

'Thursday.'

'What, *this* Thursday?'

'Yes, *this* Thursday. He could manage that, right?'

'I guess so.'

'Oh, and it's going to be on TV. But probably don't tell him that. Yet.'

So, with a turnaround of less than forty-eight hours, Al got a washboard (making him even easier to confuse with the Bottlers' Al), learned to play it and then performed two songs – 'Careless Love' and 'Number Nine Train' – on national television. By the end of the shoot, his knuckles were raw and his fingers were bleeding. But Al had gotten the washboard bug and there was no stopping him. For a while, I thought he might simply abandon his drums altogether and just stick with the kitchen appliance. It certainly made enough noise. If you've ever stood in the same room as a really good washboard player, you'll know that you can close your eyes and imagine an entire drum kit made of tin and wood and nails, big and brash and ballsy with the merest hint of violence. Even at gigs you rarely need to amplify the sound – in fact, you often need to dampen it down to stop it drowning out everything else. No wonder washboard players are so militant about their chosen instrument.

The Culture Show piece went down well, thanks in no small part to Billy Bragg's enthusiastic involvement as a spokesperson for the skiffle cause. The Dodge Brothers continued to play, and our audiences started to grow. In Southampton, we became a regular fixture at venues like The Talking Heads, The Platform Tavern and The Joiners. Aly, who had taken over management of the band, started to get us gigs in London, at The Borderline off Tottenham Court Road, and the Blues Kitchen in Camden. I kept thinking back to the days of getting banned from that 'top London venue' in the early eighties, wondering whether the manager from hell would show up and try to steal my guitar again.

By this time, I'd acquired yet another guitar; a lovely blond 1953 Epiphone Zephyr archtop which I'd found in a second-hand store in Shirley and fallen in love with immediately. Mike had fallen in love with it too, so I lent it to him on a semi-permanent basis, which meant that I only ever saw it at gigs. But I figured that an instrument that beautiful deserved to be played, and it certainly made The Dodge Brothers sound authentic. It had one single DeArmond pickup right up by the neck which produced a rich, round, bell-like ring. I remembered all those hours I'd spent as a teenager trying to wind the pickup wire for my homemade Delta guitar, and marvelled once again at the strange magnetic miracle of this extraordinary electronic invention. The combination of ageing wood and vintage pickup really *did* do something magical to the sound of that guitar. It sounded as if you were playing it in the 1950s – that musical time machine again.

The more Mike played the Zephyr, the more I became obsessed with the idea of getting The Dodge Brothers to go back in time, to get back to the roots of the music I loved. My dad, who had once attempted to write a biography of Jelly Roll Morton, had started buying me old jug-band recordings, realising that after all these years our musical tastes were finally dovetailing. He found the complete works of Washboard Sam that Document Records had issued on CD and got me the entire set, to which I listened on hard rotation. Meanwhile Al, who now had washboard fever, had agreed to use an empty wine bottle as an instrument, and we wrote a song called 'Died and Gone to Hell' on which the entire percussion track consisted of him playing the washboard with his right hand while holding the wine bottle between his knees and hitting it with a drum stick with his left hand. Together, they made an ear-splitting racket, and the song became a live favourite. We'd sit Al on a stool at the front of the stage and warn the audience that there was a strong possibility that the bottle might break, adding a hint of blood-spilling danger to the proceedings.

Gradually, an element of carnival showmanship started creeping into The Dodge Brothers' gigs. Having spent years busking with the Bottlers, I suggested that The Dodge Brothers spend some time working the pavements, which had always been an effective way of sharpening up your act. We put together a busking set, which we would often roll out on the afternoon before a gig, to drum up support and to get ourselves into shape. When *The Culture Show* organised its very own British Busking Challenge in 2008, we found ourselves back on the Bottlers' old stomping ground of Covent Garden, playing to a crowd of rain-drenched onlookers. Somehow I persuaded Mike to clamber up the side of my bass and perform the solo to 'Slow Down' while perched atop the creaking instrument. I know it sounds stupid but it looked really good, and after fifteen minutes we'd taken over a hundred quid, propelling us (albeit briefly) to the top of *The Culture Show*'s busking chart. Sadly, the next week Supergrass took twice as much money in as many minutes, knocking us off the top spot. But they turned up with a drum kit. And a PA. And a carpet! Huh?

After our moment of street-side fame was broadcast, I got a text message from rocker Richard Hawley, with whom I'd previously compared hair products (he favours Black & White, which I can never wash out) and record rarities. It turned out that he shared my love of skiffle, as did his elders and betters. 'My mum thought you were great!' he wrote. 'Some of us still know and still care!' I was so moved, I found myself wiping away a tear and raising a glass to the ghost of Charlie Poole.

By this point, I'd started to think that The Dodge Brothers should write their own material, but this clashed with our stated ethos of not playing any songs written after 1956. We'd already recorded an unofficial album of cover versions which we'd been selling at gigs, and which included a version of 'Oh Death', a gospel song with the cheery refrain 'You took my mother and gone'. The song was immortalised in 1934 by Charley Patton and Bertha Lee, although the way we played it, it sounded a lot more ramshackle. We'd also recorded a version of 'Worried Man Blues' which I loved but which Mike thought was naff because it's such a well-known standard. In the end we compromised and agreed to bury it as a hidden track at the very end of the CD. To hear it, you have to let the disc continue to play for three full minutes of silence after the 'final' song, at which point it pops up unannounced, smothered in artificial scratchy record noises. We sold several hundred copies of that first Dodge Brothers CD, and I suspect that only a handful of people have ever found that hidden track.

Then, just to make matters even more exclusive, we deleted the CD in the belief that it would become an obscure collector's item. The last time I looked, nobody was offering it as a valuable rarity on eBay. Hey-ho.

As for the songwriting, I came up with a cunning plan. I knew that composing new songs would seem out of place with our increasingly stern retro-ethic. So instead, I decided to try and write some *old* songs, and see whether I could pass them off as ageing obscurities. I started with something called 'Churchhouse Blues', which effectively obeyed every rule of old-fashioned blues songwriting. It was in A, featured only three chords, and had one basic idea which ran through the whole song. The verses were simple, moving from A to D to E, with the first line of the lyric repeated. (Readers old enough to remember the TV show *That's Life* may recall Richard Stilgoe performing 'Poppa's Blues', which memorably begins: 'The first line of the blues is always sung a second time, oh the first line of the blues is always sung a second time . . .'). I stole a line from the Tom Waits song 'Mr Siegal', about finding a book of matches which I stuck into the chorus, and then wrapped the whole thing up with a three-time repeat and a variation on the old shave-and-a-haircut finale. It could not have been any more formulaic. Then I played it on an acoustic guitar and made a recording of it that sounded like I was trying to remember an old song and getting bits of it wrong.

I gave the recording to Mike, along with a couple of other songs put together in the same duplicitous fashion. I assured him that these were old standards, and told him he could probably find some different versions of them on the internet. It never occurred to me that he'd bother to check.

Of course, he *did* check.

'Mark,' he said next day, 'are these really old songs?'

'Yes' I lied.

'Really? Because I can't find anything about them on the internet.'

'Well, that's the internet for you,' I insisted.

'Mark,' said Mike. 'Did you actually write these songs yourself?'

'No,' I insisted.

'Really?'

'Oh alright then, yes. I did write them. But they do sound old, don't they?'

'Yes, they do,' agreed Mike. In fact, he admitted, he had briefly been fooled into believing that 'Churchhouse Blues' was something written in the late forties or early fifties, which kind of proved my point.

'That should be our motto,' I said. 'We don't write new songs; we write *old* songs.'

Somehow, that silly motto unlocked something in Mike, and he suddenly started to produce new old songs at a rate of knots. Every time we got together Mike had churned out another classic that sounded like it had been gathering dust in some Library of Congress vault for decades. Before we knew it, we had the best part of an album's worth of new old material, at which point Aly insisted that we stop piddling around performing circus tricks in public and go back into the studio to record our first proper album.

Most of *Louisa and the Devil* was recorded at Active Music in Poole, although a couple of tracks (including 'Died and Gone to Hell') were recorded in Aly's front room, with just a single open mic. There was something very liberating about that experience – just getting everyone to sit around one microphone, and move nearer to it or further away from it depending on whether each person or instrument was too loud or too quiet. It was a technique which would come in very useful when we ventured to Sun Studio some years later.

By this point, The Dodge Brothers had fallen in with The Subways, whom we had supported at the Guildhall in South-ampton. It was an astonishing gig because The Subways had a mighty PA system that had scared the living crap out of me. We'd done a backline soundcheck just before they opened the venue doors, but none of us were expecting the sheer level of noise we encountered when we finally went onstage and started playing to the packed house. It was like standing in the middle of a hurricane, with everything louder than everything else. Yet somehow nothing was feeding back, and the sound balance was extraordinarily clear. And incredibly loud. Only in retrospect did it occur to me that this was the first time we'd ever heard ourselves through something approaching a modern stadium sound system. Nowadays, thanks to advances in audio technology, gigs can be ear-splittingly loud without any loss of sound quality. But having grown up with creaky Vox PAs which would shriek and howl the minute you started playing, it came as a real surprise to hear myself at the kind of volume which could loosen the fillings in your teeth. It was shocking, but also thrilling.

Anyway, after that gig we became very good friends with The Subways' main man Billy Lunn, and he agreed to sit in on the recording of 'Died and Gone to Hell', adding guitar and vocals in the middle-eight and lending a sheen of rock star glamour to the proceedings. Meanwhile, Julian 'Jules' Balme, who had designed iconic album covers for The Clash, Mad-ness and Imelda May, agreed to handle *all* the design work for

The Dodge Brothers, from logos, badges and posters to album covers.

'My advice,' said Jules sagely, 'is to keep yourselves off the album covers. You look better when we can't see you.'

This seemed sensible. I remembered a story (probably apocryphal) that seventies pub-punk rockers The Motors had been advised by their record company to remain hidden whenever possible. As someone who owned a copy of 'Dancing the Night Away' with a picture sleeve depicting the band in all their handsome glory, I thought the record company had a point. Instead, Jules found a vintage-era image of a cowgirl with a whip about to collar a rifle-wielding outlaw and used it as the basis for a gatefold CD sleeve the sheer gorgeousness of which still thrills me to this day. Jules also designed the disc itself, a target with bullet holes blown at strategic intervals, and came up with a bunch of catchy taglines which perfectly captured the mood of the record ('Death, Booze and Heartbreak *ride every trail*!'). Indeed, it was Jules who dreamed up the phrase which came to define our ethos of attempting to write 'Tunes of proven merit'.

The finished CD looked quite brilliant. As Aly observed drily: 'Even if the record sucks, people still want to own it for the artwork.'

Luckily, the record didn't suck. When we sent a copy to 'Whispering' Bob Harris, he responded enthusiastically and played the opening track, 'You Can't Walk Like a Man (When You're Too Drunk to Stand)' on his late-night BBC Radio 2 show. Listening back to *Louisa and the Devil* now, almost a decade after it was recorded, I'm still really fond of that record. One of the things I especially like is just how authentically shambolic some of it sounds. There are songs recorded in Aly's

Jules Balme's brilliant cover artwork
for Louisa and the Devil.

kitchen with just Mike playing a banjo, Aly strumming a guitar and Al tapping a pocket full of change. There are protest songs like '42 Days' on which I demonstrated that I really can't play the ukulele. There are some lovely arrangements of tracks like 'Frank Harris', with Aly's lilting mandolin riffs and some intricately shuffling washboard percussion. And then there's the epic final track, 'The Dying Ranger', an old nineteenth-century folk song which starts out with Linda playing the autoharp (I bought her the instrument for a birthday present so she *had* to play it), then segues into a section of Mike tap-dancing (no, really) and ends up with me playing the bagpipes – an instrument Linda had given me a just couple of weeks before the recording.

We pressed up a thousand copies of *Louisa and the Devil* which promptly sold out, so Aly arranged a second pressing. This was a first for me; the *Trumpeting of Mighty Jungle Beasts* EP had done OK, but we still had a few boxloads left over at the end of its run which I think Simon donated to the Green Party. Heaven knows what they would have done with them – recycled them, probably. The Bottlers had done several runs of compilation cassettes, but that wasn't the same as making up a vinyl record or a properly mastered CD. We actually thought about doing a vinyl release of *Louisa and the Devil* and, indeed, the demand for such an item seems to have grown over the last ten years. I suggested that we issue the entire album as a boxed set of shellac 78s, but it turned out that each set would cost around £150, so we shelved that idea.

But on CD, the album got some very decent reviews and it started to land us some decent gigs. On the strength of an early pre-release copy, we'd been booked to play the Cropredy Festival in August 2009, an annual event in an Oxfordshire village that Fairport Convention had hosted for decades. The festival began as a private garden bash back in 1976. By 2009, it had moved to a vast field which held something in the region of 20,000 people. It had the biggest stage I'd ever seen, complete with a giant video screen to ensure the bands were visible to those standing at the back of the crowd. Because light travels faster than sound, the video screen was slightly out of sync with the PA, with the picture delayed ever-so-slightly so that the people at the *back* of the field would hear and see things at the same time. At least, that's what I was told – maybe they were pulling my leg. But if you were onstage it really was crucial that you didn't turn and look at the screen, because it was definitely playing out of time – marginally behind the beat – and it would cause you to lose your footing, as I discovered to my cost.

Cropredy was a very steep learning curve for The Dodge Brothers, and I took two words away from our time at that festival: 'rolling risers'. Apparently, if you're festival regulars (which we weren't) you demand 'rolling risers' as a matter of course. These are large movable risers on which bands set up their drum kits backstage. Since there's usually no time or opportunity for soundchecks between acts, you just have to set up in the wings and trust the PA team to make you sound good when you finally appear onstage. If the drum kit is set up on a rolling riser, it can be miked up in advance, and you can have all your amps set and ready to go beforehand. Cometh the allotted time, the riser rolls forward with all your equipment on it, you shift the amps onto the floor, and boom – off you go.

The thing is, we didn't have a drum kit, so it had never occurred to us to ask for a rolling riser. We didn't even know what a rolling riser was. I remember playing a support gig at The Brook in Southampton where the main band very kindly offered to dismantle their drum kit to make space for ours. 'Oh, don't worry,' said Al, dumping down his small kit bag which contained nothing but a snare, a washboard and an empty wine bottle. 'This is my drum kit . . .' As far as we were concerned, the fact that we could pretty much carry all our own equipment on and offstage unaided was a strength. It turned out that, as far as festivals are concerned, it was quite the opposite.

*The Dodge Brothers onstage at the
Kings Theatre, Southsea.*

After the band before us had finished playing, the four Dodge Brothers wandered onto the huge Cropredy stage, each lugging their own instruments and amplifiers. After an entrance that made us look more like the cleaners than the turn, we all proceeded to shuffle around onstage, plugging things in, propping amplifiers on stools, connecting foot pedals to power sources, and generally shambling around as if we were in our kitchen, rather than at a vast festival – with giant video screens! The sound crew were understandably underwhelmed and decided to let us just get on with it. We were clearly a bunch of amateurs.

As for the audience, having initially raised a hearty cheer as we ambled onstage, they then grew impatient as we failed to burst into song; instead, we just crawled around on the floor, in full view of 20,000 people. To be fair, it didn't actually take us that long to set up – but as anyone who has ever seen somebody freeze up onstage knows, a few seconds can seem like several hours in the middle of a performance. So, by the time we finally turned towards the crowd and said, 'Good evening, we are The Dodge Brothers', they were understandably losing interest.

Overall we played OK – except for the moment that my ukulele literally fell apart onstage and I experienced another one of those moments in which I appeared to be living out my anxiety dreams in real life. At one point, when things were rocking along quite nicely, I made the mistake of turning to look at the video screen and was so distracted by the size of my projected ugly mug and the fact that my mouth appeared to be moving out of time that I momentarily forgot the song and had to be rescued by Aly shouting at me from the other side of the stage.

Remarkably, a number of YouTube videos subsequently appeared of The Dodge Brothers at Cropredy and we seemed to be going down very well so maybe I'm just misremembering or exaggerating. Heaven knows it wouldn't be the first time. I do know that we got called back for an encore and we sold a ton of CDs to people who'd told us how much they had enjoyed our set. But deep down I knew that we'd been out of our depth, and we needed to sharpen up our act.

'You should have had rolling risers,' said Chris, a colleague from the BBC who'd served time doing the sound at festivals and who knew the minute we shambled onstage that we hadn't done anything this big before.

After Cropredy, Aly took us all aside and gave us a stern

Top: The Dodge brothers at Cropredy.
Bottom: The jitter-inducing view from the stage.

talking to. Up until now, he explained, this had all been a lot of fun and we'd pretty much managed to skiffle our way through things on a wing and a prayer. But that wasn't going to work anymore. If we were going to continue to play gigs of this kind of size, we were going to have to sort ourselves out; we were going to have to get organised.

'Organised.' That word struck terror into my heart and fear into my soul. Up till now, my musical career – such as it was – had been anything *but* organised. Indeed, I had become stupidly proud of just how *dis*organised I had managed to remain. The Dodge Brothers had often joked about the fact that we didn't rehearse, we just learned new songs onstage. We used to tell audiences that 'We like to play songs you don't know, and sometimes songs that we don't know either.' Our soundchecks were closer to extended jam sessions, in which we'd often work out entirely new pieces rather than worry about the niceties of aural balance. As far as I was concerned, I only ever had one question: 'Are you getting enough bass?' If the audience said they were, then I was happy. If they weren't, then I'd just hit the instrument even harder.

Now, that era was coming to an end. We were about to strike out on a new chapter of our career which would take us to the Royal Albert Hall, to the film festivals of Norway, the fields of Glastonbury, and the studios of Memphis Tennessee. From here on in, we'd be playing gigs in which larger amounts of money, equipment, and people were involved and invested. What had started as two people outnumbering their audience in a Hampshire pub was about to become four (and occasionally five) people playing to audiences who deserved not to be let down.

In short; things were about to get professional.
And that felt very scary indeed . . .

The vast Cropredy video screen.

9

LAST TRAIN TO MEMPHIS

I'm the first to admit that I have a tendency to mythologise my past. But there is one thing about which I am certain; the decision to record The Dodge Brothers' next album at Sun Studio in Memphis was not mine nor Mike's, but Linda's.

Back in 2011, Mike and Linda had both been presenting erudite papers at the annual Society of Cinema and Media Studies get-together. The SCMS conference takes place in a different town each year, and Linda was regularly called upon to deliver academic papers in major cities like Los Angeles, Tokyo and Toronto. Since Linda didn't trust me not to burn down the house in her absence, she'd long ago decided that the whole family should accompany her on such jaunts. This arrangement suited me fine; I got to attend a whole bunch of interesting seminars about films like *Cruising* and *Night Moves*, the kids got to see exciting places which we could claim were broadly 'educational', and the Radio 5Live show got to be broadcast from exotic locations which suggested that I (rather than Linda) was a key cog in the world of international film academia.

In 2011, the SCMS conference was being held in New

Orleans, and Linda suggested that afterwards we take the opportunity to do the so-called Mississippi 'Blues Trail' – fly to Memphis, head to Clarksdale, and then follow the Natchez Trace north to Tupelo via the farms and railroads on which our musical heroes had first plied their trade. Although our musical tastes differ in some key areas (Linda has an inexplicable fondness for acid jazz and doesn't 'get' The Comsat Angels) we've always shared a love of old blues music, and have somehow managed to indoctrinate our kids with a similar passion. This would be the perfect family road trip – combining sightseeing, music, and a whiff of 'research'. En route, we could visit Sun Studio in Memphis, where Elvis, Carl Perkins, Howlin' Wolf, Junior Parker, Johnny Cash, Charlie Feathers and Jerry Lee had recorded in the fifties, cutting discs to which we all still listened religiously in the twenty-first century. It would be a pilgrimage.

And so in March, Linda, Mike, Georgia, Gabriel and I all flew to Memphis and checked into a motel opposite Elvis's old mansion home of Graceland. The motel was nothing fancy, but it had a guitar-shaped swimming pool out back and a waffle-making machine in front, so frankly no one cared about its shortcomings. The other residents were clearly on the same mission as us and many of them looked as if they had loved and lived *a lot*. For them, Elvis was a god, and I'd be lying if I pretended that I didn't feel the same.

The tour around Graceland was bizarre, but when we got to the rooms where Elvis's stage costumes were displayed I felt as though I was in the presence of the Turin Shroud. You don't listen to somebody's music for that long without coming to feel that they were in touch with something otherworldly. Standing in the racquetball courts where Elvis once played, I found myself as overwhelmed as the first time I watched *The Exorcist*, reminded once again that there really is magic in this world.

After the Graceland tour we headed South towards Clarksdale, following the Blues Trail to the cabin where Muddy Waters first learned his licks, stopping off at the railroad stations where lonely train whistles had first inspired those whooping harmonica sounds. I remembered the stories of Les Paul bringing home a stretch of railtrack and inventing the modern electric guitar. I thought of building that ridiculous Delta guitar back in Elstree in the early seventies, and realised for the first time that its name was not futuristic but retrospective – recalling the Delta Blues of the swamplands through which my family were now wandering.

Clarksdale is tucked into the north of the Mississippi Delta, a couple of hours' drive from Memphis, through cotton fields and cypress swamps. Sam Cooke grew up here; and it was at the crossroads just outside the centre of town that Robert Johnson reportedly sold his soul to the devil in return for the gift of playing a mean guitar. Clarksdale is also home to the Riverside Hotel, a building steeped in blues history. Bessie Smith died here in 1937, when it was the G.T. Thomas Afro American Hospital. The likes of Sonny Boy Williamson and Robert Nighthawk stayed here in the fifties and Ike Turner was said to have knocked together the structure of 'Rocket 88' (arguably the first ever rock 'n' roll record) in a room at the Riverside.

When we arrived, the Riverside's charismatic proprietor Frank Ratliff ('Call me Rat!') was sitting on the porch, sipping lemonade. 'Take any room you like,' he said breezily, 'if it's free, it's yours.' We headed into the motel, the cool darkness inside in stark contrast to the blazing bright heat outside. It was spartan but clean and welcoming and it immediately became our new favourite place.

A young New Zealander poked her head out of one of the rooms and said, 'Hi.' She was an upcoming recording star who'd had some hits down under, but who had been dispatched by her record company to rack up some 'real-life' experiences by touring around the South. She had an old Stella guitar, which she'd purchased at the nearby Bluestown Music store, and a pistol in her handbag, which she called 'my travelling companion'. She seemed extremely cool. I felt a little bit scared and very English.

Rat showed us round the Riverside, pointing out the lower corridor in which Bessie Smith had spent her final hours (now sealed from visitors) and name-dropping the extraordinary list of blues legends who had stayed there.

Sounding like the massively uncool and uptight tourist I so clearly was, I asked if our car was safe parked on the street. Rat gave me a wry smile.

'It's a rental, right?' he asked.

'Er, yes, a rental,' I replied.

'And it's insured, right?' he said, more as a statement than a question.

'Yes,' I replied uncertainly. 'I'm pretty sure it's insured.'

'Then it's "safe", ain't it?' said Rat.

I looked nonplussed.

Rat waited a beat, and then laughed out loud.

'I'm just messing with you! I have a CCTV out front. If you pull it round front, I'll keep an eye on it for you.'

Which he did.

He was lovely.

At first glance, Clarksdale can seem rather unimposing. Actor Morgan Freeman may co-own the fashionable Ground Zero club here, but much of the town remains impoverished, with boarded-up businesses and long-closed theatres a common feature. Yet scratch away at the sleepy surface and you'll find some electrifying treats, such as the legendary New York Hi-Style store, purveyors of exotic clothing whose celebrity clientele include Bob Dylan and Elvis Costello. Specialising in electric-blue suits and powder-pink ties, Hi-Style is a garment store entirely unencumbered by natural fibres. Everything here is made of weapons-grade polyester, designed to withstand the apocalypse, never to biodegrade. If a fire ever broke out, that store wouldn't burn – it would *melt*.

We spent an hour in Hi-Style, during which I purchased a pair of foot-crucifying plastic Cuban heels and Mike tried on a red suit so bright I worried we would all die of sunburn. Everything was cheap as chips, none of it the least bit 'casual'. It was like falling into a candyfloss machine and allowing yourself to be dressed with sugar and napalm.

Emboldened by our purchases, we sought out a barber shop where cutters with clippers and cut-throat razors made sure that we looked as good as we felt. Then we headed up the Natchez Trace to Tupelo to see the shotgun shack in which Elvis had grown up. Due to some tourist-friendly town-planning, that shack now stood alongside the church in which the young Presley had first learned to love gospel music. Inside interactive video projections recreated the kind of services he would have attended in the forties and fifties.

The highlight of the trip, however, was our visit to Sun Studio. Located at 706 Union Avenue on the corner of Marshall, Sun is a Memphis landmark in which a whole lotta history is crammed into one very small space. Nowadays it's a museum, with a brief tour of recording artefacts climaxing in a visit to the tiny room in which so many classic records were cut. You could lob a catgut-strung double bass from one end of the recording studio to the other without breaking a sweat.

Marked on the floor of that tiny room are three Xs where Elvis, guitarist Scotty Moore, and bassist Bill Black are reported to have stood while recording tracks like 'That's All Right' in 1954. Having failed to notice the marks when we were first herded into the room, I was delighted to find myself standing on Bill Black's spot – something I took as a good omen. When the tour was finished, I whipped out a harmonica which I had secreted about my person and played a couple of bars of 'Mystery Train' – to the embarrassment of everyone else in the room.

'What was that all about?' asked Linda as the crowd shuffled out onto the street.

'Well, now I can say that I've *played* at Sun Studio!' I replied.

Linda thought about this for a while, and then declared, 'You should record an album here.'

'What?'

'You should record an album here,' she repeated.

'But it's a museum!'

'It's a museum *by day*, but they said they still record here at night. Weren't you listening to the tour guide?'

I had to confess that I hadn't really heard anything after the bombshell about me standing in Bill Black's spot. After that, everything had been self-absorbed silence.

'Well, they still record here at night. You should record the next Dodge Brothers album here.'

'Yeah, right,' I replied, touched by the sentiment if unconvinced by the argument.

But as always, Linda was right – Sun Studio may have become a daytime Mecca for tourists who had experienced the jumpsuits and jungle rooms of Graceland, but after 9 p.m. it operated as an after-hours studio, a place where musicians would go in an attempt to recapture some of the spirit of those classic Sun recordings. This was not a cheap endeavour – unless they *liked* you, in which case preferable rates were negotiable. And as it turned out, Sun Studio liked the sound of The Dodge Brothers.

The decision was not immediate. Having returned to Southampton we swithered and dithered about going back to Memphis, finding umpteen reasons (cost, time, practicality) to put the idea on hold. But the more we pushed backwards, the more Linda pushed forwards, insisting that this was 'a once in a lifetime opportunity'. As far as she was concerned, if we didn't record at Sun Studio *now*, we wouldn't ever do it and she'd have to listen to us whingeing about not doing it for evermore. As she so eloquently put it: 'At least it will stop you from going on and on about trying to "recreate that authentic Sun sound". If you want to sound like you're making a record in Sun Studio, then just go there and do it.'

The rest of the band agreed – and so we did as we were told.

The experience was utterly surreal and not a little terrifying.

After a lot of back and forth, we came to an arrangement with Sun whereby we would attempt to cut an entire album's worth of material over a period of two nights, starting at 9 p.m. and finishing around 4 a.m. We would record everything on the equipment that was already in situ, and we would do it all live, with no overdubs – just like they did back in the fifties. The sessions would be engineered by Matt Ross-Spang who had been working at Sun since the age of sixteen and who has since gone on to become a Grammy award-winning producer.

Having learned his craft studying the techniques of Sun founder Sam Phillips, Matt had made it his mission to find and install the same vintage recording equipment that Phillips had used in Sun's heyday – from the Coke-bottle microphones to the analogue echo-loops and mixing desk. Some bands had apparently turned up at Sun with their own portable digital desks, believing that it was the room itself which had created the unique 'Sun Sound'. But Matt knew that it was the *nature* (rather than just the *location*) of the recording that mattered, and The Dodge Brothers seemed the perfect candidates to help prove his point.

On the evening we arrived in Memphis, the night before the first session, we steadied ourselves with a few stiff drinks upstairs in Earnestine & Hazel's, a historic venue located on South Main Street which looked like an overdressed set from some noirish David Lynch movie. In the morning, we had breakfast at the Arcade Diner, a local landmark since 1919, and a regular haunt of the young Elvis. During the day, we drove back down to Clarksdale to pay our respects to Rat and to pop into Hi-Style where Mike finally plucked up the cour-age to buy that eye-scorching red suit. We also paid a visit to Bluestown Music, hoping to pick up a few tips for the evening's endeavours.

'Ah, don't worry about it,' said Bluestown proprietor Ronnie Drew, pulling a few vintage Stellas out of the back room, and encouraging me to play around with an old bullet-mic which

Upstairs at Earnestine & Hazel's, Memphis.

made your harmonica sound like a train going through a tunnel. 'You'll be fine. It's just a room . . .'

And yet it was so much more than that. When we arrived at Sun that evening, just before 9 p.m., we saw another band shuffling out of the studio dejectedly. Apparently they'd booked a couple of hours before our session began and they had planned to knock off a few live recordings in that sacred space before we got going. But while it may be tiny, the Sun studio room is also very intimidating; apparently, they'd been too freaked out to play properly.

'We missed it, man, we *missed* it . . .' one of them kept saying as they lugged their guitars out into the parking lot, into the humid fog of the Memphis night air. He looked genuinely traumatised.

Yikes!

Matt Ross-Spang was waiting to meet us in the studio, seated behind the mixing desk, looking like he'd spent his entire life in that exact spot. Atop his wiry frame was an imposing beard-and-quiff combination, the slight shagginess of which suggested that he looked this rocking without any effort whatsoever. Since Mike was originally from Alabama, we let him do all the talking, figuring that he'd seem more 'authentic' to Matt who was born and raised in Memphis. The rest of us shuffled around in the background trying to look casual and relaxed. Ha!

The studio room itself looked very different without the crowd of tourists, simultaneously bigger and smaller than I remembered. I looked around the walls and saw the framed posters of those who had recorded there – Elvis, Jerry Lee, Carl Perkins, Johnny Cash. Then I noticed that on one wall hung a huge black-and-white picture of Bono, with trademark mullet

Outside Sun Studio, Memphis.

and stupid hat. Apparently U2 had recorded here some years ago – now Bono adorned its hallowed walls.

'That'll have to go,' I said, taking the poster down from the wall and hiding it behind the piano. Immediately, the room seemed much warmer.

At Matt's bidding, we started unpacking our equipment and getting ready to play. Mike had bought a new guitar which had been shipped directly to Sun; a brass Republic tri-cone Dobro made in Austin Texas by a guy named Frank Helsley. With its latticework sound-holes and visible resonators it looked more like a weapon than a musical instrument, something you might use to hold up a bank. It also made a mighty racket, the sound clanging off the studio walls like wheels of a freight train going over the points.

As for me, I'd arranged to use the double bass which I'd seen propped up in the corner of the studio on our first visit. This was the studio's resident bull-fiddle, and according to Matt it hadn't been played for years. I'd brought my own strings, and indeed my own Selmer steel bridge, and so I spent the first hour of our session restringing the instrument while the rest of the band got ready to play.

Matt's instructions had been simple, 'Set up in a circle so you can all hear each other, and let me set the microphones up around you.' There were to be no headphones and no fold-back – only the sound in the room. Anything else was cheating.

It soon became apparent that the biggest challenge of recording at Sun was keeping things quiet enough so that you could hear what you were doing. Al's snare drum was dispatched to the very back of the room so that it didn't drown out everything else; at one point I think he pretty much ended up playing out in the café in the foyer. Mike's guitar amp

The Dodge Brothers in the recording room at Sun.

presented another problem. In order to make it sound dirty, you needed to crank it up loud so the valves would overdrive slightly. Usually, you could do that within a soundproofed recording booth and just keep it low in the mix. But there was no baffling, no soundboards, no separation at all in Sun. Instead, Matt simply pulled a load of mattresses out of the backroom and proceeded to bury the amp under a pile of bedding, with a microphone stuck through a hole. It looked completely mad. I wondered how the hell it would sound.

When I'd finished restringing the bass, Matt asked us to just play something so that he could do a basic sound balance. Almost instinctively, we started playing 'Number Nine Train', the Tarheel Slim song that had been a Dodge Brothers' standard since our inception. Through the window between the studio and the engineering room we saw Matt's quiff pop up suddenly and start bopping around approvingly. Apparently, this was the moment that Matt decided we were OK; that we were not just a bunch of jumped-up chancers. As he later remarked in the Radio 2 documentary which travelling companion Nick Freand Jones and I made about The Dodge Brothers' adventures in Memphis, 'They started playing "Number Nine Train" and I thought "Man, *nobody* knows that song",' adding enigmatically, 'I mean, you can't talk to your girlfriend about Tarheel Slim.'

Winning Matt around was only half the battle; we still had to overcome our fear of the studio itself. Matt had explained that there was something about the studio room that 'pushed the mids' – meaning that however loud or quiet you played, the sound would somehow gather into a ball right in the middle of the room, compressed by the natural acoustics of the walls, the floor, the ceiling. It's hard to describe, but Matt was absolutely right – wherever you stood and whatever you played, the room conspired to scrunch everything together into a single sound, so tangible you could almost see it. If you stood within that ball of noise, you'd hear sound coming at you from every angle, as if you'd stuck your head right inside the mixing desk, or in the bass bin of one of the speaker cabinets. It was weird and warm and oddly disorientating. The trick was not to fight it but to just roll with it – to play *with* the studio rather than to battle against it. It seemed fairly simple, but it took us most of the first night to figure it out, despite the fact that Matt kept telling us to 'just play the room'.

The first song we played was hesitant and uncertain; all the right notes in all the right order, but without much spark or conviction. Since we weren't using headphones we had no idea what it sounded like in the booth. All we knew was that it was really hard to hear each other, and occasionally I found myself lip-reading Mike's vocals to see where we were in the song. Each time we finished, Matt's head would pop up behind the sound desk and he'd signal for us to do it again – '*Uno más*, boys,' was his favoured refrain, '*Uno más!*' This was fine for the first five or six takes, but by the time we were heading towards takes ten, fifteen and twenty, a certain degree of desperation started to set it. Since we'd agreed that we wouldn't do any drop-ins or overdubs, if anyone fluffed anything we'd just have to start again from the beginning. But even when we played it right, Matt remained convinced that we could do it better. And that meant doing it again, and again, and again . . .

Sometime around 1 a.m., we all took a break out in the parking lot. We'd opened up all the studio doors due to the heat and the night air was thick and damp. It felt as though you were inhaling the Mississippi itself, drowning in its swampy ambience. Someone had produced a bucket of beer and I plunged my fists into the ice, bruised and bloodied. I'd split the fingers on my right hand somewhere around the thirtieth take of that first song and had proceeded to bleed all over the neck of the Sun studio house bass (to the best of my knowledge, my blood is *still* on that bass – check it out if you ever visit Sun). Everyone else was nursing similar injuries; Al's knuckles were bruised and inflamed, Mike's right hand was going into spasm and Aly had blisters on his fingers that were starting to burst. In an attempt to keep our spirits up, Aly pointed out that Sam Phillips had reportedly made Elvis do more than thirty takes of an early track. I reminded Mike that when we first formed The Dodge Brothers, I had given him a CD of *In the Beginning* by Elvis, Scotty and Bill, with instructions to 'sound like *this*'. Now, here we were at Sun Studio, trying to do just that. I had never imagined how painful it would be.

By the end of the first night, we'd only recorded two tracks – less than half of what we'd planned to do. Now I knew how that guy felt as he'd crossed our paths earlier mumbling, 'We *missed* it, man, we *missed* it . . . ' We drove back to the motel, across the road from Graceland, falling into our beds just as the sun was starting to rise. We were anxious, exhausted and (to be honest) a little bit defeated. Had we made a terrible mistake? Had we really come all this way just to discover that we really weren't up to it? Was this the point that my luck finally ran out?

I felt numb. I tried to sleep but it was no good – the air-conditioning was noisy and ineffectual and the room was too hot to breathe. So I just lay there sweating for an hour or so before heading out into the blazing Memphis morning, waiting for a miracle. At a local drugstore, I tried to buy surgical spirit for my fingers, only to discover that in America it's called 'Rubbing Alcohol' [*readers are invited to insert the cheap joke of their choice HERE*]. I also found something similar to micropore surgical tape to bind up the open wounds on my hands. I thought about busking on the streets of Edinburgh with the Bottlers back in the eighties, and the pain which I hadn't experienced since those early days of 'slapping it'. I thought my hands had hardened up in the intervening years, but the Sun Studio bass was intent on fighting back – on giving as good as it got. I went back to the motel and swathed my hands in alcohol and bandages.

Meanwhile, in the room downstairs, Mike was writing songs – not because he wanted to, but because he *had* to. We'd planned to have ten tracks on the album, and so far Mike had written six or seven on his own, with Aly and me helping to carry the load on a couple of compositions. But Mike was still working on 'Singled Out' and he'd thought he'd have time to finish it in the studio between takes on the first night. Now, here he was, knackered and bruised, at 10 a.m., having to finish writing an album which we were already halfway through recording. What the hell were we playing at? What had we been thinking? This was a disaster!

We regrouped in the foyer and tried to figure out a battle plan for the coming evening. Clearly, at the rate we were going we'd only leave with four tracks. Perhaps the album could become an EP? We certainly weren't going to have enough material for a long player. I don't remember what happened for the rest of the day. I know that Nick and I did a couple of interviews for the Radio 2 documentary with people like Sam Charters and Preston Lauterbach – experts who could help put our experience in context. I know that we went back to the Arcade to drink our own bodyweight in coffee and attempt to wake ourselves up. At some point, we all headed over to the National Civil Rights Museum at the Lorraine Motel (the site of Dr Martin Luther King Jr's assassination), after which Linda headed to the Stax museum with Gabriel. The rest of us trudged back to the motel to get things together for the session.

And then it was 9 p.m. and we were back in Sun Studio, ready to do battle once more. But this time, something happened – something rather magical. Whether through tiredness or stubbornness, we'd all managed to park our fears of recording in the place where so many of our favourite records were made. Despite being surrounded by posters of the Million Dollar Quartet, we put the history out of our minds and instead concentrated on playing our own music. And suddenly everything seemed different.

We started the session with a recording of 'Singled Out', which Mike had finished writing in the motel that evening. Ideally, the song required a third guitar to play a lead riff which occurred three times; at the beginning, middle and end of the tune. But Matt had specifically forbidden any overdubs. So Mike grabbed an old semi-acoustic that was sitting in the corner of the studio, plugged it into a creaky valve amp, and gave it to Gabriel. 'Here,' he said, '*you* play it.'

Gabriel had never been in a recording studio before the previous day and hadn't heard this new song till right now. But he'd been playing guitar since I bought him a red acoustic when he was five and he'd since graduated to a black Ibanez on which he'd learned to play Motorhead's 'Ace of Spades' with some vigour. So now, here he was, playing the solo guitar riff to what would become the opening track on an album recorded at Sun Studio. As we've been telling him ever since, 'It's downhill from here, kid.'

We knocked off 'Singled Out' in three or four takes. We knew we'd nailed it when Matt stuck his head round the door and said, 'Git your asses in here and listen to *this*!' He ran the tape exactly as it had been recorded and it sounded phenomenal – as if it had been recorded back in 1954. The analogue slap-back was perfect, and the whole track trembled with febrile energy. In the recording area, it had sounded efficient, but here in the control room it sounded positively explosive. I couldn't believe my ears. This was what Matt had been working so hard to perfect. This was what all those 'wasted' hours on the first night had really been about – finding the sound of the band *in the room* and then recording it without fuss, just the way it was played.

We were so delighted that we ran straight back into the

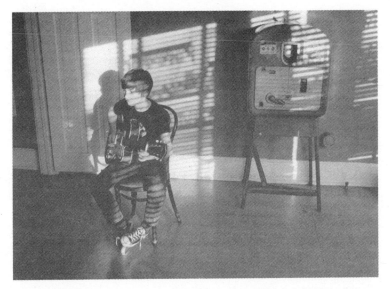

Gabriel practising the opening to 'Singled Out' in Sun Studio.

studio to record another track. This time we did 'Strange Weather', on which Aly played the mandolin while Mike used the tri-cone. Again, it took no more than three or four takes to get the song down.

Back in the control room, Matt showed us something that perfectly illustrated how the 'Sun Sound' was formed. We had five or six mics in the studio: one on the bass; one on the mandolin; one on the guitar; one on the drums; one for vocal; and one for 'roomtone'. The first thing Matt pointed out was the drum mic was turned off – the drums were just leaking in through everything else and needed no amplification. The second thing was that every single mic was picking up every single instrument in the room, all the time.

OK, so the bass mic had a little more bass and the mandolin

mic had a little more mandolin. But essentially, everything was there on every mic. Which meant that when it came to mixing the album you weren't mixing individual instruments. Rather, you were just moulding the overall sound, pushing it a little bit this way, a little bit that way, but always coming back to the sound of the room itself, constant and immutable. As it turned out, we liked the sound of those two tracks so much that we just used the raw mixes which Matt was playing straight out of the desk that night. Most of the finished album is in stereo, but those two tracks are the mono demos; unfiltered and uncluttered.

The rest of the evening went by in a haze. We'd play a track through until Matt was happy with the result, then we'd pile into the control room to give it a listen. It all sounded brilliant. While it had taken us seven hours to record two tracks on the first night, we laid down multiple versions of eight tracks in the same space of time, and even found time to stop and have a beer to congratulate ourselves on how well it was going. Matt was in his element, bouncing around between the desk and the studio, occasionally moving a mic stand, but basically encouraging us to just ignore him and concentrate on playing. Our hands hurt and our arms ached but no one cared. We were enjoying ourselves, and living in the moment.

The session wrapped just before 4 a.m. and, once again, we found ourselves out in the parking lot, although this time in considerably better spirits. When we'd finished packing up our equipment, I asked Matt if he wanted me to put Bono back up on the wall. When he laughed at the suggestion, I took it as a sign that we'd done OK. We were, it seemed, all on the same page.

Back in Southampton, we listened to the recordings we'd made in Sun. For a while we toyed with the idea of finishing the mixes in Bournemouth, but it soon became apparent that once you took the songs out of Sun, you took the Sun out of the songs. Instead, we asked Matt if he'd mix the whole album for us in Memphis, on dead time in the Sun control booth. He said he could, but it would take time – he'd have to do it *between* jobs, track by track, whenever he could squeeze an hour here, half an hour there. We knew this would mean a delay in releasing the album, but listening back to the desk-mix of 'Singled Out', it seemed like a delay worth accepting.

Looking at a copy of that album now I am still amazed by its beauty and its sound. Hell, I'm amazed by its very existence. Jules did his usual spectacular job with the artwork, finding a postcard image of the Memphis and Harrahan Bridges spanning the Memphis River for the front cover and creating eye-wateringly authentic designs for the inner sleeve. It really does look like an artefact from a bygone age – a reminder of something lost, now found again.

After all that effort, it was a relief that the album found an audience. We got blush-inducing reviews and sold out of several pressings, benefiting once again from the championing of Bob Harris who loved the fact that we'd gone to such lengths to recapture the original 'Sun sound'. In 2013, the readers of *Spiral Earth* magazine (a publication devoted to roots music) voted *The Sun Set* the Best Blues Album of the Year.

Blimey.

Several years later, I worked with filmmaker William Friedkin on the narration for his documentary, *The Devil and Father Amorth*. I didn't do that much other than a bit of a polish on the script, but Billy was kind enough to give me a credit, something which made me stupidly proud. One evening in the spring of 2018, we were having a meal together in Los Angeles and we started talking about epitaphs. Billy had once been quoted as saying that on his tombstone were going to be the words 'The Guy Who Directed *The Exorcist*' – a typically self-deprecatory comment from someone who is better known to many as the director of *The French Connection* and *Sorcerer*, and who is now enjoying a vibrant career rebirth in his eighties.

I told Billy that for a long time I'd wanted the words 'There's no such thing as a cheap laugh' written on my tombstone. But I had now revised that to something with a little more gravitas.

Here's what I now want it to say:

Married to Linda Ruth Williams
Father of Georgia and Gabriel
Once co-wrote a script with William Friedkin
Recorded at Sun Studio, Memphis

I think that just about says it all.

10
THE SOUND OF SILENTS

While The Dodge Brothers were trying to send themselves back in time musically, another retro-string was added to our collective bow courtesy of celebrated musician and composer Neil Brand. You probably know Neil from his brilliantly accessible 2013 BBC Four series *Sound of Cinema: The Music that Made the Movies* and its 2015 follow-up *Sound of Song*. He has composed gorgeous orchestral scores for films like Alfred Hitchcock's *The Lodger* and Anthony Asquith's *Underground* and become internationally renowned for his peerless ability to perform improvised piano accompaniment for silent cinema of all genres – from comedy to horror, documentary to melodrama. To watch Neil accompany a feature-length film (which he would often be watching *for the first time*) is an astonishing experience; his eyes are on the screen, his hands are on the piano and somehow music just flows out of him, accentuating and enhancing every nuance of the film.

After years of carrying entire movies on his own, Neil had decided in the late noughties that he'd quite like some company. In his research into early cinema exhibition, he'd discovered that many movie houses would rope in local bands to accompany their film programmes. Paul McCartney's father had apparently played in just such a band, called upon to play a selection of tunes while the audience watched whatever silent treats were on offer. Neil had become fascinated by the idea of a whole band improvising simultaneously. And since Mike was a silent movie specialist, it didn't take much to persuade him that The Dodge Brothers should join Neil in accompanying silent films.

'But I can't read music,' I complained when the idea was first mooted. 'So it's not really possible. At least, not with me.'

'It's OK, we're not going to use sheet music,' Mike assured me. 'We're going to use cue cards. And the rest of it we're going to make up as we go along. Like Neil does.'

'But Neil *can read music*,' I insisted.

'Yes, but he *doesn't* read music when he's accompanying silent films. He just improvises.'

'But how will we all know what to improvise? How will we know what *key* we're meant to be in? It's all right for Neil; his left hand is connected to his right hand through his *head* – so each hand knows what the other hand is doing. But with us, that makes . . . *ten* hands, only *two* of which know what's happening in Neil's head! What about the other *eight* hands? What are *they* going to do?'

'They're going to follow Neil,' Mike replied. 'And the cue cards . . .'

It sounded completely nuts, but Mike and Neil had thought it through. Between them, they'd figured out a way of everyone playing along together, without the need for sheet music. Instead, they would choose a number of key themes and motifs which seemed to fit the tone of the movie, in this particular case, the 1921 William S. Hart western *White Oak*, directed by

Lambert Hillyer. Then, Mike would transcribe all the intertitles in the movie – the bits where the cards with writing appear on the screen – and draw up cue sheets for each member of the band with suggestions for which songs might work at any particular point. This gave us a basic roadmap to follow so we'd know where we were within the movie – a necessity, since *White Oak* is a film which doesn't make a huge amount of sense. The third act involves an extended battle in which the same people appear to get killed more than once, and a comedy dog runs back and forth between scenes of brutal tragedy, requiring some alarming gear shifts in the moody musical accompaniment.

Despite Aly's insistence that we should attempt to be more professional and polished onstage ('When you've finished soundchecking your instrument, put it down and shut up!') we never actually rehearsed *White Oak* before performing it in London, in June 2009. All we did was to get most of the Dodges together in my living room (both Neil and Al were absent, as I recall) and watch the film through with the cue sheets, figuring out what we might play. It was a sobering experience, because it soon became apparent that we couldn't simply play another eighty-four bars of 'Casey Jones' without the audience getting bored and starting to throw things at us. We had three or four songs figured out that worked with the movie, but each one was only about three minutes long. So that was a tidy twelve minutes covered. Now all we had to do was figure out what we'd do for the entire hour of the film that still remained.

The venue Neil had selected for our silent movie debut wasn't some small hall or intimate low-key gathering; it was a large, prestigious concert hall in the Barbican, in London. I remember waiting backstage just before we were due to go on in a state of abject panic, thinking (once again) that I was about to walk onstage and attempt to do something for which I was utterly unprepared and asking myself (for the umpteenth time) – 'How the *hell* did I get here?'

Mike seemed to share my anxieties, which only heightened my sense of dread. I could just about deal with my own fears of inadequacy – after all, I was only the bassist, and no one really cares what happens that low down in the sound. Also, I was playing a double bass, an instrument on which it is possible to miss a note by several inches without anyone noticing. But if Mike thought we were out of our depth too, then that was really alarming.

I decided that honesty was the best policy – or rather I decided that we should throw ourselves upon the mercy of the crowd and hope that they reacted kindly.

'All you need to do,' I told Mike with what I hoped looked like confidence, 'is to say that we've never done this before, that we're very proud to be playing with Neil, that we'll be relying heavily upon *his* guidance, and that this was all *his* idea in the first place.'

'You mean we should basically blame Neil?' Mike replied.

'Yes, that's *exactly* what I mean. We should blame Neil.'

As it was, Mike didn't blame Neil. Instead, he made a lovely speech about how this was a new venture for The Dodge Brothers, and how the tradition of playing with pickup bands had been commonplace in old movie theatres. Then he talked a little about the film itself; about William S. Hart, and his place within the pantheon of silent cinema, and about the strengths and weaknesses of *White Oak*. He described some of the tunes we were going to try to weave into the performance, and explained how the cue-card system was going to work – or indeed, how it might *not* work. It was all perfectly pitched and, by the time the house lights went down and we picked up our instruments to play, the audience were firmly on our side, willing us to do well.

I really don't remember much about that first performance of *White Oak*. In terms of seat-of-your-pants improvisation, it was probably on a par with that very first Hopeless gig, minus the comedy gore. In fact, Al later revealed that he had been watching much of the movie for the first time. I recall thinking that it all made even less sense when you were trying to play along to it, and wondering when that damn dog was going to reappear and do something lovable. At some point, I figured out that as long as I could see Neil's left hand then I could tell what key he was playing in, and hoping beyond hope that he stayed off the black notes. Gradually I came to realise that we were doing exactly what Neil had said we would do – that we were making it up as we went along, all at the same time. What's most remarkable is that I'm not entirely sure *how* we were doing this. We were just . . . doing it.

The sense of relief I felt when the words 'The End' appeared on screen was matched only by the exhilaration of hearing the crowd respond positively to the performance. They whooped and cheered and made the kind of approving noises that suggested we had indeed got away with it.

'That was *brilliant*!' I said when we got to the dressing room. 'We need to do it again, as soon as possible!' The rest of the band were a little more sober, accepting that we'd pulled it off, but still aware that we'd got through the film by the skin of our teeth. As for Neil, he just beamed that big lovely smile of his, as if to say, 'I told you so.'

White Oak was a good starting point for The Dodge

Reading the cue-sheets (rather than the music)
for Beggars of Life.

Brothers' collaboration with Neil, earning us a decent rep-utation with the silent movie crowd whom I had previously considered to be utterly terrifying. But Neil was on the lookout for something more adventurous and found it when he accom-panied (sight unseen) a movie called *Beggars of Life* in Zurich. This was a William Wellman picture which had faded into obscurity (it has only recently resurfaced on Blu-ray), and Neil thought it would be perfect for the Brand–Dodge treatment. It's a wonderful film in which an outlawed Louise Brooks teams up with Richard Arlen's hobo and the two hit the rails in search of refuge and safety – somewhere to call home. Made at the end of the twenties, *Beggars of Life* had originally been released with a couple of sound sequences which were sent out on discs to be played in sync with the picture. These included a sequence in which Wallace Beery (as the gruff 'Oklahoma Red') arrives with a barrel of booze, singing the boisterous drinking song 'Hark Those Bells'. Posters for the sound ver-sion of the film were emblazoned with the words 'Come Hear Wallace Beery Sing!', which sounds like an enticement on a par with 'Come See Les Dawson Tap Dance'.

Sadly (or perhaps thankfully) all sound versions of the film are now missing presumed lost, with only a couple of raggedy silent prints remaining. The best of these was owned by the George Eastman archive from whom we licensed the movie, and with whom we would continue to work for the next decade.

Somehow, Mike tracked down some sheet music for 'Hark Those Bells' and for a theme tune which had been written specifically for the movie. He also found an old Bukka White song called 'Poor Boy' which he used as the inspiration for 'Wildflower', a haunting ballad with mandolin and harmonica

Accompanying Louise Brooks,
with The Dodge Brothers and Neil Brand.

which we'd play in the film's more melancholic moments, and which would wind up as the closing track on *The Sun Set*. Elsewhere there were punch-ups and train wrecks which suited The Dodge Brothers' cacophonous mix of washboards and percussion, with Al adding some well-timed sound effects for gunshots (a sharp snare snap) and rattlesnakes (a hand-held shaker).

Beggars of Life came together beautifully and it became our signature film. With Neil, we'd go on to accompany a growing selection of silent classics, from Abram Room's revolutionary Russian weirdie *Ghost That Never Returns* (on which I started experimenting with a vaguely historically accurate theremin) to *Hell's Hinges*, a tale of fire and brimstone featuring a climactic sequence in a blazing church which (like the train wreck in *Beggars*) was shot for real. But it was Louise Brooks and Richard Arlen falling in love in a succession of boxcars and haystacks to which we would return time and again. We played *Beggars* everywhere – from the historic hall of the Bo'ness Hippodrome in Scotland to the Verdensteatret in Tromsø ('the world's oldest cinema in use') way up in the Arctic Circle. And in July 2014, The Dodge Brothers made history by becoming the first band to score a silent film live at the Glastonbury Festival where we played *Beggars* to a tent full of people up to their ears in mud.

The Glastonbury gig was a particularly big deal for me, since I'd only been to the festival once before and it was an experience I had been trying to forget ever since. This was back in the mid-nineties, when Channel 4 had the broadcasting rights which have since passed to the BBC. Their coverage that year was to be fronted by Mark Radcliffe and Marc Riley, on whose late-night Radio 1 programme (affectionately known as the 'Graveyard Shift') I had long been presenting 'Cult Film Corner'. The TV broadcast was produced by Malcolm Geary, who decided that a B-team was needed to take the load off Mark and Marc. So, in a flash of inspiration, he decided to pluck two regulars from the Graveyard Shift and stick them together in a field. One of them was Katie Puckrik, a fantastically energetic and enthusiastic presenter with plenty of TV experience and a knack for hitting a mark and talking to camera on cue. The other was me, an awkward, uncomfortable and increasingly morbid presence with a morose demeanour which began at a point of total despair and went downhill from there. I didn't just die on camera – I festered. You can almost see me putrefying right there, live on national TV. It was horrible. It lasted all weekend. And, thanks to the miracle

38

SEE A WEIRD BAND PLAY ALONG TO A MOVIE

Look out, it's Mark Kermode's favourite combo The Dodge Brothers, who'll be providing the soundtrack to the classic 1928 film *Beggars Of Life* on Sat at 18.00 in the popcorn-friendly Pilton Palais.

Returning to Glastonbury with a 'weird band'.

of the internet, most of it is now on YouTube.

Good grief.

Twenty years had passed since that bruising experience, but still the memory sent a shiver down my spine as I traipsed back into Glastonbury in 2014. An official brochure listing '44 Things to Do in Glastonbury' placed us at Number 38, under the headline, 'See a Weird Band Play Along to a Movie'. I couldn't quite figure out if that was a compliment or an insult. I decided to assume it was the former. Incessant rain had already turned the festival encampment into something which resembled the Somme. I had been booked to make a couple of other appearances alongside the *Beggars of Life* screening which was taking place in the so-called 'Pilton Palais'. Inevitably, every single one of these other events was at the other side of the festival, which is geographically about the same size as Wales. Luckily, organiser and projectionist Michael Denner had turned up in a US army vehicle that had seen service on the Normandy beaches in the Second World War. I felt safe in the truck, and resolved to spend as much time as possible in there.

Michael drove me out to the Crow's Nest where I was doing a book talk, and where I realised for the first time that, wherever you go in Glastonbury, it is impossible to compete with the sound of the main stages. After the talk, very little of which could be heard by anyone other than me, I started to trudge back towards the cinema tent (Michael and his army vehicle were otherwise engaged). I felt like Gandalf setting out from the Shire and probably looked just as old. After an hour, I arrived back at the Pilton Palais only to discover that it was time to get back in the truck and head off to the saucily named 'Croissant Neuf' stage where The Dodge Brothers were playing a warm-up gig ahead of the *Beggars* screening. The venue was packed, and for a moment I thought we had become overnight superstars. Then someone pointed out that it was raining and everyone was just cramming into the tent for shelter.

We got back to the Pilton by about 4.30 p.m. ready to sound-check for the film. However, as is customary at a festival of this size, the stage was still under construction. As each section was completed, we occupied it with Neil's piano, my double bass, Al's drum and washboard, Mike and Aly's guitars, mandolin, banjos and other assorted skiffle detritus. By the time we were all up there, you couldn't actually see the stage – it looked like an explosion in a skiffle factory.

Yet despite the air of muddy chaos, the show got under way only five minutes after its advertised start time.

Once again, the rain was our friend, although the booming sounds of the ironically named 'Acoustic Tent' next door soon became our enemy. We promptly entered into a battle of noise with the neighbours, throwing washboards, snake-rattlers and train whistles their way. It felt like hard work, but the movie proved a diehard crowd-pleaser. Neil handled it all magnificently, cutting an eloquent path through the narrative, capturing every nuance of the action even when the projector momentarily gave up the ghost and left us all staring at a blank screen.

Everything accelerated towards the climactic train crash which saw us virtually smashing up our instruments for a riotous finale. And then it was all over. Mike made an impassioned impromptu speech about supporting silent cinema. The crowd clapped and cheered. I stepped backwards and fell off the stage, landing arse-first in a slurry of wet mud.

After the screening, we headed over to the merchandise table to indulge in the usual post-gig business of flogging T-shirts and CDs. We were all weirdly elated by how well it seemed to have gone, and I was flying high at the thought of having laid the ghost of Glasto '94 to rest.

'Have you got any of the tunes you played tonight?' asked one rain-sodden punter through the wall of his see-through plastic poncho. 'Any of the songs from the film?'

I picked up a copy of *The Sun Set* and waved it at him proudly.

'You know that ballad that we played during the haystack scene?'

'Oh yes, that was really sweet.' He smiled.

'Well, that's the final track on *this* album.'

He looked suspiciously at the cover of the CD.

'*The Sun Set*? That's not the soundtrack to the film? The one that you just played?'

'No,' I said, 'but it *does* feature *one* of the songs we played. And we recorded it at Sun Studio in Memphis!'

I waited for him to be overwhelmed with admiration. Instead, he just stared at the CD for a while, turning it over in his hands.

'That's Sun Studio in Memphis, where Elvis recorded with Scotty and Bill. And Jerry Lee. And Carl Perkins . . . '

'Hmm,' said the punter with the poncho, still eyeing up the sleeve. 'Does it have the thing you played at the end, when the train crashed?'

I looked at him, baffled.

'You mean, the bit where we all basically smashed up our instruments onstage before I fell over in the mud?'

'Yes!' he replied. 'I liked that bit. Is that on there?'

'Er, no, because that wasn't really a tune; it was just us making the noise of a train crash. But the thing is, *this* was recorded at Sun Studio. In Memphis.'

'Yes,' he replied. 'So you said. But it doesn't have the train crash song?'

'Not as such.'

'Righto, I think I'll leave it then,' he said.

And with that, he marched off into the mud, in search of pastures new.

I haven't been back to Glastonbury since, but at least that festival no longer haunts my nightmares. It's a demon that has been duly exorcised from my anxious mind. I would no longer wake up in a cold sweat dreaming about dying on my feet in that muddy field. I was done with that nonsense now.

And besides, I had other things to worry about . . .

OUTRO

TOUCHEZ PAS AU GRISBI

So there I was, onstage at the Royal Festival Hall, with the BBC Concert Orchestra behind me, a packed house in front of me, and a chromatic harmonica poised at my lips, waiting for me to blow my career. Again.

Stop me if you've heard this one. I know *I* have . . .

The omens were not good. The day before, Robert Ziegler had called me to the legendary Abbey Road studios, to run through the piece that I was due to perform. I'd been practising it over and over and over again, but the theme from Jacques Becker's 1954 French–Italian crime classic was simply way beyond my paltry talents. It began with an eye-watering, minor-sixth ascension which recurred at regular intervals throughout the piece, and which you had to hit *on the nose* or everything fell apart. 'Just hit that opening phrase nice and clear,' Robert had instructed, 'and no one will notice anything else.' Which was basically a nice way of saying, 'If you fluff the first line, you're stuffed.'

A professional harmonica player could doubtless do this in their sleep. But for me, the combination of minor jumps and precise semi-tonal slides was the equivalent of trying to solve a Rubik's cube underwater.

In the dark.

With your mouth.

The first few times I had tried to play 'Le Grisbi', the noise was so horrendous that the dog hid under the kitchen table, while the cats scarpered through the flap in the kitchen door. After days of trying and failing to play the damned thing, I figured the only way I could pull it off would be to cheat. Since the problem with the chromatic harp was that it played *all* the notes, maybe it would be possible to disable the ones that I didn't need, thus reducing the risk of hitting a howler. I'd already had to buy a new harp since I couldn't find the old one – the one on which I had finally conquered the theme from *Midnight Cowboy*. Sort of. But that John Barry tune was a piece of cake compared to what composer Jean Wiener had cooked up and I was no Larry Adler. So, despite having shelled out a small fortune on a new Yamaha chromatic, I decided to take the instrument apart and start blocking up the pipes I didn't need.

This was a tricky business, and it felt more like bomb disposal than musical tuning. The insides of a chromatic harmonica look like some infinitely miniaturised Heath Robinson contraption – full of tiny screws and fragile metal reeds, with air holes covered by spring-operated levers, all of which are small enough to be screwed up by a single grain of sand. By the time I got the thing dismantled, its contents covered the whole of the kitchen table. Putting it back together again would have been a nightmare under normal circumstances. But attempting to do so after strapping thinly sliced lines of Sellotape over a selection of carefully chosen air holes added a whole new level of complication. The process took several hours, but amazingly it worked! The next time I attempted to play the piece, I had managed to reduce the accidental wrong notes by about a third. It still sounded terrible, but at least it was a third *less* terrible than before.

I carried that clumsily customised harmonica with me everywhere I went, and whipped it out to practise at any and every opportunity. The effect was startling. Friends started to avoid me. My family decamped to the furthest corners of the house. Even the dog didn't want to come out on walks with me. By the time of the Abbey Road rehearsal, I was still struggling to hit that opening salvo – something which became apparent to Robert when we ran through the piece on the piano. I sounded squeaky and awkward and (worst of all) chronically under-rehearsed. I remembered failing my Grade 4 French horn exam, and thinking that my stumbling sight reading had probably sounded more prepared than this.

If things seemed bad at the piano, they became even worse when I was called upon to rehearse with the orchestra. Now, the notes simply vanished into the air. My mouth was dry, my palms were sweaty and the harmonica sounded like it was dying of a broken heart, but not in a good bluesy way. In fact, it turned out that I'd rehearsed the piece so much I'd actually blown out the upper reeds, and it was now *impossible* to hit that minor sixth even if I could actually play the instrument. Which I couldn't.

It was horrible. The orchestra were shocked. Robert was alarmed. I was so embarrassed that I simply fled the building and didn't stop till I got to Southampton.

'You'll be OK,' said Linda when I told her to get ready to sell the house – again. 'You've been here before, and it all worked out fine.'

'Yes, but the last time I actually *could* play the piece,' I replied. 'This is different – I *really can't play this*. Plus, I have busted the reeds on the new chromatic.'

'You can replace the reeds,' said Linda.

'But not in time – the concert's *tomorrow*. You have to send it away to get that done. That'll take a week, minimum.'

'What about the old chromatic? The one you played "Midnight Cowboy" on. That was working fine. Where's that gone?'

'I don't know,' I bleated. 'I think it's in there, somewhere.' I gestured towards the chaos of my office – a vast mountain of toppling boxes and stacked old newspapers into which entire search parties could disappear, never to return. 'But I really don't know. Maybe I left it somewhere else. And now I don't have the time to start trying to clear through that mess – it'll take days! I'm ruined!'

Linda smiled and shrugged. 'You'll be fine,' she said again.

The next morning – the day of the concert – I got the first train to London with the intention of heading straight to Hobgoblin on Rathbone Place, and buying a new chromatic. I knew they stocked them; after all, I'd bought the Yamaha there only a couple of weeks before. And it worked fine . . . until I broke it.

I arrived outside Hobgoblin at 9.30 a.m., only to discover that the shop didn't open till 10. It was cold and raining, but I had no option other than to wait. Maybe someone would show up early. Inevitably, the opposite happened; the weather was so foul that central London had ground to a standstill, and it wasn't until about 10.15 that someone arrived to let me in.

'Sorry we're a bit late,' said the assistant affably. 'Terrible traffic today. I hope you haven't been waiting too long. What can I do for you?'

'I need a chromatic harmonica in C,' I said, 'exactly like the Yamaha I bought here a couple of weeks ago. I need another one of those.'

'Ah, yes,' said the assistant. 'We had one of those, but I think we sold it.'

'You did,' I replied. 'To me. And now I need another one.'

'Oh really? Why's that?'

'Because I've blown the reeds on the first one.'

'Oh, well just bring it in and we can get it fixed.'

'No, I don't have time; I need one that works *today*. Do you not have another one?'

'Well, we did,' said the assistant, trying really hard to be helpful, 'but like I said, we . . .'

'Sold it. I know. To me.'

We stared at each other in silence.

'Sorry,' said the assistant, as if this was somehow their fault, which it clearly wasn't. 'I could order another one.'

'Would it arrive today?' I demanded, a note of panic in my voice.

'No, not today, but maybe tomorrow,' replied the assistant, before apologising once again.

'Is there anywhere else I could get one? Anywhere nearby?'

The assistant thought about this, and then said, 'You could try the music shop on Wardour Street. They may have one.'

'Great!' I said. 'Where is it?'

'It's . . . on Wardour Street.'

'Of course,' I said, and legged it out of Hobgoblin, turning West down Oxford Street, onto Wardour Street. As I ran, I googled the shop that Hobgoblin had suggested. The number came up. I rang it.

'Hello, how can I help you?'

'Hi. Do you have a chromatic harmonica? In C? In the store?'

'Hold on a moment, I'll transfer you downstairs.'

A pause.

'Hello, how can I help you?' (Same phrase, different voice.)

'Hi. Do you have a chromatic harmonica? In C? In the store?'

'Hold on, I'll check.'

Another longer pause.

'Yes, we have one.'

'Great. I'm on my way. Can you put it aside?'

'Certainly. When are you coming in?'

'About . . . now!'

I burst through the doors, jumped down the stairs, and bounded up to the man behind the counter who still had the phone to his ear.

'Chromatic harmonica in C?' I barked alarmingly.

'Er, yes,' said the assistant, putting down the phone and holding out the instrument.

'Great!' I pulled the box from his hand, whipped out the instrument, put it to my mouth, and tried to play the opening line from 'Le Grisbi'. He looked aghast.

'Sir, you cannot *play* the instrument!' he spluttered.

Suddenly, everyone's a critic. I looked at him indignantly.

'What do mean, I can't play it. How do you know I can't play it?'

'You can't play it *in the store*,' he explained. 'Not until you've purchased it.'

'Well how do I know if it works?' I asked exasperatedly. The assistant pointed at the desk on which sat a set of bespoke bellows.

'You use *this*,' he explained, taking the harmonica out of my hands and wheezing some air through it with the hygienically configured (but musically rubbish) contraption. Clearly this upmarket store's regular clientele were more concerned than me about the transmission of germs. The folkies at Hobgoblin had never been this squeamish.

'You're kidding?' I said. Evidently, he wasn't; he was deadly serious. So, keeping the harmonica away from my filthy mouth, I checked to see if the slider button was working. It wasn't. It was jammed.

'The slider button's jammed,' I said, handing it back to him. 'Do you have another one?'

'I'm sure this one's fine,' he said, pushing the button which refused to budge. 'Maybe it's just locked.'

'Can you unlock it?'

'I'm not sure, I'm not really a harmonica specialist. Perhaps if you come back tomorrow . . .'

'No good, I need it today!' I shrieked. 'Do you have another one?'

The assistant took a deep breath, put the harmonica back into its box, and headed off towards the store room. After about five minutes he came back with two chromatics. They were both of the same make, although in two different models, with two distinct sounds. I tried both of them on the bellows. They sounded exactly the same. Of course they did. You wouldn't hear the difference until you actually *played* them. Which I was not allowed to do.

I tried the slide buttons on both; they both worked. I had no way of telling which one was more suitable. So I took a punt and chose one at random.

'This'll do,' I said, and handed the assistant my credit card, hoping I'd made the right decision.

It wasn't until I got to the Festival Hall that evening that I was able to check out my purchase. I'd gone straight from the music store to the BBC on Portland Place to do the 5Live Film Review show with Simon Mayo which had long been a Friday afternoon fixture. From there I went straight to the BBC News Channel to do my weekly TV broadcast with Jane Hill, and then cabbed it to the South Bank where I arrived at about 6.20 p.m. The concert wasn't due to start till 7.30, so I had an hour to kill in my dressing room, attempting finally to nail 'Le Grisbi'.

The new harmonica sounded infinitely better than the one I had broken, although it didn't have the custom stops which I'd built into the previous instrument. So although the notes were now clearer, there were a lot more of them – many of them wrong.

There was a knock at the door. It was Robert. He was his usual enthusiastic self – reassuring and upbeat – although he confessed that he'd wondered if I was actually going to turn up after my disappearing act the previous day. I told him that I'd been wondering the same thing.

'You'll be fine!' he said. 'Just like with "Midnight Cowboy". See you onstage . . .'

And that was that. There was nowhere to run to. Nowhere to hide. I had no choice but to keep going forward.

How hard could it be?

The first half of the show went well. I introduced a selection of film noir pieces which were brilliantly performed by the orchestra under Robert's trusty baton. The music sounded electrifying and the audience went wild; the show was a hit.

The second half was equally well received, although I could feel the weight of 'Le Grisbi' approaching – looming ever nearer. I looked around at the musicians, marvelling at how effortlessly they seemed to play such complicated pieces. I wanted them all to know how much I admired them, and how sorry I was for what was about to happen.

And then the moment arrived. I stepped up to the microphone, looked out at the audience, heard the orchestra strike up the introduction to 'Le Grisbi', lifted the deadweight of the harmonica to my lips, saw Robert point his baton towards me, took a deep breath, and . . .

I got away with it. Just about . . .

As with 'Midnight Cowboy', it wasn't perfect. Far from it. There were moments of hesitancy and uncertainty, and one very clear notational wobble. But I hit that opening minor sixth out of the ballpark and after that everything just fell into place – just as Robert said it would. For the one and only time in my life, I played the theme from *Touchez Pas au Grisbi* with most of the right notes in most of the right order. Don't believe me? Then go listen to the programme on the BBC iPlayer. 'Le Grisbi' is there in its entirety and, against all expectations, it is not terrible. It may not be *great*, but it is definitely passable. And frankly, that is way more than I was aiming for.

The minute the concert was finished, I headed straight to the bar and sank three large whiskeys before coming up for air. By the time Robert joined me, I was ploughing into my second pint, yet my hands were still shaking. Torn between tears and euphoria, I seemed to be going into shock, with only the alcohol keeping me grounded. I felt like Arthur Dent, downing several pints of bitter to soften the trauma of teleportation

– the difference being that Arthur (at the instruction of his friend Ford Prefect) had done the drinking *first*.

'See?' said Robert, with a twinkle in his eye. 'I told you you'd be fine.'

Someone from the orchestra came to say goodbye to Robert, and then turned to me and said, 'Nice job on "Le Grisbi".' I grinned at them like an idiot, feeling the soothing effects of several adult beverages coursing through my veins.

My head was starting to spin, my nerves were finally subsiding. And then, just like before, I started to convince myself that I had always known it was all going to be alright in the end. Sure, there had been a few rough moments – that rehearsal at Abbey Road the day before had been a bit hairy, hadn't it? But everyone knew it would work out on the night, right? The outcome was never really in question, was it? I'd been here before and it always came together in the end. I had always gotten away with it.

And the next thing I knew, I was back where I started – convinced (despite plentiful evidence to the contrary) that I could pretty much do anything, musically speaking, ready to repeat the same mistakes, over and over again.

A few weeks later, thanks to the miracle of the internet, I got a message from Henry Priestman, former frontman of Yachts – the band which I had loved as a teenager. Henry had read something about me stealing his name when I was in college and wanted to know if the story was true. I assured him that it was – that I had spent several years in Manchester passing myself off as 'Henry' because of my admiration for his music, and that to this day several old friends (including most of the

Bottlers) still consider it to be my 'proper' name. Mr Priestman thought this was absolutely hilarious and asked if I would write some liner notes for the forthcoming CD box set reissue of the entire Yachts back catalogue. I said I'd be honoured, and set to work on them immediately.

Then Henry mentioned something else. He was recording a new album with Les Glover and he'd planned to do a new version of an old Yachts hit, 'Love You Love You'. Would I like to play bass on the recording? Again, I said I'd be delighted, but pointed out that getting the two of us in a studio together was going to be logistically difficult. We lived at different ends of the country and time was tight for both of us. Instead, Henry said he would email a sound file of the track and I could just record my bass part in isolation, down on the south coast, and then email it back to him.

About ten seconds after I'd agreed to do this, I realised that I had once again overstretched myself. I had no idea how to record the bass track on my own. So I called Aly and asked if I could come to his house and record it there – like we'd done with a couple of Dodge Brothers tracks on *Louisa and the Devil*. Aly said that would be fine, but it would make much more sense to just book the Active Music studio in Poole for a couple of hours.

'OK, but will you come with me?' I asked, sounding a bit needy and pathetic.

'Sure,' said Aly, realising that I was already freaking out about this whole 'working with Henry Priestman' business and understanding that I had a history of getting myself into scrapes like this.

So the next week we drove to Poole and checked into Active Music, where Martin (who had engineered those early Dodge

Full circle. Filmmaker Mark Jenkin took this shot of me busking in a former fish merchants in Newlyn, shortly before it became a cinema. Really.

Brothers recordings) was as friendly and welcoming as ever. Aly and Martin set me up in the sound booth, and we ran through the track a few times, with Aly giving me instructions by remote control from the mixing desk. When it was done, Aly emailed Henry to download the hi-resolution sound file and told him to pick the take he liked best.

A few months later, a copy of the finished album arrived in the post. Entitled *Six of One & Half a Dozen of the Other*, it contains twelve songs, one of which is 'Love You Love You', with me playing bass. I couldn't quite believe it – me and Henry Priestman *on the same record*!

Bizarrely, at the time of writing this book, I have still never actually met (or spoken to) Henry Priestman. I have, however, agreed to join him live onstage in Camden later this year, to play bass on a couple of old Yachts tracks.

Modern life is weird – if rather wonderful.

Anyway, I have to go now. The Dodge Brothers are recording a new album, and I have to drive a carload of equipment down to Poole and get set up for this afternoon's session in Active. By the time you read this book, the album will be done and dusted, so you have the advantage of knowing whether or not it's any good. I haven't actually heard most of the songs we're going to be recording yet. Mike and Aly have been on a writing binge and they've assured me that it's all going great and I can learn my parts in the studio. And if that all sounds a bit ramshackle, then that's entirely appropriate. After all, that's just how it's always been.

I'm sure it'll all be fine in the end.

How hard can it be?

ACKNOWLEDGEMENTS

First and foremost, this book is for Linda, Georgia and Gabriel, without whose love, support and companionship I would be utterly lost. You have brought harmony to the discordant chaos of my life, and I love you all, with all my heart.

I also want to dedicate this book to my mother and father, both of whom, in their different ways, nurtured a love of music from an early age, for which I am profoundly grateful.

At the risk of sounding like someone receiving an Academy Award, I'd like to thank my agent, Hedda Archbold, who has stood by me through thick and thin, and without whose time-management skills and sage career advice I would never have been able to write anything at all. And my editor Jenny Lord (aka Fab Jenny) at Weidenfeld & Nicolson, who championed this book from the outset, and who effectively willed it into existence. I owe you both, big-time.

A number of people who appear in this book were kind enough to give up their time to read all or part of the manuscript, and to offer suggestions, corrections and advice. The responses I received were, without exception, terrifically positive and helpful, with the added bonus that I got to rekindle some old friendships. I am especially grateful to: Alison Armstrong-Lee, Charlie Baker, Danny Baker, David Baddiel, Jules Balme, Kevin Big Hair, Simon Blair, Simon Booth, Neil Brand, Duncan Cooper, Steve Fellows, Olly Fox, Phil Gladwin, Alex Hammond, Mike Hammond, Aly Hirji, Steve Hiscock, Simon Mayo, Matt O'Casey, Suggs, Rick Wakeman and Robert Ziegler for their help, guidance and patience.

Many people also provided photos and memorabilia from over the years, and it's been a delight trawling through the material they unearthed. Some of that material is reproduced in this book (thank you to Holly Harley at Weidenfeld & Nicolson for organising it so beautifully!). Much more of it helped with my research and fact checking. Thanks to everyone who sent me pictures, posters, tickets, diary entries, set-lists, cassette tapes and more.

Finally, I'd like to say the biggest thank you to all those people with whom I have been privileged to play – in bands, on streets, in theatre productions – over the years. From childhood to adulthood (and now encroaching old age), making music with friends and colleagues has been one of the greatest joys of my life. I am very grateful to everyone who has tolerated my ineptitude and played along with me, in whatever capacity. Thank you!

Now, in the words of Marty McFly; 'It's a blues riff in B; watch me for the changes, and try to keep up, OK . . .?'

ILLUSTRATION CREDITS

Pages 7: Julie Edwards; 19, 23, 33, 45, 47, 57, 72: Mark Kermode; 29: copyright Wimborne Publishing Ltd., www.epemag.com; 44: Lyrics by permission of Duncan Cooper; 49: Simon Booth; 76: Courtesy Phil Gladwin; 97: Photo by Jeff Flowers, used with permission of Denise Hodgkinson; 109, 113: Charlie Baker; 132: Tamsin Larby; 136: Matt O'Casey; 139, 180: Olly Fox; 142, 204: Linda Ruth Williams; 145, 159: Michael Pollard; 150: noddy/Alamy; 171: Shakeyjon/Alamy; 190: Alison Amstrong-Lee; 217: John Ralph; 229, 247, 249, 255, 258: Jules Balme at Vegas Design; 232, 234: Adam Prosser; 236: Chris Knight; 245: Aly Hirji; 264: Susana Sanromán; 266: Sara Porter, www.saraporterphotography.co.uk; 284: Mark Jenkin